THE DVD REVOLUTION

THE DVD REVOLUTION

MOVIES, CULTURE, AND TECHNOLOGY

Aaron Barlow

Westport, Connecticut
London

Library of Congress Cataloging-in-Publication Data

Barlow, Aaron, 1951–
    The DVD revolution : movies, culture, and technology / Aaron Barlow.
        p. cm.
    Includes bibliographical references and index.
    ISBN 0–275–98387–0 (alk. paper)
    1. DVD-Video discs—Social aspects. 2. DVD-Video discs—History. I. Title
PN1992.945.B37   2005
384.5' 58—dc22   2004018109

British Library Cataloguing in Publication Data is available.

Library of Congress Catalog Card Number: 2004018109
ISBN: 0–275–98387–0

First published in 2005

Praeger Publishers, 88 Post Road West, Westport, CT 06881
An imprint of Greenwood Publishing Group, Inc.
www.praeger.com

Printed in the United States of America

The paper used in this book complies with the
Permanent Paper Standard issued by the National
Information Standards Organization (Z39.48–1984).

10 9 8 7 6 5 4 3 2 1

To

Brooks Landon

Who started me down this road

and

Will Brooker

Who set me back upon it.

Thanks.

Only the art itself can discover its possibilities, and the discovery of a new possibility is the discovery of a new medium.

—Stanley Cavell, *The World Reviewed*

Any account of the cinema that was drawn merely from the technical inventions that made it possible would be a poor one indeed.

—André Bazin, *What Is Cinema?*

Films are like Persian rugs: You keep them at their best by using them.

—Henri Langlois

CONTENTS

ACKNOWLEDGMENTS		ix
INTRODUCTION		xi
1	HOME VIEWING OF FEATURE FILMS IN AMERICA	1
2	*CINÉMATHÈQUE FRANÇAISE* AT OUR HOUSE	29
3	DVD FAN CULTURE	55
4	THE SPECIAL EDITION DVD	75
5	THE DVD AUDIO COMMENTARY	109
6	THE DVD, THE FILM SCHOLAR, AND THE CLASSROOM	127
7	THE QUESTION OF OWNERSHIP	143
AFTERWORD		157
NOTES		161
SELECTED BIBLIOGRAPHY		167
INDEX		171

# ACKNOWLEDGMENTS

Like anyone writing on film these days, I owe a debt to the Internet Movie DataBase (http://www.imdb.com), the best source anywhere for information on the particulars of any movie. Thanks to Dulcie Barlow, Gina Rosencrantz, Aubrey Heimer, Richard Conklin, Lianne Towbes, Sonja and Syron Martin, and all of the other people at Shakespeare's Sister in Brooklyn, New York, where a great deal of this was written. Thanks also to Jan Stern and Ann Hergenrother for the support they have given me. Three writers kept my nose to this grindstone by their example: Elizabeth Gold, Helene Stapinski, and Lol Fow. My students at Pratt Institute in the spring of 2004 patiently endured my explorations and musings and even added to the project through their own work (Reuben Kleiner and Keith Eng were particularly helpful). Finally, and most importantly, I must acknowledge the contribution of my editor at Praeger, Eric Levy, who guided this project from its inception. If not for Eric, this book would never even have been started.

INTRODUCTION

In 1994, video stores offered only VHS tapes and a few laserdiscs. There were rumors of new technologies for home viewing on the horizon, but few took them very seriously. Film connoisseurs cherished their lovingly-prepared laserdiscs; everyone else seemed satisfied with VHS tapes.

What a difference a decade made! By 2004, the videotape had lost most of its shelf space and the laserdisc was but a fading memory; the Digital Video Disc (or Digital Versatile Disc) has replaced them in one of the fastest and biggest technological changeovers ever seen.

Having completely defeated its competing media, the DVD is now fundamentally changing the way we interact with movies. Indeed, the DVD has thrown us unprepared into a whole new cinematic possibility where, among other things, the integrity of the film is of higher importance than ever before and its life is immeasurable. Starting with videotapes—but accelerated since the introduction of the DVD—movies are no longer fixed in time but are now fixed in boxes, few even indicating the year of release, removing them from the competition of the "new," raising them above mere trendiness. Thanks to the DVD, our classic movies are beginning to be treated as respectfully as classic books.

This is only one of the changes the new technology is sparking. Home DVD viewing has become such an integral and powerful part of the American film experience that it is likely to soon achieve in perception what it already has in fact: dominance over the filmmaking world. What does this mean for the industry? For the film scholar? And for the viewer? How are classic movies improved so much by the DVD? This book examines these questions and more: What is it about the DVD that has made its victory so complete? What need in American culture is it responding to? Is it the ease of use? Is it simply fascination with the newest technology? Is it because its costs are competitive with owning and using a VCR? Is it the DVD's compatibility with home computer and video game technology? Is it the "extras" savvy marketers quickly started adding to their DVD offerings? Is it the improved picture quality? Is it the options the DVD provides, for example, with letter-boxing, language, subtitles, and sound? Is it the audio commentary tracks that so many of the DVDs now provide? Or is it a culture that has become attuned to the visual in ways never before seen?

Of course, it is all of these things. Together, they present an irresistible technological change, altering the way we watch movies at home even more than the advent of the audio CD changed our music-listening habits. And just as the CD altered the way music is made, the DVD is changing not only the movies but also our viewing habits.

To really understand why the DVD is having such an impact, it is neces-sary to examine the cultural changes the technological changes are connected to, contributing to them as well as being influenced by them. If we follow the model of the cultural shift that followed the introduction of print technology, we can see that the new technologies are having comparable impact—with the videotape perhaps being analogous to penny dreadfuls, dime novels, and even cheap paperback editions of classic literature. Not quite the real thing, these responded to—and increased—a demand for written entertainment. The DVD, though perhaps not purely for *cineastes*, provides a commodity of high enough quality to satisfy all but those very few. They make it possible to watch a movie at home confident you are seeing an authoritative version, just as you are when you read a quality edition of a novel.

Today's best film DVDs certainly aren't merely videotapes in another medium. Some are duped (or duplicated) from carefully restored or pre-served master reels, taking advantage of the DVD's high-quality picture and the expectation attendant to the proliferation of high-definition viewing technology. Many DVDs include commentaries, biographies, and other types of extras; some interactive, others requiring connection to the Internet, all intended to entice the home fan who might already own the movie on videotape. Most DVDs allow for viewing in the Original Aspect Ratio (OAR) and not just in the "pan-and-scan," corrupted form that had become the television and videotape standard.

A quick look at Amazon.com shows the success of this repackaging strat-egy: 20 of the 57 feature films on the top 100 DVD list for 8/18/03 were an extended edition, special edition, or collector's edition. That's 35% of the total. Obviously, there's a thirst for the extras and for films that can be viewed with the knowledge that what is seen is close to what their makers intended. Consumers, after all, now see their films as more than merely things-in-themselves: the movie experience now includes after-market products, Internet discussions, fan meets, and more. Yet fans want the artifact at the center of all this to have as much integrity as possible.

Many of the films that are appearing in new DVD editions developed their followings as videotapes. Some of them were certainly blockbusters in the theater, but others were not. They have coalesced into a body of films that has become part of the conversation on cinema that almost anyone interested in the art form, from fan to director, has become familiar with, whether they approve of the choices or not. DVD packagers, who are careful observers of cultural trends, have begun taking these films, presenting the restored or well-preserved versions, and building extensive apparatuses around them. In this way, a film that was a relative box-office failure, such as *Buckaroo Banzai's Adventures through the Eighth Dimension* (W.D. Richter, 1984) can find itself on DVD with commentaries, an alternate opening, and deleted scenes. Such DVDs are often released with the ballyhoo of special theatrical showings and promotional tours. Special editions of legitimate classics such as *Casablanca* (Michael Curtiz, 1942) and *Singin' in the Rain* (Gene Kelly and Stanley Donen, 1952) are forming a body of *great movies*, akin to annotated *great books*, and will become the backbone of many a home library. Warner Brothers has even asked fans to vote on classic films for release in special-edition DVD form.

With the DVD now firmly established as the dominant home-cinema medium, the outlines of its possibilities are starting to be filled in. Over the next few years its impact in the home, on film scholarship, and on filmmaking will certainly increase. It is already evident. Nelson Coates, the production designer for *Imposter* (Gary Fleder, 2002), says that one of the goals of today's moviemaker is to "end up with a stronger movie on first, second, and third viewings. . . . These days, with movies living so much longer, everyone has time to stop and look and see that scene over again on their DVD."[1] Coates's comments are on the minds of everyone involved in the movie industry: The opening weekend's gross receipts still dominate film-industry thinking, but recognition of the importance of eventual DVD sales (and the multiple viewings they engender) grows daily. *Imposter* itself had a poor run in the theater, but will have a long life as a DVD.

How exactly, beyond requiring a new attention to detail and fear of anachronism, has this growing exposure to movies at home affected the films of today? What is there about new films that shows the impact of home viewing? By looking closely at how some films of the past (and not-so-past) have been constructed and reconstructed, we can begin to create a picture of the changing impact of older films (due, in part, to their restoration, increased availability and, now, presentation with expanded features) on the more contemporary ones. A film like *Pulp Fiction* (Quentin Tarantino, 1994) exists in large part because of films on television and the videotapes its creator grew up with. The films of today are beginning to reflect a new type of knowledge about film on the part of the viewer as well as the filmmaker.

Because of the DVD, movies are becoming personal in unexpected ways, and this is further impacting the ways in which films are made and talked about. Eventually, it will even change how films are studied. But none of the changes are happening without concern. Just as in the early days of videotape, some observers worry about the loss of the theatrical experience. Others feel that the new digital possibilities will make filmmakers forget the possibilities inherent in film (just as something was lost when sound came in). Anxiety in the face of a changing future is to be expected; but there is excitement, too, and it seems that this has been the dominant emotion.

Excitement and fear—these have been the emotions surrounding the DVD ever since it was first heard of as a new form for home viewing. The fears have eased as the DVD has been integrated into the cinema industry, but the excitement remains. Today the potential of the DVD is much clearer and less worrisome than it was a decade ago. In fact, some are already finding it passé, predicting its demise in favor of movies downloaded and stored on hard drives, following the pattern we have been seeing with music—and with concomitant concern over piracy and file sharing.

Other anxieties remain, however, especially among *cineastes*. How real are their worries that film has seen its day in the sun setting? After all, video has always been a degraded medium for movies originally shot on film. But, by the same token, music on cassettes (or even on vinyl or CD) is just as degraded, as are works of art on slides or reproduced in textbooks. The existence of these has not stopped people from attending concerts and going to museums—people recognize the place of copies in the hierarchy of art and appreciate that, in many cases, they would never get to experience the art at all if it weren't for the degraded forms. They use the reproductions because the originals aren't often conveniently available—and because they are better than nothing. If it weren't for the videotape, and now the DVD, few people would have any chance at all of experiencing the films of years gone by or those from foreign cultures. In fact, film's past would be the province of the elite only.

To put the question more clearly, let me ask, "Would we be better off if we ignored *Beowulf* because we know the texts we have are corrupt?" We could ask the same question about most of Shakespeare's plays. What about the *Odyssey*? What Homer recited is probably quite different from what we read—even without the problems inherent in translation. Fortunately, the value of any work of art manages to seep through even a degraded version of it. Yes, we would like the best version possible—sometimes the best isn't very good, but it might be all we have available so we should avail ourselves of the value that it does have.

Despite the fears of film purists—and they *are* real (for example, we may be losing close to the entire history of the 16mm *avant-garde* as a result of careless institutional switches to digital)—the impact of new technologies on cinema will, on the whole, be positive. Moreover, it will affect film positively in many more ways than we can currently imagine. The more people who can experience any art, ultimately, the better for art.

One of the most obvious problems with a book like this is that I am talking about something that has a strong moving-image component—and I am doing so without access to those images. That makes my task somewhat difficult; sometime in the future, a technology may even make books and DVDs one—but that time is still a little bit away. Nonetheless, I hope I can open up discussions that will follow into new media. What I am ultimately attempting to do is to join a broad cultural dialogue, one that will help us all to understand more fully our own relations to the changing visual, virtual, or informational culture we inhabit. We are at the beginning of a transformation that will be as invigorating to discussion as it already is for viewing, and I hope I to provide a small contribution to it.

Another problem I faced when planning this book was how to deal with world cinema. Certainly, American cinema—Hollywood, really—has dominated world cinema for almost a century, but that is changing, and the DVD is part of how it is changing. The trouble is, there is just too much out there for me to expand my brief to include the ways in which the DVD is affecting cinema in Africa, China, or India (where Bollywood may be on the verge of making a run at American hegemony). The cultural impact of the DVD on these nations will be different from its impact on the United States, but others will have to provide its description.

One of the perplexities I have faced in preparing this book is in assessing the audience I am addressing. Study of something like the DVD is not a program that can be kept within a specific field, not even if cultural studies can itself be clearly defined and delineated and accepted as an academic discipline. In addition, I have not been attempting to write a book of interest only to the academic; in keeping with what the DVD is doing, I want to open discussions up, not cloister them in an ivory tower. My own formal training has been in literature, but I have always approached it from the point of view of a fan, not a scholar. In the last few years, I have turned my interest toward film, learning about it because I love it. Yet for this book, I have had to go beyond both these enthusiasms, to combine a bit of philosophy, a pinch of sociology, a dose of linguistics, and pieces from a dozen other fields just so I can understand this new technology that has so delighted me. My purpose here, then, is to present avenues for exploration for others like me, people finding the DVD the best of the presents under the technological Christmas tree and wanting to know more about it.

It is for this reason that I have written this book in discrete parts; not as separate essays exactly, but as differing approaches to distinct discussions. I do not expect that every reader will find every chapter of interest. So, given that there is no inalterable progression through them, I encourage readers to start where they will, taking what they want and moving on to their own positions and participation in the debate on the meanings and forms of the recent turns our culture has taken.

Chapter 1

HOME VIEWING OF FEATURE FILMS IN AMERICA

Maybe it was America's passion for movies that killed the Betamax. Sony's home video system played one-hour tapes that just weren't long enough for feature films. The Video Home System (VHS) tapes that soon came onto the market were 2 hours long (and more) from the start, encompassing whole movies. Fans flocked to VHS when it was introduced in the mid-1970s and ignored the Betamax; almost immediately, home VHS libraries blossomed, first through tapes recorded from commercial broadcasts—or duped (duplicated) from other tapes—and later through prerecorded commercial products.

The popularity of watching movies at home has not slackened since. On the contrary, as the millennium loomed new technologies began to make home viewing analogous (in some respects) to theatre viewing: projection systems, widescreen High Definition Television (HDTV), DVD, and surround sound. Along with an ever-increasing number of computer possibilities (including the Internet) and new listening devices, they have become among the most obvious manifestations of what might be called a new "virtuality" (or however it may ultimately be known), a culture that threatens to supercede the literary culture of past centuries.

Of course, home viewing of commercial films was possible in America long before VHS and Betamax battled it out, even before television burst upon American culture in the late 1940s. Home viewing goes at least as far back as 1923 when Kodak introduced its 16mm Kodascope projector. This, coupled with Kodak's new "safety" film on a cellulose acetate base that was not nearly as volatile as the standard 35mm film of the time, made it possible for the well-to-do to set up a home-viewing apparatus. Kodak marketed the Kodascope with the Cine-Kodak Motion Picture Camera, and the system proved immediately successful for taking and showing amateur movies. The popularity of these cameras was important to the fast growth of Kodak and Kodak developing labs, but it was an expensive and unwieldy method of home viewing. Professionally made 16mm films for home viewing appeared at almost the same time, including Kodak's own Cine Kodograph series. The films were short and fragile, though—it took time and a certain amount of skill to set up the showings.

In the early 1930s, Kodak began experimenting with the smaller and cheaper 8mm format, which soon replaced 16mm as the prime home-viewing possibility, lasting in popularity well into the television era and only losing favor with the introduction of the home video camera in the mid-1970s.

Though home film viewing grew in popularity as 8mm costs dropped, it really was not until the advent of television in the late 1940s that home viewing became both affordable to the vast majority of Americans and of real commercial interest (either positively or negatively) to the film industry. Earlier, home viewing was seen more as an oddity, a vehicle for hobbyists, and for the most part it was hobbyists and amateur filmmakers who kept 8mm and later Super 8mm alive. Though there were quite a few short commercial films available for home viewing, the home movie was seen by most people as home shot, as well.

The most successful distributor of commercial movies for home viewing early on was Castle Films, founded in 1924 as a distributor to schools and, after 1935, providing short films for sale to the general public. The company was best known for its short cartoon and music films (*soundies*) on 16-millimeter stock in the 1940s. After World War II, Castle was bought by a division of Universal Studios and changed its focus to abridged versions of feature films, dropping the soundies but keeping the cartoons that had also long been one of its staples. Castle flourished up through the mid-1970s, when the introduction of VHS technology tolled its death-knell, too.

Though it clearly had some success, Castle's promotion of home viewing represented little more than a minor sideline to Universal, and its model was generally ignored by the other studios. Television, on the other had, as it grew in popularity during the late 1940s and early 1950s, certainly caught their eyes. Though profits from home viewing may have been strong for Hollywood almost from the first commercial TV broadcast (at first through provision of production facilities and B-movies and, later, via feature films), relations between the film and television industries were never comfortable in those early years. The film industry started out feeling threatened by this technological innovation, only to embrace it as the money poured in—a pattern that would be repeated a number of times over the next half century as further home-viewing innovations appeared and moviemakers once again incorrectly sensed their doom. It is only recently, in fact, that the studios have begun to accept that home viewing and theater viewing work to enhance each other.

The initial public enthusiasm for television sent much of the Hollywood film industry into an actual panic. Studios scrambled for alternative technologies and gimmicks that would keep people in theater seats and away from their couches. Widescreen formats and 3-D movies were just two of the innovations developed to distance the movies from the home screen, as was a renewed emphasis on color that all but killed the black-and-white film (television, after all, was completely black-and-white in those early days).

Although House Un-American Activities Committee hearings seeking subversives in Hollywood scared the film industry away from approaching very many controversial topics and the older Hayes Code and Breen Office had stifled sexual topics, the movie studios of the 1950s did feel that they could walk a little closer to the edge of "respectability" than television could—and did so. Hollywood also turned a great deal of attention and money to the spectacular film, reasoning that its scope could never be effectively reduced to the small screen.

When the filmmakers decided this, they took "scope" quite literally. At the same time that television was emulating the aspect ratio of movies of the 1930s, new technologies were allowing films to be shot in wider formats than ever before. Earlier films (and television) were approximately four units wide for every three tall, expressed as the ratio of 1.33:1 for television (some films were a touch wider at 1.37:1). The new technologies allowed films to be shot that were almost twice as wide without losing clarity or focus—more than seven units wide to every three tall—while still using 35 millimeter film. Filmmakers quickly found that this could provide a much more dynamic picture. Widescreen soon became the standard for theatrical release; today, most films are produced in an aspect ratio of either 1.85:1 (called *academy flat*) or 2.35:1 (*Panavision* or *CinemaScope*). Television is only now catching up, with widescreen generally limited to the new digital sets which have an aspect ratio of 1.78:1; standard televisions still require a *letterbox* effect of black strips at top and bottom of the screen to show widescreen films in their full aspect, or Original Aspect Ratio (OAR).

With an eye to the changing aspect of the television screen, DVD producers have developed *anamorphic enhancement*, which allows widescreen viewing without loss of any part of the picture and without distortion on either traditional TVs or on the new widescreen models. The only difference between the two images is the size of the image and the height of the black strips, which will be lower on the widescreen TVs (they are hardly seen when the original aspect is academy flat, but are certainly noticeable for Panavision and CinemaScope films).

From a point where home viewers actively resisted the black strips of letterboxing in the 1970s and 1980s, widescreen has become the accepted standard for the DVD—and even for the remaining videotapes. This change is part of the wider movement of growing popular respect for film as an artifact. So strong is this heightened regard for the integrity of film that in 2003 Blockbuster Video announced that it would give preferential placement to OAR versions of movies where before it had featured pan-and-scan fullscreen.

One of the reasons movie producers of the 1950s felt that the spectacular was safe from the small screen was that these new widescreen films tended to concentrate on composition within the shot (*mise-en-scène*: the visual design of the film)—utilizing to as full an extent as they could the widescreen possibilities, and not so many editing devices—to further the plots and meanings of the films. Because of the reduced clarity and size of the television screen, such *realism* had a hard time being recognized and appreciated when presented on the televisions of the day. Instead, an increased use of editing, cuts, and a *montage* sensibility, was quickly found to work best for viewing on television.

The tension between realism and montage had been around since the early days of cinema (with Auguste and Louis Lumière—who filmed scenes of everyday life—perhaps representing realism and Georges Méliès—with his fantasies—representing montage even before the turn of the twentieth century, although it has been argued that Méliès was more realistic than the Lumière's were, for his fantasies are clearly and "really" fantasies whereas the Lumière scenes are composed, and so do not present "reality," even though they pretend to). Within a couple decades of that beginning, director and critic Sergei Eisenstein had become the first significant writer on film to promote montage, or formalism, claiming that the art of film rests in the editing, in the transformation of reality into a created, formed artifact (he was followed in this by Rudolph Arnheim, among other writers). In the montage films of a formalist approach such as those that Eisenstein promoted, images are juxtaposed to meet the needs of the filmmaker, to create a meaning not out of the images alone, but out of the ways in which they are combined. Quick cuts and soft focus are often associated with montage.

One of the factors pushing toward the adoption of a formalist approach was a desire among early filmmakers to disassociate themselves with the theater. A concentration on simply presenting what is happening on a stage or a set could lead to the assumption that the cinema is only an adjunct to the theater. By positing montage as the center of their work, filmmakers could quickly demonstrate the weakness of this view.

The musical *Chicago* (Rob Marshall, 2002) provides good contemporary examples of effective use of montage. In the movie, Marshall is able to create the effect of continuous, skillfully effected dance—though the dancers he used were, for the most part, not professionals. In fact, of the principal actors, only Catherine Zeta-Jones has an extensive background in dance. By skillful editing, Marshall was able to make Richard Gere seem a confident tap dancer, certainly effective enough for the courtroom song where he "razzle-dazzles 'em."

Before Eisenstein and the institutionalization of Hollywood narrative production (the studio system) with its continuity style in the 1920s, the silent film often featured a different perception of movies, a realism in which meaning resides in the things the camera "sees" and it is the job of the filmmaker to ensure that this is available to the viewer. An extensive depth of field and long takes are hallmarks of this type of cinema. The fact of framing the picture is somehow ignored to some degree in realism in a way that it is not in formalism, where the framing is considered a crucial part of the art.

A good example of the use of realism in a film is *Broadway Melody of 1940* (Norman Taurog, 1940)—a movie that may, at first glance, seem to contain no realism at all (it is, after all, a fantasy). The realism of the film certainly exists, however, and it is the realism of the dance. The camera, the sets—everything about the film itself—is formatted to best exhibit the very real skills of the principal dancers, Fred Astaire and Eleanor Powell.

Unlike *Chicago*, in which the skills of the filmmaker are used to make the dance, the filmmaking skills of the creators of *Broadway Melody of 1940* are used to showcase the dance. The difference here is as stark as that between a painting and a photograph. A ballerina executed on canvas by

Edgar Degas is not dependent on a model as much as she is on Degas' own skill, and she need not exist external to the picture at all. Though he skillfully lighted them, accenting their graceful arms and long legs, Maurice Seymour's photographed dancers necessarily existed outside his own artistry. This, then, is the critical difference between formalism and realism: The former places the artist at the forefront, whereas the latter concentrates on the subject.

Hollywood, never a place to leave possibilities untouched, at first took from both realism and formalism as it developed what has come to be called a *continuity* style that attempts to highlight action while hiding device. The intent was to mask identification of filmmaking style or mechanism in favor of allowing the narrative to provide the overt impetus toward resolution. Emphasis was placed firmly on making sure that the tale stayed in the foreground, the telling itself remaining as unnoticeable as possible. Jean-Louis Baudry explains the way it works:

> We know that the spectator finds it impossible to notice that the images which succeed one another before his eyes were assembled end to end, because the projection of film on the screen offers an impression of continuity although the images which compose it are, in reality, distinct, and are differentiated, moreover, by variations in space and time.[1]

Taken from the frame to the shot to the scene and the entire movie, this idea of continuity encourages concentration on the *what* over a focus on the *how*.

In part because of the demands of dialogue early in the sound era, in part because of cultural shifts between the devil-may-care 1920s and the much more careful 1930s of the Great Depression, Eisenstein's severe viewpoint seemed even more appropriate to the developing sound-film medium, and montage (as part of a continuity approach) soon began to dominate both the changed cinema and the developing ways of talking about it. Cuts from one speaker to another in scenes of dialogue also eased filmmakers' fears that they might create a visually boring scene, for the cuts kept an emphasis on visual movement. In America, it wasn't until the end of the decade, perhaps not even until *Citizen Kane* (Orson Welles, 1941), that realism began to return to a prominent place in filmmaking.

After World War II, André Bazin, perhaps the most important film critic after Eisenstein, began to seriously promote realism. He felt that realism was a return to a higher level of filmmaking and that directors like Welles, Vittorio Di Sica, Jean Renoir, and William Wyler were allowing their subject matter to speak for itself, a virtue from Bazin's point of view, providing viewers the chance to look out upon reality through the medium of a film window, rather than framing reality for the viewer through montage. Bazin was followed by Siegfried Kracauer, who expanded upon this realist position.

Though these two views of film were seriously contested, one against the other, by film writers and scholars up until the 1960s, we now recognize that they needn't be prescriptive or even in competition. Among its many contributions to film and our understanding of it, the French *Nouvelle Vague* (New Wave) effectively demolished the montage/realism distinction as significant to film appreciation by pointing out that realism contains formalist aspects, and vice-versa. Realism and montage, however, remain useful terms in talking about trends in filmmaking.

Television, especially with its technical limitations of the 1950s, did not fit well with a realist filmmaking strategy. Detail was lost perforce; the promotion of a few salient items became the center of television-oriented cinematography, making montage the logical tool for creating something that could replace the lost subtleties of realism. The lines of a television screen couldn't carry the detail that is found in the grain of silver-oxide film, and the television image was, of course, tiny, especially when compared to the screen of even the smallest theater. In addition, television is rarely viewed in a darkened environment like that of a movie theater, further diminishing perception of detail on the screen. Also, the rhythms of television viewing, interrupted by advertisements and other viewer distraction, require repetition and a quick pattern of conflict, resolution, and conflict again, something easier to accomplish through montage. The reasoning, therefore, that the spectacular film using a realist approach could keep people coming to the cinema by offering something not possible on the small screen does not seem to have been ill-thought.

Because the image is so much larger and more central in a theater than it is in a living room, it is possible for the filmmaker to rely on image for narrative movement in a way that a television show's creator could never manage. This provides a freedom that television cannot duplicate, for the producer of a television show must assume that some "viewers" are not even watching at all, but are listening while they are involved in another task. Especially early on, certain movies were seen as not transferable to television because the very nature of their reliance on image would not fit with the distractions accompanying television viewing.

Intent on keeping movies distinct from television, throughout the 1950s most of the major studios also tried to keep their best films from the small screen, relegating mainly B-Westerns, science fiction, and horror to television (with an unforeseen impact on an entire generation of filmgoers for whom these became sentimental favorites). A few feature films, such as *The Wizard of Oz* (Victor Fleming, 1939) and *It's a Wonderful Life* (Frank Capra, 1946) soon became associated with holiday viewing (the former with Thanksgiving, the latter with Christmas). However, it wasn't until the early 1960s, with the advent of *Saturday Night at the Movies* on NBC, that films cracked prime time and fairly recent and successful Hollywood films reached television, though in edited and pan-and-scan forms that are anathema to cinema purists, sometimes with good reason. In one instance in the 1970s, a station in New York City cut the long Paris flashback from *Casablanca* (Michael Curtiz, 1942)— much to the outrage of viewers. In that showing, Rick and Ilsa never did have Paris! *Casablanca*, at least, was shot with a 1.37:1 aspect ratio that transfers relatively seamlessly to television. Widescreen films, on the other hand, had to be copied onto a print of 1.33:1 aspect ratio by the system—pan-and-scan— of editing out up to half of the initial movie and altering the original camera movement by moving the transfer camera over the frame to capture the part of it considered most important.

As early as the late 1950s, unwillingly capitulating to the reality that a good part of their present and future profits were going to come through television, filmmakers began to construct their shots with an eye toward eventual television showings, toward a facilitation of pan-and-scan. Soon, indicator lines in film camera viewfinders were telling filmmakers what part of their frame would be carried on a small-screen aspect, keeping the reality of future television showings always before them. The impact of this in the 1960s, of course, was the start of a reversal of the move toward spectacle and a renewed tendency toward montage in filmmaking, for cinematographers began to avoid edge framing, to group important items toward the center of the frame or to at least use only one extreme edge at a time, a tendency that continued into the new millennium. Of necessity, this reduces reliance on *mis-en-scène*, forcing filmmakers to do more of their work in the editing room. Today, however, as a result of further advances in technology (including the DVD), this trend appears to be receding.

The growth of montage can be easily illustrated through a comparative examination of a contemporary film and one made 40 years earlier. Almost any two films would do, but I have chosen to concentrate on two that have at least a few elements in common: *Mutiny on the Bounty* (Lewis Milestone, 1962), made within a year of the commencement of *Saturday Night at the Movies* (just as filmmakers were on the verge of finally accepting that home viewing would be the fate of their work), and *Master and Commander: The Far Side of the World* (Peter Weir, 2003). Though the latter is a war film and the former is a tale of conflict within a crew, both focus on the workings of a ship of the pre-steam British navy. *Mutiny on the Bounty* is set in 1787 and *Master and Commander* in 1805.

Though they are extremely different, both *Mutiny on the Bounty* and *Master and Commander* are part of a postclassical film world. That is, they were made after the fall of the old Hollywood studio system and with the small screen in mind (although from completely different perspectives). They come from a period during which the cinema had been shifted from its seat at the center of popular culture, moved out of the way by television. In 1962, film was still searching for its new role; by 2003 it was much more confident of its position, though once again finding itself threatened by technological changes in the small screen.

Master and Commander displays more than just the growth of technical possibilities over the years between release of the two films; it was made at a time when its creators knew quite well that more than two-thirds of their income would come from the small screen (small-screen revenue would have been a negligible concern to the makers of the earlier movie) and the result shows this. Consideration of eventual DVD release is evident in every frame of the film. Though few filmmakers would be willing to admit it, a look back like this one makes it clear that the change in income sources is having a tremendous impact on how films are made.

Not only had special-effect possibilities matured (to say the least) in the years between the two films, but so had technologies particularly suited to the small screen, including the handheld cameras initially developed for television news. These can be used—and are in *Master and Commander* and many other films—to give the viewer a sense of being right in the midst of an action sequence, bringing the details of battle, for example, close up. This is a technique particularly suitable to the small screen and its lack of sweep. Earlier films tended to draw back when lots of action was going on before the camera, encapsulating as much as possible in any one shot, secure in the knowledge that all would be visible in theater viewing.

The quick cutting of montage is rare in *Mutiny on the Bounty*; the camera movement is slow, almost stately. In *Master and Commander*, shot replaces shot in quick succession, keeping the viewer on edge throughout almost the entire movie. There is a classic realism/montage distinction between the two movies, but one brought about by the particular needs of particular times as much as by the specific choices made by different directors. Weir clearly wanted to use montage to further his narrative, but his reasons for this certainly had to do with recognition of their effectiveness on the small screen. Reflecting the older mindset, Milestone wanted his wide vistas to move the film behind its dialogue, keeping the film "above" mere television.

Nothing at the start of *Mutiny on the Bounty* is hurried. The first two shots are each twenty seconds long, the third lasts more than a minute, and they all serve the purpose of exposition, culminating in an explanation by the narrator, a botanist named William Brown (Richard Haydn) on the possible importance of breadfruit. Contrast that with *Master and Commander*, where a series of quick cuts through the ship, instead of the voice-over narration of the 1962 film, sets the stage for the action that will quickly come; cuts showing items whose import often isn't at all clear until later in the film. The implication, unlike that of the earlier movie, is that there isn't time to admire the view.

The Bounty (Roger Donaldson, 1984), made halfway between the other two films, has also moved halfway from *Mutiny on the Bounty* to *Master and Commander*. Its first two shots after the credits are 10 and 18 seconds long, respectively, and are followed by leisurely scenes of exposition, showing only a little more sense of haste than is seen in *Mutiny on the Bounty*.

Where *Mutiny on the Bounty* and *The Bounty* rely on dialogue to set the characters and, often, to further the plot, *Master and Commander* utilizes action. All three movies are presented in an aspect ratio of 2.35:1 in their 35 millimeter versions (though *Mutiny on the Bounty* is somewhat wider in its 65 and 70 millimeter versions), but *The Bounty* and *Master and Commander* make little use of the extremes of the frame and linger less on wide shots. In action sequences, *The Bounty* and *Master and Commander* often rely on quick cuts to show the action, whereas *Mutiny on the Bounty* lets events take place within its shots.

The changes in how film is edited have led to the increased importance of certain aspects of the *mise-en-scène* even in montage. The extensive use of the close-up, which goes along with montage, combined with recognition that repeat viewers of DVDs are liable to point out any inaccuracy, has made contemporary filmmakers almost obsessive in their desire to "get it right" with the details of their movies. As *Los Angeles Times* reviewer Kenneth Turan points out, *Master and Commander* pays

> attention to getting the smallest of physical objects right. Buttons were ordered from a button-caster who's been in business since the 1770s; shoes were based on a well-preserved 1806 model; and Monmouth knit hats were made by a Welsh woman whose family has been making them since the 1700s.[2]

Such detail certainly wouldn't have mattered in the days of *Mutiny on the Bounty*, when movies were watched once or twice and then discussed ad infinitum from memory—and many of those movies are *still* loved and discussed, lack of verisimilitude notwithstanding. It certainly didn't make any difference to *Mutiny on the Bounty* whether or not Marlon Brando's buttons, shoes, and hat prove to be perfectly authentic. Today, however, even the smallest anachronism can be easily caught by the vigilant fan—though an occasional larger historical *faux pas* still does appear. There could never have existed a 44-gun French privateer with long 18s that had been built before 1805 in an American shipyard, yet one devils the *Surprise* throughout *Master and Commander*.

The distinctions between filmmaking styles—whatever their origins—occasion no reflection on the relative merits of the films. Nor does the fact that only one style accounts directly for eventual small-screen viewings, including this in planning and execution (rather than trying to exclude it, as the earlier film does). Great films are made under all sorts of restrictions; their value is determined by how well they utilize the possibilities they do have, not on the relative merits of those possibilities. What should be clear, from a look at these films, is that there has been a progressive change in the ways that filmmakers see their products over the last 40 years, a movement stemming in part from a growing recognition of the importance of the small screen.

On the audio commentary track of his *Catch-22* (1970), director Mike Nichols responds to a question posed by Steven Soderbergh relating to the change in his style between that movie and his later film *Silkwood* (1983):

> I didn't consciously make a change. The long takes began to seem to me more self-regarding and the cutting a lot began to excite me and began to give me the pleasures that most directors have right away. That's how you start. And I came to it very later, and love montage, of course, because its

one of the newer things for me. I think that, with all the advantages that [long] takes like this give you, it brings a certain theatrical quality that isn't always desirable.[3]

The pressure toward montage was certainly subtle, and it just as certainly did stem, in part, from a desire to avoid theatricality by using techniques that cannot be accused of being simply examples of stage on film. *Catch-22*, coming at the end, as it did, of the time of the stately spectacular, must have seemed somewhat old-fashioned by the 1980s, when concentration on montage had surpassed the realist approach. Nichols, it seems, did not himself consider the needs of the small screen, but was responding to the general trend. His change does arise from other factors than this: he was one who had himself moved from stage to screen and he had developed, over time, a clear understanding of the difference between the theatrical and the cinematic.

Of course, for every example such as this there is a counterexample, although these do not necessarily obviate the argument first put forward. While films certainly have moved toward the fast cut over the past 40 years, there are significant examples of movies that have moved in the opposite direction. Perhaps the most notable of these from the 1990s is *Reservoir Dogs* (Quentin Tarantino, 1992), where the long take is a part of a deliberate aesthetic of filmic simplicity that takes advantage of the restrictions of a low budget.

Changes in the small screen, however, may be helping change the movies once again in this first decade of a new century—and it may even be that Tarantino was simply more than a decade ahead of the newly emerging sensibilities. In addition to the demands of style, HDTV and digital technologies are making it possible to capture much more of the *mise-en-scène* on the small screen, furthering what may become a rebellion against the contemporary montage aesthetic. Some filmmakers have already taken advantage of this change and are tailoring their films to the new possibilities. Chief among them is Peter Jackson, who combines realism with computer-generated imagery (CGI) in a way that allows him great latitude in shot length and composition in his *The Lord of the Rings* trilogy (2001, 2002, 2003).

Just as the introduction of television changed the movies, so America's growing passion for movies at home continues to change the ways in which films are made as well as how they are seen. The sustained fondness of the baby-boom generation and its children for horror and science-fiction films exists in part because it was the cheaper versions of these, along with Westerns, that were first presented with any regularity on television. One of the reasons the Western survives, though its death is often reported, is that its well-understood genre conventions (reiterated through constant television showings) provide a venue for directors to work without the necessity of establishing certain conditions, confident that their audience will be cognizant of the genre background.

Hollywood, as might have been predicted, panicked when the VCR was introduced in the mid-1970s, once more expecting theater viewership to decline in favor of the small screen. The VCR was seen in the industry as a parasite stealing cinema's nourishment, gnawing away at it from within. Yet people kept streaming to the theaters, watching new movies there, their old favorites at home. Notwithstanding the attitudes within the industry, the distinction between the two ways of watching films was well understood by the viewing public: "Real" viewing happened at the cinema; the VCR, a poor substitute, was best for seeing a movie for a second time. By 1985, the frightened film studio heads were sighing with relief. Box-office revenues continued to be strong even in the face of the 60 million VCRs sold in that first decade of their existence.

The children of the baby-boomers, the ones who have grown up since introduction of the home VCR in 1975, have, like their parents (the first television generation), had the ability to look at movies in a way never before possible—in the living room, yes, but now they could watch the films as often as they desired. Those who have since become filmmakers themselves benefit from a newly available breadth of understanding of the history of the medium. Their sensibilities were fashioned by the VCR much as those of George Lucas and Steven Spielberg's generation were by Lash LaRue and Buck Rogers on the Saturday afternoon small screen; they had accessible viewing to an extent possible to only a very few of the earlier generation.

Even though the small screen was instrumental in their own development, today's filmmakers continue to be protective of the large-screen medium and the unique aspects of cinema showings. Robert Zemeckis, one of the most successful directors of the 1990s, commented (before the introduction of the DVD) on his own feelings:

> I'm in a constant conflict about having to make a movie for the big and the small screen at the same time, stylistically. So I just basically make it for the large screen. And I actually have a hard time watching videotapes at

all. I can only watch laser discs now. Because it's getting that I can't stand... the degradation of the image.[4]

He goes on to admit that watching films in cinemas, especially exploitation films and others made for downscale audiences, could have its drawbacks, including rolling wine bottles and careless projectionists. But, as he also says, it is the theatre that most films are made for, so any small-screen home viewing, no matter how technologically advanced, will never provide exactly the same experience—and it will not be the one the filmmaker intended.

Even Zemeckis has finally had to find ways of coming to terms with the differences between home and theater viewing. For his *Cast Away* (2000), he presented his final film in a widescreen, academy-flat aspect, but made sure nothing would be taken away from his picture when it was transferred to small-screen media. He did this by essentially shooting in a "super 35mm" mode (with an aspect ratio closer to television's) and then masking out part of the top, bottom, or both top and bottom of his larger frame to create the aspect he wanted for theatrical release. This allowed him to concoct a later version of the film in the television 1.33:1 aspect ratio by *adding* image rather than by taking away, as is done in pan-and-scan. Another film that used this technique is *Air Force One* (Wolfgang Petersen, 1997). Though this is not likely to become a standard methodology for small-screen presentation (it still plays havoc with the framing), it does demonstrate that there are more creative ways of making the transfer from one aspect ratio to another than past practice has shown.

Though it will always be true that home and theater experiences are different (sharing the film with a large audience would be hard to reproduce in a living room), the differences in the quality of the showings themselves are evaporating (although a distinction will always remain). The growing acceptance of—and even insistence on—OAR possibilities for home viewing and demand for enhanced (Dolby 5.1) sound are two of the most obvious signs of this. These changes are occurring not only because of the changes in viewing possibilities at home but also because of changes in the theaters themselves.

One of the objections to home viewing—that it cannot match the experience of seeing a film in a theatre—arises from memories of movie houses of a sort that haven't been seen for a long, long time, from a nostalgia for the huge and ornate edifices of the 1920s and 1930s. These were places of splendor and awe, telling audiences that they were about to experience something marvelous, something well beyond the commonplace. Few of these remain, and those that do have often been split up into multiplexes (in part because of the fear of decreased viewing at the onset of the VCR). And unfortunately the newest multiplexes, with their surround sound and stadium seating, are built to be unobtrusive. This may be because the cinema chains don't want their facilities to compete with the product shown, mistakenly feeling that the cinema experience consists only of comfortable seating, surround sound, and a large, wide screen. Such insensitivity has partially removed the movie-going experience from the realm of the special, taking it into the kingdom of the commonplace, making it harder for most people to answer the question, "Why go to the theatre when we could see it at home?" Now, with the DVDs dressed up with all sorts of extras, including enhanced sound and carefully-transferred picture, the experience of watching one becomes something much more special than a mere movie on television. The DVD encourages careful viewing of a sort not normally associated with home viewing; its very presentation announces something much more "serious" than television, a videotape, or even a cable movie showing.

The move of the theatre structure toward the banal has also affected the place held by cinema in courtship. Since the earliest days of film, the cinema has a center of dating. If the cinema was palatial, so much the better for romance. Today, the home can often be much more impressive than the cinema. After all, the home, since the advent of television and air conditioning, has become much more central to our lives and, therefore, much more reflective of our personalities. To impress someone, then, we might well wish to take them home, where they can see us amongst our "things," rather than taking them to a sterile multiplex. "Would you like to see a movie with me?" has been replaced with "Come over to my place and watch a DVD." For many viewing purposes, the DVD has superceded the theater—so it is no surprise that it has taken over financially as well.

For just about a decade after the introduction of the VCR, Hollywood resisted incorporating home viewing into its vision for its products, seeing videotape as an incursion on profitability, as competition, instead of an extension to the life of its films. By the mid-1980s, however, the industry had realized three things: It could not stop the growing rental and home ownership of movies phenomenon; it was actually making tremendous amounts of money off of it; and it held properties (its older films) that were already beginning to prove extremely profitable within this new milieu.

Some of these films, such as Stanley Kubrick's 1971 movie *A Clockwork Orange*, developed their reputations on videotape more so than in the theaters. *A Clockwork Orange*, with its original X rating, did not get extensive theater distribution. As soon as the VCR appeared, however, it became one of the favorites for home viewing, acquisition of pirated copies becoming the occasion for viewing parties all over the country. So much was the film associated with videotape that its crisp appearance on the DVD release surprised many, most of whom had never seen the film in the cinema and had always associated it with muddy videotape images.

It's not surprising, then, that the film companies were soon jumping enthusiastically into the home-video market, creating the first director's cut videos, and special editions of popular older films, enticing viewers to jettison their home-recordings of their favorite movies for higher quality prerecorded tapes that came with everything from featurettes about the films to collectible extras such as the mounted frame of 35-millemeter film that came with a Deluxe Collector's Set of *Blade Runner* (Ridley Scott, 1982).

Still wanting to protect their films and profits, the studios developed a two-tier pricing structure for videotapes, introducing the movies first on tape for rental only and charging the outlets a substantial price for the purchase. Later, once it was felt that the rental market had been nearly tapped out, the price would be reduced and the tapes would be offered for purchase by home viewers. The demand for—and profit from—DVDs of recent movies (along with Internet purchase outlets), however, has largely undermined this system, as has the extremely low production cost of the DVD (each one costs less than one dollar to manufacture—much less than it costs to produce a videotape). Today, it is possible for the home viewer to buy most films as soon as they are available for rental.

One of the prime motivators behind the push for the development of the DVD in the 1990s was recognition that the flaws of the then-current and popular delivery technology (the videotape) would be magnified as new home viewing and audio technologies were introduced. Even before HDTV began to be developed, broadcast and videotape images on projection TV and on new large-screen televisions showed a muddiness (both in sound and picture) that would not long be tolerated. Even so, demand for improved home viewing was continuing to grow, convincing the entertainment industry that it was going to have to pay attention to the development of new methods of delivery.

Before 1995, the best possible alternative delivery system to videotape was the laserdisc, based on technology available since the 1960s. But the laserdisc, expensive and as large as a long-playing (LP) record while holding only a limited amount of information on each disc, never caught on. Though a number of lovingly created laserdiscs had become available for rental or purchase by the 1990s, only serious movie buffs ever became enthusiastic about the medium. Other media were developed, including RCA's Capacitance Electronic Disc in the early 1980s, but, even when brought into the market, they sold poorly. Neither the time nor the price nor the technology was quite right.

Continuing its phobia that new technology would undermine profits, the film industry sought ways of ensuring its continued profitability in recognition of the inevitability of digital technology for home viewing. By 1995, two DVD standards had been proposed for the looming technology: the Toshiba consortium's Super Density format and the Multi Media Compact Disc that Philips and Sony had developed. The possibility of a new and expensive Betamax/VCR competition was averted by the creation of a new consortium of film studios and electronics firms to establish a single standard, which was agreed upon in late 1995. The standard covered a range of read-only, recordable, and rewritable applications on discs that would hold much more information than a VHS tape. Also, with proper care, they could be expected to last ten times as long. Because their size was to be identical to that of a CD, new carriers did not have to be developed (although CD readers cannot read DVDs), yet the DVD can store as much as 24 times as much information as a CD, if both sides are used. In a smart move, the DVD was designed to be compatible with extant technology. That is, DVD players can read CDs.

The video DVD was first offered for sale in the US in 1997. Today, the DVD-ROM (also first seen in 1997) is replacing the CD-ROM on new computers and shows up as a game-console possibility (both X-Box and PlayStation2 incorporate the DVD-ROM). In home viewing of movies, computer usage and data storage, and games, the DVD has become the vehicle of choice.

Almost as soon as DVD players became available, Blockbuster Video began offering them for rental along with the DVDs to play on them, phasing out laserdiscs at the same time. By the end of 1999, thousands of titles were available on DVD and millions of players had been sold (making machine rental relatively unnecessary). By 2001, it was possible for a film to outgross its first-weekend theatrical release during its first weekend in DVD release. In just four years, the DVD had muscled its way to the center of home viewing and quite possibly to the center of the film industry as a whole. In fact, small-screen viewings (dominated by the DVD) now account for nearly three-quarters of the global revenues of the film industry, almost exactly the reverse of the situation 25 years ago. This shift has completely reordered the priorities of the studios. It could even be said that theater showings today—and the panoply of cinema awards—are nothing more than a gigantic advertising campaign meant to stimulate the arena of real profit—home viewing. Look at the timing of the annual Academy Awards: The ceremony, fortuitously, takes place months after all of the nominated films have been released and when few are still in the theater—and when almost all are just becoming available on DVD.

From a marketing point of view, there is an almost perverse side to the promotion of home viewing. In an age saturated with advertising, the DVD can actually work as a way out of advertising bombardment, out of a world where the number of commercial images seen by the average American on a daily basis has doubled in just 20 years. Other new technologies are doing the same thing, placing more and more control over viewing in the hands of the viewer, much to the consternation of the entertainment and advertising industries. The general pervasiveness of advertising makes DVDs and these others (such as the TiVo digital video recorder that allows viewers to effectively delete all broadcast advertising) all the more enticing to many customers: control goes to the viewer in more ways than one, for it moves them further from direct interaction with the advertising inserted into broadcast and cable media.

The attraction of the DVD depends heavily on viewer control for other reasons as well, just as the videotape did. Quentin Tarantino, for example, explains this by describing what he calls the "hangout movie." These are the movies that fans watch many times, movies whose characters become something like those friends one can call at any time, friends one can relax alongside without the need to meet any expectations.

There's more than just that emotional aspect to the hangout movie. Such films go hand in hand with the video viewing habits that developed in the decades after the advent of the VCR, with the most important aspect being that complete control the viewer assumes over the movie. If one likes, it is possible to change the contrast or color of the film or, on DVD, even zoom into one corner of the frame. Don't like the songs but want to watch Bollywood films? Fast-forward past them; no one will know to fault you. Hungry? Hit pause and go rummaging in the kitchen. Answer the phone, if need be, or switch to television mode to keep track of the basketball game. Certainly, films viewed at home are rarely given the same rapt attention one can find in the theater, where distractions are limited, and audience members enforce a certain code of silent conduct. But, seen over and over, the hangout movie becomes more familiar to viewers than films seen only once in the theater can ever be—even if watched with concentration. No individual hangout movie viewing instance, then, requires rapt attention.

Such a freedom with film as viewers take with hangout movies offends a certain class of film buffs—the ones who call themselves *cineastes*—but the positive role that home viewing has played in the development of contemporary film culture cannot be underestimated. Also, as the film studios discovered, the fact of increased home viewing has yet to undermine the importance of the cinema experience to American viewers. Yet it remains that, as Tarantino echoing Zemeckis points out:

> you make these films for the theater experience, and outside of that you're left with this rather unglamorous presentation of your films. You don't even want to have to think about the fact that people are having conversations and doing the crossword puzzle while your movie's playing. . . . I've made a case for the benefits that access to video gives, but the availability devalues films at the same time. . . . In an ironic way, by making art available we make it more disposable.[5]

Disposable in an immediate sense, yes. But increasing film availability through home viewing has also ensured that the films will live—and be viewed—for a much longer time.

In addition to the ways it has changed our relations with films, home viewing has developed into a financial safety net for Hollywood. Films that flop on theatrical release—or that never even make it to that exalted state—can now prove profitable through longer-term video and DVD sales. A certain (growing) number of films are even developed as *direct to video*, sequels to children's films prime among them.

The growth of direct to video came not simply because it was seen as an avenue to make money from box-office flops, but also partly because of the difficulty small, independent films were having with finding distribution. At the same time the VCR was changing home-viewing habits, Hollywood, thanks in part to *Star Wars* (George Lucas, 1977), was beginning its fascination with *high concept* pictures (feeding audiences known vehicle types with familiar faces). The studios were also focusing more than ever on opening-weekend grosses, using that as the standard for film success, even in the face of the increasingly lucrative video market. In effect, this led to a shutting out of filmmakers whose films did not seem to have the wherewithal to sustain a big opening-weekend push. That is, filmmakers whose films could not be easily encapsulated for placement into the studios' promotional machinery were left out of the mix.

Lack of entry into studios and their funding mechanisms led would-be studio filmmakers in the 1980s to cast about for other backing sources, leading to what have now become classic urban legend stories of family credit-card manipulation, outright theft, and even the selling of blood in order to get films made. Though these desperate filmmakers did not recognize it at the time, they were developing what is now seen as the independent film movement that would counterbalance the bloated studio productions of the time.

Soon film companies were beginning to recognize the serious value of what had come to be known as *ancillaries* (videotape, cable, and broadcast television), especially in relation to the film libraries they owned. This, in fact, may be the start of the really significant impact of home viewing, for it was then, in the early 1980s, that Hollywood, for all its continued fascination with box-office returns, began to realize where its future income lay. Since that time, an increase in the abilities of a variety of media to interact with each other in new and often surprising ways has tied ancillaries more closely to each other and to the films and the industry that spawned them. This is also partially why the balance has shifted, moving profits so heavily to the ancillaries.

With film distribution becoming increasingly globalized, especially with the ease of access to home viewing possibilities, the movie studios have acted to try to maintain their profit centers while still opening up new markets and combating piracy. Videotape piracy has long been a billion-dollar business; to control DVD piracy (or to at least keep pirated versions from filtering into the United States and Europe where the film studios can expect to get higher prices), the world was divided into regions when DVD standards were established. DVDs meant for one region could not be played on players meant for another. This way, piracy in Asia, for example, could be restrained from spreading to other regions.

Not surprisingly, this reflects a two-tiered film distribution system that has been around for almost a century. Because domestic audiences could sustain higher prices, Hollywood would release its films in the United States first, and would recoup its costs at home, even making some profit. International distribution, when it came after the end of the first American run, was gravy, though admission prices were reduced (making the films competitive with locally-produced films). Only recently, and in the face of the threat of the pirated versions that were becoming available before a film was released internationally, has Hollywood begun to open films at the same time elsewhere in the world as it does in the United States.

Though the film industry wants to regionalize DVDs, one of the technology's greatest areas of promise is in a real globalization of cinema that will, ultimately, reduce the influence of Hollywood and give national cinemas a great deal of improved exposure. Some of these cinemas operate on unique presumptions, ones that outsiders have a hard time accepting. The most notable of these is Bollywood (also the biggest film-producing center in the world), which uses formulas that American audiences, for example, have a hard time adjusting to. The song and dance sequences in Bollywood films tend to be long, and are stylized in ways almost inaccessible to people not habituated to them. Because of their portability (regional restrictions notwithstanding), DVDs from Bollywood are bound to show up more and more frequently all over the world, and viewers outside of India are going to begin to learn and accept Bollywood style. The same will probably happen to the national cinemas of other countries, brightening and widening the possibilities for film experience everywhere.

There well may never have been a successful independent (or Indie) movement if it had not been for the demands of home viewing. The rise of video rental led to a rise in demand for product to fill the store shelves, a demand that the studios, as usual, were slow to meet. Thus, Indie films such as *The Return of the Secaucus 7* (John Sayles, 1980), *My Dinner with André* (Louis Malle, 1981), *Eating Raoul* (Paul Bartel, 1982), and *Repo Man* (Alex Cox, 1984) could find more viewers than they had found through their (comparatively) small theatrical releases, and so through video could also sustain their makers for a much longer period of time. The rising popularity of the videotape rental (and cable) also allowed slightly older outsider directors such as John Waters (*Pink Flamingos*, 1972) and David Lynch (*Eraserhead*, 1977) to gain currency—in more ways than one.

The growing success of Indie films in the 1980s, and, a little later, the correspondingly increased interest in the Sundance Film Festival (formerly the U.S. Film Festival), has led that movement away from being an outsider by any definition. The Indie movement has developed its own system of distribution (through festival exhibition and the ensuing bidding for rights by "independent" distributors) and gate-keeping. No longer is there the free-for-all that could allow Spike Lee, the Coën Brothers, Joseph Jarmusch, Gus Van Sant, Steven Soderbergh, and Quentin Tarantino to become industry heavyweights. Instead, the Indie movement has moved towards a codification as ponderous as that of the studios it was initially reacting against. In fact, it could be argued that the Indie movement of the 1980s and early 1990s was effectively dead by the year 2000, its death throes beginning in 1994 with the release and huge success of Tarantino's *Pulp Fiction*. The shoe-string Indie film, picked up by a distributor and bringing in millions at the box-office was no longer a possibility—unless it had a gimmick like Daniel Myrick and Eduardo Sánchez's 1999 movie *The Blair Witch Project*. The outside found itself once more kicked . . . well, *out*.

With the festival system no longer as open to the really new and untried, the DVD and direct to video may well begin to supplant the film-festival system for promotion of independent films and the work of as-yet-unknown directors. Already festivals have become more elitist and celebrity driven, and filmmakers who feel shut out are increasingly turning to DVD technology for distribution. With accessible and simple transfer technology making them more and more common, independent DVDs may even start to show up in their own sections of video stores, for both sale and rental. As viewing technology improves and prices fall, venues for public viewing of these DVDs are bound to grow, venues that may serve the same purpose that the church basements and coffeehouses that nurtured the avant-garde 16mm filmmakers of the 1950s and '60s.

A new Indie movement, in other words, may result from the possibilities offered by the DVD. This one might be distinct from the older movement, in that it won't be dependent on traditional distribution networks. The Internet may offer distribution possibilities not yet fully explored by filmmakers, or that may work in conjunction with DVDs.

Perhaps the most subversive possibility of the DVD is just this: It could conceivably supplant the film and video distribution systems that are at the heart of Hollywood profitability. While the film industry concentrates on piracy, this separate threat may be making those fears of piracy moot: If viewing starts to move from home to theater through exposure to independent DVDs (reversing the earlier trend), the entire structure of the industry will be altered with centralized control of distribution becoming a fading memory.

Currently, few theaters are equipped to show digital movies—even films made digitally, such as *Star Wars II: Attack of the Clones* (George Lucas, 2002) have had to be transferred to 35mm stock for most theater showings. This will change, though, for the cost of a digital copy is a tiny fraction of the cost of a 35mm print. From the point of view of the film companies, however, this has a downside: It will be possible for these same theaters to show cheaply made independent films without a huge cost to the filmmakers. Still, the savings are so great that the studios will risk the competition.

One of the most persistent clichés about the movies is that it is mass art, and that the aim is always to find as large an audience as possible, that art cinema is nearly an oxymoron. In today's Hollywood thinking, this seems to mean targeting teenage boys, who then pull others (girlfriends, parents) into the theaters and who are likely to see the films two or more times. Like the people who think it takes less talent to produce a book for children than one for adults, certain viewers feel that movies for children (including teenage boys) are not film art at all. Most of the films aimed at teenage boys suffer from this viewpoint. As a result, older audiences often try to avoid them (though that is increasingly difficult, if one is interested in movies at all), forgetting that the fact of the intended primary audience has little relation to the film's artistic value—or the interest it can hold for other audiences.

On the other hand, it has also been argued that, to reach the widest audience, a work must be generic, with no unique expression, catering to the broadest (or lowest) standard of taste. Hollywood accepts this to some extent, using focus groups and surveys to make decisions about movies that really should be taken in relation to the art. Take that to its logical extension, and it is clear that all movies should be the same movie. Obviously, that's not true; audiences complain when the movies are too much like others; they insist on a certain degree of originality.

It is clearly quite possible for a movie on a narrow, unusual topic to find a wide, diverse audience. *The Blair Witch Project*, in black and white, with low production values, and with a juvenile premise, attracted audiences everywhere it played, and of every demographic. Mel Gibson's *The Passion of the Christ* (2004), a distinctly personal film from an idiosyncratic viewpoint, has proven incredibly successful. Michael Moore's political outsider film *Fahrenheit 9/11* (2004) became, within weeks of release, the highest-grossing documentary ever. None of these succeeded simply because of critical acclaim or a huge Hollywood publicity campaign. Quite the contrary, for the most part. Each of these, like many, many others, shows that mass audiences can and will accept distinct expression. If the movie studios cannot accept that audiences are not easily led, easily satisfied sheep and fail to act on it, alternative distribution outlets will. DVDs may prove to be at the heart of this distribution, providing the means for finding new directors and actors involved in intriguing, individualistic projects. Though there may be plenty of good movies aimed at teenage boys, audiences are there for a wider variety of film products. DVD technology may make it possible for them to be found.

DVDs are already being used to distribute amateur films, instructional material, and more. Because they are inexpensive to produce, easy to mail (and cheap, for they qualify for a Post Office media mail rate), DVDs are popping up all over the place for numerous purposes. NetFlix, a subscription DVD library that uses the Internet and the mails, has become a huge success. Soon, independent filmmakers will find ways of using the mails to promote and distribute their films, further undermining the current distribution system. One Internet service, Film Movement (at www.filmmovement.com) offers a different independent DVD per month to subscribers in an attempt to establish its own successful alternative distribution system.

It is certainly true that the studios are interested in the lowest common denominator, but—even in Hollywood—niche movies still manage to get produced. The studios are learning that what is meant by "as large an audience as possible" can be a number of different things, and that what should be classified as an audience is changing as a result of home viewing. A film that can endure beyond its theatrical showing may ultimately find a much larger audience than the blockbuster of the week—and make more money (though not all at once).

Even so, the studios still think in terms of theatrical gross, with ancillaries as mere gravy. As more time passes and the strength of home viewing becomes more and more apparent, this will change. If it does not, if the studios continue to think only in terms of huge, immediate gross (as they are now doing even with DVDs, pushing DVD releases the way they do theatrical releases), an alternate means of access to movies on DVD may arise, a real independent distribution system that is not based (as the studio system is) on recouping a huge investment as quickly as possible. Some argue that such a system will even bypass the DVD itself, that it will be a Web-based system. If retro individuals want personal copies, they will download the original, burning their own DVD and copying a cover from the web.

Already, creative new ways of using DVDs to cash in on theatrical release are appearing—just as they are for the DVD releases themselves. For example, an animated DVD prequel to *Van Helsing* (Stephen Sommers, 2004) called *Van Helsing: The London Assignment* (Sharon Bridgeman, 2004) was released on DVD just days after the longer film appeared in theaters, with members of the *Van Helsing* cast providing voices for the shorter film. A new DVD issue of Roland Emmerich's *Independence Day* (1996) was scheduled to coincide with the theatrical release of his *The Day After Tomorrow* (2004).

In addition, filmmakers are coordinating more closely than ever with game makers, scheduling the release of games to fit with both theatrical and DVD release of the films that inspired them. *King Arthur* (Antoine Fuqua, 2004), *Starsky & Hutch* (Todd Phillips, 2004), *The Punisher* (Jonathan Hensleigh, 2004), and *Around the World in 80 Days* (Frank Coraci, 2004) all had video games planned for DVD release even before the movies appeared in the theater.

Other aspects of the film world are changing because of the DVD as well. For decades, films have been identified in academic writing by title, director, and year of initial theatrical release (or, sometimes, just by title and year of release). This system worked fine as long as all ancillary releases reflected that initial version or looked to it as the standard, the original. Today, however, with DVD versions being released that are substantially different from the initial theatrical version and that are sometimes more authoritative, this method of identification is becoming unwieldy. When talking about *Blade Runner*, for example, it is important to distinguish between two quite different versions, both of which had theatrical releases (though the second was as much ballyhoo for the videotape as a release in its own right), but the old system has no way of satisfactorily dealing with the two versions as legitimate yet competing versions of the movie. Soon, there will be a new, probably changed, version of *Blade Runner* on DVD. Will a way be found to refer to it that doesn't make the DVD subservient in discussion to the theatrically-released film? These days, films as they are released on DVD may actually be purposefully more authoritative than the theatrical release. The directors, knowing the restrictions on running time that need attention when preparing a film for the theater, may make longer, more complete versions for eventual DVD release, cutting their films down temporarily for the theater. Which, then, is the "real" film? Other filmmakers are reworking their older films, taking advantage of new technology. Should George Lucas's *Star Wars: A New Hope* be a 1977 film, or should its date be considered 1997, when it was released again in a remastered and expanded version?

As of yet, no standardized way of indicating edition has emerged within the cinema world, though no doubt one will eventually. The Internet Movie Database (imdb.com) lists Charlie Chaplin's *The Gold Rush* with a 1925 release date. Yet a later version, edited by Chaplin (it is substantially shorter than the earlier version) with both a soundtrack composed by Chaplin and a narration—written and read, not surprisingly, by Chaplin—and released in 1942 is given primacy of place on the DVD release of the movie (though the DVD does contain both versions). *Vertigo*, in its restored version, differs from the movie Hitchcock saw released, especially in its soundtrack (a long-forgotten stereo recording is used in place of the one Hitchcock had chosen—a small difference, but a change, nonetheless). Should it be listed as a 1959 movie? And is the date of theatrical release of the restored version of *Vertigo* more important than the release date of the DVD, given that it is the DVD that carries the film into the future?

Though these questions may not seem tremendously important, they do point to the fact that the DVD is changing the movies—literally. The tendency is—and will likely remain—to give primacy to the theatrical versions of films, but this may not always be appropriate, and will be less so as time passes. As more films are released first on DVD, some of these will certainly show up later in theatrical runs. If this happens more than a year after the DVD release, which date should be given for the movie?

Quoted in *The New York Times*, Hollywood talent agent John Lesher reflected a common view in the industry about the DVD: It may be making money for the studios now, but "in five years when you can download a movie as fast as a song, that will go away."[6] The same has been said of books, but it hasn't happened. And the argument that it is downloading that has hurt the sale of music CDs is suspect, at best. Whatever its ultimate fate, however, the DVD, clearly, is already changing the film world in myriad ways.

What we now call the DVD may be completely altered at some time in the future. It may become something akin to the holodeck of Gene Roddenberry's *Star Trek* television and movie series, where it becomes a room that can mimic the entire universe of a story, putting the viewer right in the middle of it, making the viewer even an actor in the scenario. Or it could develop into the *SQUID* (Superconducting Quantum Interface Device) of *Strange Days* (Kathryn Bigelow, 1995), a recording and playback device that makes the viewer experience the situation exactly as the recorder did.

It is unlikely, however, that the DVD will disappear as a discrete item, replaced by Internet access to movies. Americans are more comfortable with things than with access. They want to have what they see as their own, not communal rights to something stored far away—just try to get a city dweller to give up a car, even if mass transit is available, even if the occasional rental is cheaper and more convenient.

Finally, the DVD, more than just being a conveyance for movies, is becoming a whole new means of viewing films, of interacting with them, and learning about them. This is a technology where the medium is certainly changing the message it conveys. Over the next few years, even the medium will change—but it will probably remain, like the videotape and the DVD, a discrete, physical item that can be collected and stored at home.

Chapter 2

CINÉMATHÈQUE
FRANÇAISE
AT OUR HOUSE

It didn't take long for a clichéd image of the videotape collector to appear in the public consciousness. Soon after the VCR appeared on the market, it was the harried film buff, the one who always had to set the timer before going out, to record a particular movie off of television, hoping to gain a clearer tape this time than the last one. He or she always said it really was preferable to watch films in theaters, but so few of the really good ones were being screened. Later these same people were the ones with the dual-cassette machine and the separate rewinders, now more relaxed, who were always willing to let someone tape from their collection—as long as they could tape one of yours, as well—but who always said you really should see the movie in the theater, too. Even, later, when prerecorded tapes flooded the market and these collectors had abandoned all those home recordings for commercial versions, the collectors still only sheepishly admitted to the fact that their passion was, in fact, home viewing as much as it was films. They knew only too well the weaknesses of their videotape collections in comparison to what could be seen on a theater screen.

The image of the DVD collector appeared just as quickly after the introduction of that technology. This time, however, there was no need for the collector to hide or excuse the addiction. In fact, DVD owners were quickly demanding that the packagers set the bar higher and higher for home viewing. The theater was no longer even mentioned. Packagers quickly recognized that they could issue more and more DVD editions of the same movie, and that the collectors—if the extras and the quality were sufficiently expanded and higher than the older editions—would gladly shell out money for a movie they already owned. Widescreen and anamorphic quickly became bywords for the cognoscenti. Collecting DVDs developed a snob appeal that collecting videotapes never managed. Home viewing of movies finally became a recognized, viable method of viewing and learning about movies.

Though there remain a few film purists who even now think of it as an abomination, home viewing of movies has an ancient, reputable pedigree. It has been around at least since 1922, when the Pathé-Baby was first introduced in France, not long before Kodak's 16-millimeter systems came on the market in the US. The Pathé-Baby, hand-cranked, showing 9.5 mm film with sprocket holes in the center between the frames, made it possible for French audiences to see Chaplin films, Felix the Cat, and even feature films such as *Napoléon* (Abel Gance, 1927) at home.

Though cumbersome and (at first) relatively rare, the Baby stayed on the market for a long time, even past World War II. Its fans delighted in seeing films at home (just as DVD fans now do) and were collectors—just as are the growing number of people with a hundred or more DVDs lined up in their living rooms. Clearly, the history of the DVD has to take the Baby into consideration, for it was certainly the equivalent technology of its generation—though more limited, of course, and not as cheap or easy to use.

Just as a history of film on DVD has to look back to the Baby and to Kodak's Kodascope in the United States, it also has to look at the history of film itself. Though the temptation is to define film reductively (through a definition of the word), we have come to understand that film covers a great deal more than an image projected on a screen through celluloid. It does include movies as they are viewed in milieu well beyond the theater and by means quite different from a projector. A history of film also includes a great deal more than its creators. Films are created by their viewers almost as much as by the filmmakers, for filmmaking is a corporate art, for the most part. It is the work of a group of people who rarely operate without consideration of the commercial possibilities of their products—and, therefore, they keep the potential audience always in mind as the product is made. The idea of a movie as simply the result of an individual vision and sensibility has long been abandoned. Writers, actors, producers, directors and, yes, even audiences are involved.

So, the history of film has been forced to expand, to include a history of viewing and different means of viewing. As Tom Gunning, a historian of film at the University of Chicago, writes, there is no question that cinema now means something very different than it did even a generation ago. Is video a form entirely different from cinema, or simply a new means of distribution . . . ? Are the technological differences between film and video strong enough to determine an aesthetic disparity or do they simply represent alternate modes of exhibition? . . . [A]n enormous transformation of movie watching has taken place, from a public theatrical event to an increasingly private act of domestic consumption.[1]

This transformation is continuing, of course, and it is forcing a different look at the past in terms of the movies, at the place of home viewing (and there certainly was one) even before television, and the first "transformation" of film viewing. Home viewing in the 1920s sowed the seeds for the phenomenal growth of private viewing later. Television watered and nurtured the shoots. Videotape was responsible for sapling growth, and the DVD is helping move it to maturity. This thriving aspect of the movies is forcing that expansion of our conceptions of film history.

Though it is easy to talk of revolutions and change, all "overnight sensations" come from years of preparation. This is no less true of the DVD. Though it may seem to have appeared out of nowhere, it really comes from the confluence of a number of factors, many of which had been building for years. The interest in classic films, for example, has been growing for decades, frustrated only by technological limitations. And home viewing itself, as we see here, goes back to the 1920s.

Since the introduction of the Pathé-Baby, home film viewing has usually been associated with collecting (with the exception, of course, of the television film-viewing in the first decades of television). People have long wanted to own their favorite films, cherishing them as though they were mounted butterflies when they did get them. So, a history of the film on DVD also has to look at the history of the collector—which, of course, is tied up with the history of film itself, and of the technologies that have driven it and changed it.

Paradoxically, the present-day collector will also change perceptions of the history of the movies, even as far back as Georges Méliès and the Lumière brothers. History, after all, is based on contemporary conceptions of the past, not simply on the past itself. As of now, DVD releases of old films are, perforce, selective. Maybe, one day, there can be complete editions of the works of early filmmakers, but even such collections will be missing the films that have disappeared completely over the years (and these are many). As it is, most of us can only see old films through the lens of a packager, someone who has already made decisions about what we can and cannot obtain. Packagers respond to demand, and demand often comes from what the public perceives that technology can provide. Consumers won't long accept, for example, the poor transfers on DVD from worn prints of John Wayne's Republic Westerns of the 1930s that are currently available. Skill, money, and time will be spent restoring these to something akin to their original state—and this will be done to Wayne's movies even as better films (perhaps) languish in tatters. Restored, these Westerns will be considered even more important than they had been, the very act of restoration having given them a sort of historical imprimatur. Similar cycles have occurred throughout the history of film, starting even with the Pathé-Baby. A film released for home viewing would have had a certain cachet with some—but others would have considered it, by virtue of that release, merely the film version of pop pulp.

Though small and simple, however it might have been viewed, the Baby clearly had possibilities far beyond the viewing of home movies of birthday parties. It was developed specifically to tap the craze for commercial movies that had been growing extraordinarily since the end of the World War I, not as might be assumed, simply so that amateurs could show the films they had made themselves. That, for the most part, came later, as the cost of amateur filmmaking came down, allowing enthusiasts room to play without bankrupting themselves.

The Baby—with, of course, no accessory sound apparatus—was introduced at the height of the popularity of the silent film, a form of motion-picture art soon to be swept almost to oblivion by the advent—and the astonishing, unexpected popularity—of sound movies. Though the cinema has gone through a number of revolutions since (each, including this first one, decried as the ruination of the art), none had as extensive an impact—at least not as quickly. Sound brushed away the silent film so completely that even now we have not managed to reconstruct with any accuracy or extent the body of pre-sound filmic work.

As early as 1925, just as home viewing was gathering steam, the movie studios were experimenting with a variety of methods for including sound as part of their pictures, including Western Electrics' system of matching records to film tried out at Warner Brothers. Soon, as possibilities clarified, the Vitaphone Corporation was formed by Warner Brothers and Western Electric. Warner Brothers began its work on sound with short films showing musical performances and then progressed to *Don Juan* (Alan Crosland,

1926), the first successful film to utilize a recorded soundtrack and sound effects, though it still relied on dialogue cards for speech.

Not only was it found to be relatively inexpensive to convert theatres to sound capability but the new system actually cut costs also (upscale theaters sometimes employed full orchestras; mid-scale, an organist and maybe more; the low end, at least a pianist—all more expensive than a recording). Because the projector and the Vitaphone sound system were almost completely mechanically separate, there was always the danger that any problem with one would throw it out of synchronization with the other. Glitches of this sort are most obvious with speech, so it is not surprising that the first sound films stuck to dialogue cards. *Don Juan* did quite well at the box office; other films, such as *The Wedding March* (Erich von Stroheim, 1928), were begun using the same technique and the stage for the coming revolution was set. All that remained was to acquire a little more confidence in the synchronization—and that came soon.

So, despite misgivings in the rest of the film industry, it should not have been all that surprising when, in October of 1927, Warner initiated the era of the spoken word in the feature film with Al Jolson's words, "Wait a minute, wait a minute: you ain't heard nothing yet," introducing the song "Toot-Toot-Tootsie" in *The Jazz Singer* (Alan Crosland, 1927). Within just a few months, *Lights of New York* (Bryan Foy, 1928), the first "all-talkie" and another Warner release, had made it clear that there was no going back. MGM quickly followed suit. It's first musical, *Broadway Melody of 1929* (Harry Beaumont, 1929), even won the 1930 Academy Award for Best Picture. By the end of 1930, sound films had become the only acceptable medium for feature films—and thousands of reels of silent films quickly headed for oblivion. Lost was a whole film language based, in part, on camera movement that was now impossible (for the moment) due to the constraints of ponderous sound technology.

As Norma Desmond (played by Gloria Swanson) puts it in *Sunset Boulevard* (Billy Wilder, 1950), "There was a time when this business had the eyes of the whole, wide world. But that wasn't good enough for them. Oh, no. They had to have the ears of the world, too. So they opened their big mouths and out came talk, talk, talk." Talented performers were brushed aside (including Swanson herself), as were great directors (one of these was later a Swanson co-star in *Sunset Boulevard*, Erich von Stroheim). Almost unnoticed, a stylized and sophisticated way of presenting and seeing film disappeared, drowning in that "talk, talk, talk." Not even Charlie Chaplin, then the world's biggest star, could completely buck the trend. For *City Lights* (1931), his last silent film, Chaplin recorded the soundtrack he had written and added it to the film, accepting that theaters were no longer equipped for live musical accompaniment.

To make way for sound, and the equipment for sound recording (which took up a tremendous amount of room), the studios needed to create space. As the silent films had clearly lost their economic value, they became the victims of sound for a second time, losing their space in the studio vaults. Well over half of the total number made has never been recovered; the past was swept away in the excitement over the new sound possibilities. The studios should not be vilified for this: not only were the films now seen as worthless, but they were dangerous and quite likely to deteriorate anyway. Film stock of the time (it wasn't until the 1950s that acetate replaced nitrate for feature films) was made with a nitrate base that was extremely flammable (even able to burn under water) and susceptible to changes in temperature. Opening an old film canister could be quite an adventure even under the best of circumstances: it was quite as likely that the contents would be a putrid amorphous goo—or a mass with the solidity of a hockey puck—as they would be a viewable film. There was not even a way to accurately judge the state of a film's deterioration, to estimate how much 'life' the film had left in it.

Though sound's triumph was complete in the marketplace, film fans in all sorts of places recognized the non-economic value of their old favorites. A few of these fans set out to save the silents, amassing libraries, sometimes even off the backs of dump trucks, some of which later became the starting points for formal *cinémathèques*. As late as the 1980s, caches of films from the 1920s and earlier were occasionally turning up, making up for the old loss, if only in a small way. The people who put together those collections were the first heroes of film preservation.

Just at the time when sound was beginning its move toward domination, one of these heroes, then a young boy in Paris who had been a film fan since even before his tenth birthday in 1924, became fascinated with the Pathé-Baby. As his teens progressed, he started collecting silent films to show on the one his parents had finally bought for him. He certainly wasn't the only one to do this, but Henri Langlois's home viewing and love of the disappearing silent films would lead him to become the most important film collector of his time—perhaps of any time. He would prove to be responsible for the salvation of more silent films than anyone in the world, and his contributions did not stop there. His focus on film itself, not on its place or means of

showing, led to the start of a world-wide film preservation movement. So
great was his contribution that, in 1973, he was the recipient of an honorary
Academy Award "for his devotion to the art of film, his massive contributions in preserving its past and his unswerving faith in its future."[2]

By the 1930s, with sound film taking over the cinema world and many
of the silent films that he had learned to love moldering in forgotten ware-
houses, Langlois already knew what his mission would be; he had to find a
way to save what, even then, was clearly being lost, films whose achievements
no longer counted when measured against the standards of sound or profit.
He joined with others like him in the French *ciné-clubs* (which showed films
in small venues, even in homes) that tried to fill the gap when the commercial theaters converted to sound, zealously seeking out the silent films that
they saw as examples of art beyond what the sound stages were producing,
showing them and collecting them with equal zeal. These clubs sowed the
seeds for the movement that would eventually save a portion of what was
already often thought lost entirely, a movement that would make possible the
film-restoration projects that, almost half a century later (and partly as a
result, once again, of home viewing of films), began to bring these films to
life once more.

The library of film Langlois eventually founded in the mid-1930s, *Cinémathèque Française*, would become a repository for films of all sorts, from all
nations and all periods. Langlois had taken to heart the lesson of the end of
the silent era, that films are cared for by the studios only when they retain
economic value. He understood that the film stock of the time was unstable
and needed great care for preservation, that the film studios were not interested in preservation, and that no one else was as dedicated to film preservation as he was. Langlois also recognized the importance of film culturally; he
wanted the films he loved to be seen, not merely preserved. He reasoned that
his showings would promote preservation, too, as more people learned to
appreciate the older films. So he worked always in a twofold manner: preserving film and making sure it was shown.

Langlois's passion was further inflamed by the German occupation of
France during World War II. The Nazis, for the most part, wanted to destroy
all films exhibiting ideas anathema to them—and that was most films. With
the complicity of at least one understanding German army officer and film
enthusiast, Frank Hensel, Langlois was able to collect an astonishingly large
number of movies from those the occupiers themselves had seized—at the
same time that he was hiding others from them. In one famous photograph,

he is seen pushing a baby carriage, the blanket covering films instead of an infant, taking movies from one safe house to another. War or no war, Langlois never stopped collecting and preserving, continuing to amass films under the noses of the Nazi occupiers. He even managed to get films out of Germany, where they were in greater danger, to the relative safety of France.

Perhaps it was his understanding of the role film can play in people's lives that led to Langlois's peripheral role in the *Resistance* during the occupation. Morale, of course, is always critical in war time, and the secret home film showings that Langlois provided were most certainly important to keeping up the spirits of those who were invited—if for no other reason than that the showings were mud in the occupiers' eyes.

Because of his hidden stockpiles, after the war Langlois was immediately able to help satisfy the pent-up demand for movies on the part of the French public. Because he returned films, no proof required, to their pre-war owners, those grateful owners, including French distributors of Hollywood films, quickly found ways of getting recent films to Langlois, placing him in a central position in the French cinema world that he would hold for the rest of his life. Cinémathèque Française exploded in importance as the French drank in the huge backlog of movies that had been denied them during the occupation. Because of the Cinémathèque, France also quickly stepped into the forefront of both film scholarship and European film production, providing leadership for film the likes of which has not been seen since.

Though Langlois's contribution is to film as a whole, home viewing clearly played an important part in the development of both his passion and his knowledge. Yet many cineastes argue that film cannot be appreciated if it is not seen in the theater. Home viewing is a mere distraction, a diversion, and not a place for "real" film appreciation. Even if this were true, the example of Langlois makes it clear that home viewing can have a positive impact on film culture as a whole, just as it did in his case; just as it did when the home videotape player was introduced and cultural knowledge of film exploded throughout America. Just as it is doing now, with the rise of the DVD, which is allowing film buffs to build libraries of their own, thus making film restoration more financially viable than ever before, with these fans providing a huge market for the renewed movies.

Not only was Langlois able to secure current films for viewing after the war, but his retrospectives and presentations of non-Hollywood foreign films spawned even greater interest in world cinema and in cinema's past, an interest in cinema unlike anything the world had ever seen. His screenings at the

Cinémathèque, along with the work of André Bazin and the journal *Cahiers du cinéma*, inflamed an interest in film that was responsible in large part for the beginnings of a real, sustained world-wide film scholarship and, later, for the *Nouvelle Vague* or New Wave that influenced cinema everywhere in the 1960s. This movement was heavily dependent on knowledge of earlier film, especially in its promotion of attempts to combine elements of both formalism and realism and its frequent referentiality and homage to favorite, often forgotten *auteurs*. No less than François Truffaut and Jean-Luc Godard were able to learn about cinema made before their time and shown beyond their local theaters in large part because of the passion and dedication of Langlois and his Cinémathèque.

Truffaut and Godard, along with other future directors (including Eric Rohmer), came to be called "les enfants du Cinémathèque" (the children of the Cinémathèque), so great was its influence on their future careers. Rohmer describes the basis of its importance: "Can you imagine a budding musician who was unable to listen to the works of Bach and Beethoven, a young writer who was not able to read the works of the past by going to a library? . . . For the cinema to have a future, . . . its past could not be allowed to die."[3] The Cinémathèque had kept old films alive. In terms of the history of film, the importance of this preservation cannot be overstated. As Truffaut has said, "The Cinémathèque was really a haven for us then, a refuge, our home, everything."[4] It was the heart of the cinema. The ability to find access to films and to study them without undue difficulty was extremely important to the Nouvelle Vague, for this was a movement based in part on the very scholarship that was exploding as the movement began. Both Truffaut and Godard wrote about film before they made films. The heated discussions on the way home after Cinémathèque showings are still mentioned reverently by film fans born long after they had passed into memory. A new film nightly, a Cinémathèque reality, was a heaven that could only be entered into in America when videotape rental became a reality a generation later.

The Cinémathèque offered something to France that is only now becoming available in the United States, and that is a way of linking passion for film, an avenue for watching and studying numerous films from a wide variety of times and places, and a forum for finding others who share that passion. It is the DVD that, along with the Internet, is making possible a new generation of "les enfants du Cinémathèque" in America. Maybe, one day, once they, too, have produced great filmmakers, they will be known as "the children of the DVD."

At one point in the 1950s, Langlois was responsible for the showing of over 30 different films per week, sometimes up to 2,000 a year. Nothing in the United States has ever equaled that viewing possibility—and nothing outside of the introduction of the VCR (continued by the DVD) has even approached its influence on film viewers and filmmakers. Nothing else, certainly, ever provided the "home" for director wannabes that Truffaut found at the Cinémathèque.

To really comprehend the extent of the impact of Langlois (and to imagine what the impact of the DVD may be one day), we need only look to the *affaire Langlois* of 1968, sparked when André Malraux, at that time the French Minister of Culture, tried to have Langlois removed as the head of the Cinémathèque, whose funding, more and more, was coming from the government. Though the world knows of the May 1968 troubles in France, not many know that the confrontations really began to heat up months earlier, in February, when Langlois's ouster was orchestrated and film fans took to the streets.

Bernardo Bertolucci's film *The Dreamers* (2003) uses the events that ensued upon the attempted removal of Langlois as the backdrop for its own action, even incorporating into the movie news clips of François Truffaut and the actor Jean-Pierre Léaud (who played Antoine Doinel in a series of Truffaut films) leading the protests. It was amazing, really: on February 14, 1968, thousands of protesters assembled near the Cinémathèque screening room to support Langlois—only to be charged by club-swinging police!

At no time before or since has a bloody confrontation occurred in defense of film preservation and showings, and probably nothing like it will ever happen again. The protests went on until the middle of April, when Langlois was reinstated. A few weeks later, protests resumed—this time for serious political reasons, though the experience of the *affaire Langlois* protests certainly contributed to the perception that change could be made through the streets. Richard Roud, a follower of Langlois and one-time Director of the New York Film Festival, paraphrases filmmaker Jean Rouch speaking to the February 14th crowd, saying that this was "the beginning of a cultural revolution, the first consciousness-raising among youth, and a rejection of the government's increasing attempts to regulate and control French life."[5] Though it is unlikely that the DVD will ever spawn such sentiments, its impact may be just as great.

The example of Langlois, along with recognition of his contribution to film studies and film appreciation, should make it clear that film, to be fully understood, needs to be considered as more than a creature of the theater. Though certainly limited, home viewing can lead to the development of film aficionados of the best sort, ultimately helping protect and enhance even the large screen. It can also lead directly to the preservation of older films, as it did in Langlois's time and as it is doing now, when the demand for classic films for home viewing is making it economically feasible for studios to put up the money for careful restoration.

Fifty years after Langlois first encountered the Pathé-Baby, another boy, also already passionate about film, also discovered a new technology for home viewing—though this time it was the VCR. This boy grew to be a man who, like Langlois, is proving to be an important force for film preservation, though he is best known right now as a director. He is Quentin Tarantino. It isn't yet clear how extensive Tarantino's effect will prove to be on film preservation—and he is not alone as a preservationist: the concerns of others, including fellow director Martin Scorsese, are helping change our cultural attitudes toward film preservation. These have led to the creation, among other things, of the Criterion label, which has become a locus of intelligent film preservation and presentation via laserdisc and DVD—but the enthusiasm Tarantino shows for films of all sorts, as a collector and film-festival sponsor, is certainly a good sign for the future of cinema—especially if we look back and judge what he is doing by the enormous contribution of Cinémathèque Française to film and film culture before him.

Tarantino has at least one important similarity to Langlois: to both, any film is important (an attitude that seems to go hand-in-glove with collecting and with home viewing). *New Yorker* writer Larisa MacFarquhar heard this as she watched Tarantino address the filmgoers at one of his Austin, Texas festivals: "They may not be the world's best movies, he tells the audience, but they are movies and, as such, are worthy of respect."[6] Langlois, who dedicated his life to the preservation of *all* film, would have agreed wholeheartedly. Both would understand the film scholar Stanley Cavell when he writes, "in the case of films, it is generally true that you do not really like the highest instances unless you also like typical ones."[7] And unless you respect not just the typical ones, but even the bad ones. As a proponent of the *auteur* theory of film creation (stating that the director is the center of a film's vision and being), Langlois might actually argue that a certain director is not worth considering, but he would never make such a judgment about an individual film. A film can surprise one, after all, leading to a new appreciation of its director.

Significantly, the attitudes of the two collectors both side-step or ignore the arguments that claim a superiority for artistic endeavors meant for a small, appreciative audience over those aimed at a mass audience. They saw that art could be found in unexpected places and that it did not have to be specifically aimed at elite, artistically-aware audiences. In fact, Langlois promoted—and Tarantino promotes—talents who have never been seen as part of the elite, bringing new appreciation, in particular, to nearly-forgotten actors. Langlois brought Louise Brooks back to familiarity for millions, just as Tarantino has done for Pam Grier. Both believe that mass art can be great art, that the extent of the target audience (or even the perceived value of that audience) has nothing to do with the artistic quality of the work itself.

Both also changed perception of earlier genres of film. Langlois forced film scholars to reconsider pre-World War I Italian film (among others) just as Tarantino has been making it difficult to ignore the cheap genre films that he references so frequently in his own movies. In both cases, the breadth of the cinema has been expanded by the interest of an individual collector.

Collectors who do not share the attitude toward film of Langlois and Tarantino are ever destined to footnote status in the history of cinema. Sure, there is always an avant-garde trying to attract an elite audience through experimental film, and a place for the "middle brow" film of the Merchant/Ivory sort, focusing on the viewing yens of the college educated (just as there will always be other niche genres from time to time, such as Blaxploitation films or Hong Kong action movies)—but the greatest films, like the greatest plays (such as Shakespeare's), manage to rise above any genre, even the most elite. Tarantino and Langlois are important collectors, in large part, because they never lost sight of this fact. Their love is (and was) for the whole, not just a part. So far, serious DVD collectors—at least, those who share their enthusiasm over the Internet—exhibit this same attitude.

One of the criticisms constantly leveled against the film industry is that it is controlled by faceless "suits" more interested in the reactions of focus groups than on the creation of art, more interested in turning a profit than in creating something with lasting artistic value. A film enthusiast of the Langlois/Tarantino ilk may acknowledge this, but will concentrate on the real and exciting art that manages to get made despite the obstacles, and there is plenty of it, no matter the genre or the intended audience. The individual vision (if that's what is required for real art) still comes through—cinema is nothing if it is impersonal.

There is room in the cinema universe for all sorts of movies: The creation of a thoughtless chase movie does not mean that some other, more serious work of art is not getting made (the people involved in the one project would not likely be interested in the other—and someone interested in funding the one would rarely be interested in the other). On the other side, that someone collects Roger Corman films does not mean that they might not also own films of Jean Renoir. A look at the DVD collections on DVDAficionado.com or guzzlefish.com (two of the websites where collectors can list their DVDs) shows that serious contemporary collections, for the most part, extend well beyond any sort of genre boundaries. Though they may never have heard of Henri Langlois and the words *Quentin Tarantino* may be nothing more than a name they want or don't want to collect, the growing clan of DVD collectors is following in the footsteps of these two men. The DVD, as a collectible, is showing the real, untapped strength of cinema as a popular, enduring art form.

Like Langlois, Tarantino has been accused of trivializing cinema by a concentration on films that others see as kitsch, on movies that are merely imitation and not art in their own right. The type of film collecting Tarantino does, in this view, would be no more involved with art than, say, collecting beer bottles would be. Yes, some could be said to present beauty, but, from this perspective, few rise to the level of art. Tarantino's serious consideration of the films he loves, and understanding of them, of the ways they build their narratives and characters, however, shows that his interest in them, at least, rises above the level of camp. The same can be said of DVD collectors.

In many ways, Tarantino has become the exemplar of the modern film viewer and collector even though he is best known, right now, for writing, directing, and as a Hollywood personality. An enthusiast, he focuses on film even as his subject matter (much as did the filmmakers of the Nouvelle Vague), often angering those who prefer to see film centering on explication of the experiential world unmediated by prior movies—or, at least, not explicitly. But film has become Tarantino's vocabulary and he speaks it fluently, even casting actors through past films before any current contact. He speaks film so well because he grew up with it, learning film as he learned the world.

Tarantino's early experience of film at home likely came through such broadcast presentations as *Thriller Theatre*-type showings late at night, movies in the afternoon on *Dialing for Dollars*, and Saturday-afternoon war movies and Westerns. The quality of these films might not have been the highest even before their adaptation to the needs of television, but they helped develop in the future director (as in many others) his love for all films, no matter their reputations or perceived level of excellence. As a child, like many of his generation, he certainly badgered his mother into taking him to the cinema as often as possible, but television viewing of films had to have had just as extensive an effect upon his developing aesthetic.

In some respects, the impact of the introduction of the home video player in the 1970s certainly *was* muted by the limitations of the medium (its degraded image was nothing like what could be seen on a cinema screen)—even though it opened up viewing possibilities for so many. Though there are many filmmakers like Tarantino whose knowledge of cinema can be traced directly to home viewing, viewing limitations make it hard to examine a film on videotape with any care or to get overly enthused about a collection of tapes. Videotapes, to many viewers, served only as poor reflections of the real thing, the "actual" movies. At the same time, through their limitations, they contributed to the romanticizing of the theater as the "only" place where films could legitimately be seen, a romanticizing that has contributed to the sustained disdain, in some quarters, for home viewing even in the face of the DVD—analogous to a situation in which it would only be deemed proper to read books in libraries or special reading rooms, and never at home!

One of the side-effects of the introduction of the VCR may have been a contribution to the death of the small revival house and the loss of vitality in many campus film societies, thereby contributing to the death of the dialogues that had surrounded their showings. The small amount of information that can be carried on any one videotape makes it hard for the tape to adequately provide any sort of apparatus that could serve as a substitute for the type of discussions that surrounded these or the Cinémathèque Française showings. Furthermore, due to the limitations on their quality, promotion and even release of video editions rested primarily with recent popular productions and not with classic films (though release of these on video did pick up as the 1980s progressed).

Tarantino was twelve when the VCR was introduced. To a boy already addicted to television as well as movies, the introduction of the machine into his house must have seemed a godsend, whatever its limitations might have been. The movies available, however, would not yet be the classics or even the big box-office hits. A few years later, the video store, Video Archives in

Manhattan Beach, California, where he then worked, must have also appealed in an almost religious way to this young fanatic. There, the variety of the film selection would have been greater than anything that had been available to him before. Tarantino just wanted films and, at that time in his life, was probably willing to sacrifice accuracy and visual quality for quantity. And he wanted to *talk* about film. As he said in a 1994 interview with Charlie Rose, "what that store was, more or less, is not a film school. It was… like my *Village Voice*…. And I got to be J. Hoberman. I got to be Andrew Sarris at the store."[8] It wasn't filmmaking that he learned at the store, clearly, but movies, film language, and the language of film criticism. Tarantino was elsewhere teaching himself filmmaking by directing a film (never completed).

As opposed to those film-school students who might be, in a certain view, learning about film, but not learning films, Tarantino and those like him focused on the movies, not on theories explaining movies. As Roger Avary, once one of Tarantino's co-workers at Video Archives and later his writing collaborator, puts it:

> When video came along, all of a sudden you had a database of 20,000 titles. One day I realized, What am I doing? Why go to film school to listen to someone lecture about film in the old style when you can sit around for 8 or 10 hours a day and discuss movies with your friends. That was the greatest film school any of us could ever have.[9]

True, but one needed hands-on experience as well to become a filmmaker—and Tarantino was getting it—just not at Video Archives. There, like Avary, like thousands of others, he was learning to speak the language of film.

Though youths like Tarantino and Avary certainly did spend as much time as they could in movie houses, clearly a good deal of their time was spent in front of the small screen—and the situation surely continued while the two worked at the video store. Their interaction there with films was, of necessity, different from the one that they experienced when they went to the theaters. Scan lines, lack of projection, and poor sound quality affected the way home viewers of the time interacted with the movies. Tarantino, Avary, and the like certainly chafed at these limitations, but they weren't even the worst of the problems with viewing films at home.

Since the advent of the VCR, it has been is easy to ignore the fact that the purposes and uses of the theater screen and the television are quite different. Even so, the VCR immediately affected the way *all* viewers saw all movies—literally. Scared of the letter box effect when widescreen movies are shown on a television set, video producers borrowed the pan-and-scan approach that had been developed for broadcast television, presenting images that lop off up to one-third of the original picture and violate the camera movement of the original in order to make sure that the "important" parts of the scenes remain on screen. Sometimes the films were edited for content, from fear of offending certain customers of the video stores. Most viewers—already habituated to such desecrations through their television experiences—accepted these alterations without a murmur, watching the notices at the beginnings of their tapes go by, the ones alerting them to the changes, with hardly a concern. The possibility that the videotape could be seen as a legitimate vehicle for film viewing was further diminished by this reality; fans like Tarantino certainly pined for a more accessible large screen.

Whether consciously or not, filmmakers responded to the limitations of home viewing more and more in their productions, particularly as it became obvious just how much money there was to be made there. So, just as the threat of television had changed the movies two decades earlier, the lure of the videotape release changed it again. Take a look at the movies made since 1975: the broad stroke of so many of them, the emphasis on extended action sequences, the lack of cinematographic subtlety, and the continued move toward montage at the expense of realism—all of these are responses to the growing need to make films that transfer easily to the small screen.

The VCR changed the viewers, too. By the mid-1980s, the videotape had become both a babysitter and an educator. Films like *Star Wars* (George Lucas, 1977) and *The Rocky Horror Picture Show* (Jim Sharman, 1975) sparked new interest in the previously obscure science fiction and horror films that had been available on *Creature Features*, if at all, but that had entertained an entire generation growing up in the late 1950s and early 1960s. The aisles of the video rental store, growing daily with new releases of classic as well as recent films, now led a new generation to discover, for example, the John Ford westerns and Alfred Hitchcock suspense films that they may never have encountered otherwise. A cinema literacy that had been nascent in the slightly older baby-boom generation began to explode from the realm of the *cineastes* into the broader culture.

Before the advent of the videotape, only a few films really had a broad and lasting cultural impact. The most obvious examples are *Casablanca* (Michael Curtiz, 1942), *Gone With the Wind* (Victor Fleming, 1939), and *The Wizard of Oz* (Victor Fleming, 1939), though there are certainly others.

Since the introduction of the VCR, however, films both new and old have been shouldering their way into the general consciousness in a manner never before seen. The most obvious of the recent films to do this comprise the first *Star Wars* trilogy. The film, which had primarily been a creature of its immediate time, now became something with a life that could extend beyond generations, exactly the thing that Langlois had dreamed of; exactly the thing that Tarantino promotes.

Filmmakers began to recognize that they had another problem as they slowly became aware of the power the videotape was developing: How do you film with your eyes turned toward the big screen, the only arena where critical acceptance could be achieved, and yet keep from ignoring the burgeoning market of small-screen viewing? The VCR was changing the taste of home viewers, not only in what they rented, taped, or bought, but in what they were willing to see in the theater. It has been popular for years to blame the changes in the movies during the 1980s on *Star Wars*, but *Star Wars* was itself a response to a pent-up demand within the viewing public. By 1990, the aesthetic of home viewing dominated even production of films ostensibly meant only for the theater.

For all this concern, video has its advantages as well as its problems in the world of cinema. One of the most important results of the home video revolution that began with the VCR was that thousands of viewers suddenly had the chance to see many more films of their own choosing, be they genre films or foreign films or Hollywood blockbusters, and at their own pace. Viewing control had decentralized. Viewer knowledge about the particulars of films began to grow, and this, too, began to show up in movies. In her *New Yorker* profile of Tarantino, MacFarquhar wrote that his "characters do not all have psychological substance; some . . . are made, instead, out of history—out of predecessor characters whose clichés they inhabit and twist."[10] Filmmakers of Tarantino's generation understand that their audiences can catch the references they make to earlier films, allowing them a kind of shorthand for character development, if you will, and quick acknowledgement of influence. They are following Jean-Luc Godard, who was operating within that earlier milieu of such extensive film knowledge, the one generated by Cinémathèque Française, and who commented on similar criticism toward him: "People, in life, quote what pleases them. We have therefore the right to quote what pleases us."[11]

One of the most apparent similarities between the work of Quentin Tarantino and the work of many of the artists of the Nouvelle Vague is this penchant for references to earlier films. There is an assumption in each that the audience has experienced a wide range of films. This can be seen as a narrow focus, a making of films about film rather than about the world, but it need not detract from the worldliness of a film—certainly not if done well— any more than a literary allusion need detract from a novel.

By these references, both the Nouvelle Vague and Tarantino are continuing something that began with the inception of the movies. Sometimes these are merely in-jokes, but they often serve larger purposes of varying degrees of importance. The in-joke has been a part of film since it began and continues unabated. Stanley Cavell provides a wonderful listing of some from the classical Hollywood era:

> Groucho Marx came across a snow sled with the name "Rosebud" . . . and remarked . . . "I thought they burned that"; . . . Katharine Hepburn in *The Philadelphia Story* . . . cradling a sheaf of long-stemmed flowers, saying . . . "The calla lilies are in bloom again" (see *Stage Door*); . . . Cary Grant's response, on being introduced to Ralph Bellamy in *His Girl Friday*, "Haven't we met someplace before?" (they had . . . in *The Awful Truth*).[12]

These examples don't even begin to plumb the depths of these particular films: It is in *His Girl Friday* (Howard Hawks, 1940), after all, that Cary Grant ad-libs, "the last man who said that to me was Archie Leach, just a week before he cut his throat"[13]—using his own birth name for a suicide. These particular instances, however, are not really very significant. In fact, they fall to the level of trivia. In other situations, such referentiality can be much more important.

One of the most interesting uses of reference in film is that of *Once Upon a Time in the West* (*C'era una volta il West*) (Sergio Leone, 1968) where, for one thing, the entire film history of Henry Fonda, who plays the villain, is turned on its head in order to destroy the immediate viewer desire to categorize characters—something especially true when Westerns are watched. There is a great deal more of cinema's past in this movie. Bernardo Bertolucci, who co-wrote the story for the movie, remembers first seeing it:

> I was . . . happy to find in the film all the quotations that I sneaked into the treatment without Sergio knowing it. It was extraordinary, because I was coming from this French *Nouvelle Vague* kind of ideology. In our movies, the quotations were there just to prove our love of cinema . . . Now, things were becoming much more complicated. Now, here we are: You have a

great director of commercial cinema who does a beautiful film and . . . he's filming quotations, which means sequences similar to other movies, without knowing he is doing it, without the perversion that we young experimental directors used to have. . . . Now, I was seeing the film, a moment of *The Searchers* [John Ford, 1956], a moment of *Johnny Guitar* [Nicholas Ray, 1954], without Sergio knowing. Of course, when I told him, Sergio denied it, saying "I knew exactly what I was doing."[14]

With a lesser director, such extensive use of quotation might have ended up as only pastiche. Leone, however, whether or not he recognized the quotations he had been given by his writer, incorporated them into a film that is rated by fans on imdb.com as the #2 western ever (as of 7/19/04), behind only Leone's own *The Good, the Bad, and the Ugly* (1966) and ahead of the two films Bertolucci mentions, *The Searchers* (#4) and *Johnny Guitar* (#34).

The casting of Alan Hale, Sr., as Little John in *The Adventures of Robin Hood* (Michael Curtiz and William Keighley, 1938) connects that movie directly to Douglas Fairbanks's *Robin Hood* (Alan Dwan, 1922), in which Hale plays the same role. He reprises his role as Little John *again* in *Rogues of Sherwood Forest* (Gordon Douglass, 1950) providing a significant continuity with the universes of both earlier films. A scene in *The Lord of the Rings: The Two Towers* (Peter Jackson, 2003) shows three of the characters looking down over a great gate while a column of soldiers marches in. A soldier notices something amiss, and goes with a fellow to investigate. The visual allusion is to a scene in *The Wizard of Oz*, where the three heroes approach the castle of the Wicked Witch of the West. Jackson uses this to heighten the suspense: In the earlier film, the "good" characters overcome the soldiers and, disguised in their uniforms, make their way through the gate. Though nothing similar happens in *The Two Towers*, the possibility that it *might* helps keep viewers on the edge of their seats. Tarantino certainly deserves and demands the right to the same tradition of reference. Just as books come, in part, from other books, he might argue that movies are most certainly made with other movies in mind. As the DVD grows into a home staple, more and more referentiality and quotation will appear, filmmakers gaining confidence in the audience's ability to incorporate the borrowed material into their developing view of the newer film.

The videotape placed demands on the film industry that it was slow, at first (and as usual), to meet, although these eventually developed into a new standard for film success. Cinema box office (though it took Hollywood a long time to recognize this) is no longer enough of a basis for decisions concerning a particular film product. As Tarantino says:

> It was so much different before video. Now some movies that didn't do so well have entered the consciousness completely, even as little as five years later. I always had a theory that if they had ever done a sequel to *Buckaroo Banzai* [W.D. Richter, 1984]—not now, but 4 years or so after the first release—that film could've done really well, because by then a lot of America knew who Buckaroo Banzai was![15]

America knew who Buckaroo Banzai was almost exclusively because of the videotape. Another movie, *The Shawshank Redemption* (Frank Darabont, 1994), which grossed less than $30 million during its domestic release (hardly more than it cost to make), has since become one of the most popular films in the country, a perennial home-viewing favorite and ranks #2 (as of 7/19/04) on the Internet Movie DataBase's (imdb.com) user-voted list of the top 250 films of all time. These are but two of dozens of examples of the power of home viewing's contribution to ultimate film success.

Because of the decentralized control that home viewing represents and the dramatic increase in choice it provides, viewers can now affect movies in a more direct manner than ever before, and in a manner unmediated by the experts who feel they are able to determine just what it is the public wants, or by any other single determining factor, such as gross theatrical receipts.

The DVD continues this decentralization in a number of fashions, many beyond the expansion of viewer choice. In the family—in the home—it is becoming something different from what the videotape was. Like TV before it, the VCR was most often a creature of the living room and generally a vehicle for familial viewing. Because it can be played on personal computers and game systems, the DVD is becoming the center of a much more personal viewing situation, pulling film even further from its roots in communal viewing, but also bringing it back to a focus on concentrated viewing that is lacking in the family room. Negotiation over what to play, and when, is reduced to zero when there are myriad devices throughout the home that can support DVD technology, and interaction between the viewer and a computer or game system is significantly different from television-style viewing. Among other things, the use of a keyboard or game control is different from use of a remote control, and the user of a computer or game system sits much closer to the screen. Even these simple, physical differences contribute to a new type of viewing experience. Terry Flew, a communication specialist, writes that television

> has an association with shared leisure and entertainment experiences that audiences collectively "immerse" themselves in. By contrast, personal computers are more commonly associated with individualized forms of work, instrumental and particular forms of use, and "surfing" across multiple Web sites. It is commonly said in the media industry that users "lean forward" to the personal computer, and "lean back" to television.[16]

The effects of this change in focus and the further fragmented new form of viewing will not be known for years, but it will certainly be measurable. If nothing else, the new, more private viewing possibility allows for a concentrated viewing that is much more difficult to sustain in a family room where people may be coming and going, watching for a moment then moving on to something else.

The age of a child's individual control of viewing is also dropping because of the proliferation of computers and video game systems. In many American households, children have access to PCs and game systems in their bedrooms, and the children have control over their use—including when and how often DVDs are viewed—to a degree unimaginable just a decade ago. Left to their own devices, these children will develop their own new relationships to film, eventually even seeing the experience of a movie in a theater from an entirely different perspective. Certainly, the movies will continue to be a refuge, a time-honored use of them by the young, both as an escape and as a way to create their own spaces. But they may develop into something more as this new generation grows up and, perhaps, a new Langlois or Tarantino appears.

Though our relationships with the movies will change as a result of new technologies, clearly some other aspects of those relationships will remain the same. We will still love the movies as we saw them when we were younger and remember fondly the ones that comforted us as we dealt with adolescence. Theaters will still showcase new releases and provide a viewing venue outside the home, and not just because of nostalgia. Rather than losing by the advent of new technologies, then, we may be gaining by them on the whole—as long as we do pay attention to preservation of the manifestations of older technologies.

As we have seen, the greatest tragedy of the advent of sound was the destruction of an untold number of silent films, movies no longer considered

important or collectible in the new sound age. It took people with the vision
of Henri Langlois to ensure that anything was saved at all—yet the loss was
incalculable. In addition, a developing artistic vocabulary based on the image
itself was stymied and stunted, with a great deal of the films that used that
vocabulary actually lost. Today, people like preservationist Scott MacDonald
are trying to raise awareness of comparable loss, especially for the less-recognized
aspects of film such as the avant-garde on 16mm film, and others, like Martin Scorsese and Quentin Tarantino, are making sure the saved and restored
35mm films are seen and appreciated—be it at home in digital from or in
the theater, either digitally or on film. Yet it is still possible that we will wake
up a decade from now to discover that our move to the digital also created a
great loss, one as nearly impossible to recover as the loss of silent films has
proven to be. So far, it doesn't appear that this will be the case. In 1930, it is
worth remembering, few saw any irreparable loss in the destruction of all
that antiquated silent film. Today's film appreciators do seem more vigilant.

As a result of the technological developments of the past decades, film
viewing is changing as radically as it did at the end of the 1920s. The significance of the large cinema screen has certainly eroded since the advent of
television. Today, because of the digital revolution and advances in home-
viewing technologies (the DVD and HDTV), the distinction between theater viewing and home viewing is smaller than it has ever been, and an
entirely new way of interacting with movies has developed: the computer
connected both to DVDs and the Internet with its attendant "lean forward"
impact.

As usual, concern for the survival of the big screen has risen as the new
technologies have proven themselves. This happened in the 1950s, with the
advent of television, and in the 1970s, when the VCR was introduced. And
just as in the past, it is likely the cinema in theaters will survive. Still, it is
important to keep in mind while assessing this concern that the experience of
film is not centered simply on the means of conveyance. As this chapter
attempts to demonstrate, the various means of viewing can assist each other,
doing so in part because each is distinct, offering unique possibilities to the
viewer, ultimately complementing each other and not encroaching on one
another.

One of the arguments for seeing the computer as the evolving central
focus of cinema is that the computer is interactive ("lean forward"), and that
viewing on television or in a cinema is passive ("lean back"). Of course, this is a
simplistic and flawed contention, based on the idea that the film experience

(before the advent of the computer, and aside from it) is simply a focus on the screen and an acceptance (without processing) of the incoming information. In fact, each viewing possibility requires interactivity, though of a differing sort in each case—and it is for this reason, at the very least, that each will survive.

There is a focused interactive process going on each time a viewer watches a film in a theater. This process includes an ongoing evaluation based on expectations and on the unfolding narrative (or, if there is no narrative, on the temporal progression of the images) with an expectation of coming to a decision on the value of the film that will itself be a part of later discussion. For the most part, watching a film on television is a different experience (though this experience can be broken down into a number of different types, depending on whether the film is available through broadcast television—with advertisements interrupting—cable, videotape, or DVD), one of less focus and less expectation of after-viewing discussion. As a more personal experience, TV viewing is less dependent on the opinions of others and more on the individual viewer's past experience. TV viewing may be slightly more technically interactive than theater viewing, simply because of channel-changing options—and computer viewing certainly has a stronger technologically interactive aspect—but technology isn't the only basis for judging interactivity. Certainly, both Henri Langlois and Quentin Tarantino interacted with the films they saw from their youngest days, as have the billions of others who have watched and loved films, no matter what the conveyance.

Because of the widespread popularity of the videotape and now the DVD, there may never again be a single figure as important to film preservation as Henri Langlois. The huge film library he established is, even now, becoming merely a focus of historical interest. No longer is it really a lively participant in the world of film. In fact, the idea of a film library—outside of the personal—may be fading in significance as home viewers build their own collections and digital editions continue to improve in quality. If anything, film libraries may, in a few years, exist solely on the Internet or to ensure that the technology of the past is preserved.

Even Quentin Tarantino, with his huge collection of movies, may no longer be notable as a collector. He owns a large number of movies on all media, from 35mm to DVD. But, as other collectors find that the ease of storage and use of the DVD are more important considerations than the slightly higher values of film itself (especially as HD-DVD comes to prominence), the variety of media may become a curiosity and little more.

In the 1970s, as we have seen, videotape collectors were almost apologetic about their passion. They knew that the tapes they owned (tapes they had, for the most part, created themselves from broadcast and cable television or had copied from those of other collectors) poorly reflected the movies they stemmed from. Some of these people embraced the laserdisc as soon as they could, developing collections that reflected more accurately the intent of the filmmakers. Today, these collectors augment their collections with DVDs. Others eventually replaced their collections with commercial tapes of their movies as these became available, now replacing them once more with DVDs. In both cases, collectors have moved to the DVD virtually without complaint. The quality and flexibility of the medium are giving home viewing a cachet it has never before had, allowing collectors greater pride in their collections than they previously could have imagined.

The enthusiasm of DVD collectors has led to the creation of a number of Web sites where it is possible to create a catalogue of personally owned DVDs, view the collections of others, find out what DVDs are available in what editions and find sources for their purchase, create wish lists, and participate in bulletin-board discussions. Some even provide information on "easter eggs" (hidden extras on DVDs). DVDTalk.com is representative of these; it is a site that encourages collector interaction and discussion.

Future Tarantinos, both as directors and film buffs, are now learning film through DVDs and Internet discussions of them. Just as the introduction of the videotape has had surprising results in the world of cinema, the DVD and the Internet will, too, as time moves on. Certainly, the decentralization of control over film viewing that has continued and improved will make individual explorations more frequent and, likely, more interesting. Though it is easy to decry the quality of the big-budget films that invade the theaters, the scope and quality of home viewing is a completely different thing. Judging by the collections presented on DVDAficionado.com and guzzlefish.com, DVD viewers seek far beyond the contemporary Hollywood releases, showing that they are learning film in ways that will certainly have unexpected—and positive—results for cinema arts. The threads for discussion on another site, film_talk.com, include looks at the favorite DVDs of individuals, confessions of embarrassing favorites, commentary on specific movies, and a great deal more. Internet sites of this sort are becoming the cafés and bars where movies—particularly on DVD—are discussed. Though a great deal of the commentary is simplistic or even silly, much of it is serious and insightful enough to attract all sorts of movie fans, from those just

coming down with the bug to others who haunted college film society showings in the 1960s.

In the 1960s, Richard Griffith, head of the film department at the
Museum of Modern Art in New York, complained about Langlois: "That
man . . . he's not an archivist, he's not a historian, he's just a . . . just an *enthusiast.*"[17] Langlois, when told of this, was amused by the idea that enthusiasm
could be a pejorative. He was right to be amused. It is enthusiasts who have
made cinema the great art it is, and enthusiasts who will make it the greater
art it will become. For many of these, the center of their enthusiasm will be
home viewing and the possibilities around it that continue to expand. For
each, a Cinémathèque Française will be built on his or her own. It may be
that no one, ever again, will be able to have the influence of a Langlois; the
DVD, however, may allow each of us to become our personal expert pro-
grammer.

One of the issues surrounding the *affaire Langlois* of 1968 was what was
perceived as unwarranted intrusion of government, and this helped spark the
spring uprising of that year that changed France. It may be that today's "children of the DVD"—collectors and fans who are finding themselves faced
with corporate intrusion in their home relationships with film—will find
that they, too, will be using film as a spark for greater changes in their culture.

Whatever happens, the cultural impact of film, through the DVD and
related technologies, will only continue to grow.

Chapter 3

DVD
FAN
CULTURE

Though media fan culture predates the Internet, it has been through the Internet that fan culture has found its muscle. So strong is the fan presence on the Web that no one involved in "franchise" activity (the official aspect of the initial art) can afford to ignore what fans have been doing—but they cannot try to dominate it, either. There is a tension between the two: The franchise wants to control its copyrighted material (its economic lifeblood) while the fans want to manipulate that same material without restriction. Though some still fight fan culture, most franchises have realized that they need to work with it—for their own benefit.

When the estate of the science-fiction writer Philip K. Dick, for example, wanted to establish a Web site, a deal was made with the most prominent fan site, essentially establishing sister sites. One is official, dedicated to the author, his works, and news about the films being made from them. Essentially, it is a proprietary site. The other (the fan site) includes a forum, criticism and scholarship, fan art, and more; it works in response to the fiction of Philip K. Dick. It is an open site. The two sites work in tandem, neither controlling the other, providing an example for other instances where the franchise wants to intersect successfully with the fans. Unfortunately, more often than not, the tensions between franchise and fans have generally been exacerbated through the Web, not eased.

The impetus behind fan art is simple: love leads to the creation of tribute. Significantly, the creativity involved can lead to new art, even within the universe created by the old—so it needs encouragement. Ultimately, as Harold Bloom argues in his *The Anxiety of Influence*, the creative spark will lead to a break with the original, an attempt to get out from under the influence of that devotion. That's where new art, originality, and new artistic movements come from. So, as a necessary precursor, the art created in the meantime should not be demeaned or simply treated as derivative. Though it takes its inspiration directly from another work, it can be skillfully crafted, surprising, and even original within its restrictive framework. Unfortunately, when the original work is a source of income, the new art can be seen as threatening—and this can lead to problems.

Derivative art as creative fan activities goes back in media culture at least as far as the *Star Trek* (Gene Roddenberry, producer, 1966–1969) television show with its ensuing panoply of responsive creative activities; these activities often occur in conjunction with the fan conventions and amateur fan magazines that sprang up. Fan endeavors ranged from costumes designed to follow show originals to new scripts for show episodes that the authors knew would never be filmed (or even considered). A case can even be made that the ensuing series of *Star Trek* movies (not to mention the numerous spin-off television series) was a direct response to this fan activity, in the sense that fan art had been interpreted as a threat to the franchise. One way or another, the series was going to live. So, its creators decided, it might as well live officially, controlled by its originators but responsive to its fans.

Fan fiction was also a part of this creative response to *Star Trek*, and has been spawned by many other works since. Privately produced and distributed, these works utilize themes, characters, settings, situations, and occasionally even plots from the originals. Significantly, *fanfic* (as it has come to be called) remains distinct from franchise fiction, which also uses the original for inspiration. Franchise fiction has an authority, even among fans devoted to fanfic, that fanfic cannot match. *Star Trek*, *Star Wars* (George Lucas, et al., 1977 and following), and even *Blade Runner* (Ridley Scott, 1982)—among many others—have spun off new authorized fiction. Such authorized works have a "reality" within the universe of fandom that fanfic cannot match (for *Star Wars* fans, for example, the closer in origin something is to George Lucas—the fewer people between him and the new work—the more validity it has), but such works, operating under control of the copyright holders, are restricted, unable to travel the more expansive routes taken by fan fiction.

Technological possibilities have progressed to the point where film and video, as well as fiction, can be used to create significant fan art. DVDs are becoming a part of this, both as a source for material that may be manipulated into new art and as a means of distribution, circumventing proprietary controls appearing on the Internet. The use of the moving image in fan art, however, is still in its infancy, so a look back at fan fiction can be instructive, showing what might come to pass with the newer forms of fan art.

Though it really cannot be classified as fan fiction, the history of Alice Randall's novel *The Wind Done Gone*, a 2001 utilization of the world of Margaret Mitchell's 1936 epic *Gone With the Wind*, can help clarify the distinction between the possibilities open to fan fiction as opposed to those open to franchise fiction. An authorized sequel to Mitchell's novel, *Scarlett: The Sequel to Margaret Mitchell's "Gone With the Wind"* by Alexandra Ripley, had appeared in 1991, carefully vetted and sponsored by the Mitchell estate, but Randall's purpose was to do something other than merely expand on the lives of the principal characters. She wanted to show the world of Tara from another point of view, from that of the slaves whose servitude and bondage made possible the lives of Mitchell's primary characters. So, she did not feel she could ask for estate approval.

Mitchell's estate tried to stop the publication of *The Wind Done Gone*, claiming copyright infringement, but the attempt ultimately failed. The novel skates close to a line that much of fan fiction crosses, dealing with issues that the copyright holder, for whatever reason, wishes to avoid, but Randall circumvented copyright problems by avoiding the actual names given in Mitchell's work, something fanfic does not do. In fan fiction, the issues that might be restricted by the franchise are often of a sexual nature, but they are not only that. Randall wanted to open up a fictional world that she saw as confining and dishonest, but a world that clearly fascinated her and also one that allowed her to present her own point of view. For her own political and cultural purposes, she wanted to write within a context that fans of the original could countenance. Fanfic does much the same thing; so do the fan films that are now appearing.

The tradition of derivation that Randall was working within, linking to another's created world for one's own purposes, is old, of course. Virgil's *Aeneid*, just one example out of hundreds, draws directly on Homer's *Iliad* to create a new story with Roman—rather than Greek—connections and implications. Henry Fielding parodied Samuel Richardson's *Pamela* by setting his parody *Joseph Andrews* within the same family.

Richardson didn't have effective recourse to copyright protection (the Copyright Act of 1710 did not protect him from this sort of usage). The *Iliad*, of course, arose at a time when everything was in the public domain, and the world of Tara now sits quite close to the commons. Margaret Mitchell, after all, died in 1949. Not only will the copyright held by her estate expire in 15 years, but, thanks to the 1939 movie of the book, aspects of Tara have bled into common American culture. They have almost become commonplaces to such an extent that they could never be completely retrieved by the estate, no matter what exercise of copyright prerogatives might be utilized. Randall, again, was careful not to trespass explicitly on the Tara domain (she made her references oblique enough to satisfy the law) but, because Tara has become such a cultural symbol, it is clear to any reader of *The Wind Done Gone* that it is Mitchell's universe that Randall is describing, though from a fresh perspective.

Fan fiction and film, because they operate outside of copyright (whether legitimately or not), don't scruple to avoid the landmarks of the franchise. Though there is plenty of fanfic that deals with racial or social issues, like Randall does in her book, for the most part the taboos ignored by fanfic are of a sexual nature. Commercially-produced media tend to elide sexuality or to touch on it only briefly. This leaves many fans dissatisfied. They recognize the importance of sex in their own lives and in those around them, and they want to see it explored (even if they have to do it themselves) within their favorite fictional worlds. To date, sex has not become an important part of fan film—but, if the past is prologue, it will.

The DVD, with its large storage capacity, offers distinct possibilities for fan art, but it also has one major difference from the Internet that can become extremely important to fan art of all types. That is, it can be used in reaction both to fan culture and as a means to circumvent attempts at franchise control. Internet cultures move beyond the personal to a wider discussion. It is on the Internet, however, that means of circumventing copyright proliferate—but also where they can be traced. Not so, the DVD.

Because of its discrete nature, the DVD can bring back a smaller, more personal focus to fan art, something certain fans yearn for in the face of the huge arena of Internet fan activities that has grown up over the past few years. It also keeps users under the radar of franchise holders. As long as those users can obtain software allowing them to alter DVDs, or copy portions of DVDs to other DVDs, they will be able to create their own new artifacts without raising any eyebrows, for their unconnected activity will have no Internet trace. In the end, the DVD allows the user who is participating in Internet fan culture to develop and hold something completely personal and safe from Recording Industry Association of America (RIAA)-like copyright infringement lawsuits against people who have downloaded copyrighted material from the Internet. And all the while they may participate in the Web.

While permissions are getting dangerous to assume and harder to guarantee, software that allows a user to manipulate any media is getting cheaper and easier to use. When someone starts out to create a work of art using the tools available on a computer or on the Internet, that person will find it quite simple to grab something from another work for inclusion in the new one—and it's getting simpler. Yet, what the artist is doing is now often called piracy by the large copyright holders, especially (but not only) if that artist later tries to make money from it.

It is understandable that the corporations are investing in what they hope will be inviolable Digital Rights Management (DRM) schemes, devices, and software that control access (including type of access) to the material and to copying. This control, however, extends even to the end user and could begin to trample on rights in the home. It could conceivably even limit the number of viewings, control the order of viewing or place of access, whether the article can be viewed in certain area, or insist on sequential viewing. This violates the end user's sense of ownership, exacerbating the conflict between the producer and protectionism and the end user and personal freedom.

Part of fan culture is a natural banding together to defeat what the fans see as a threat: Often this is corporate control of something that fans feel they now own themselves. For them, it is a question of freedom of speech for users, of shrinking public domain and "fair use," of limiting options that should (given the new digital possibilities) be opening up. Instead, they see options disappearing due to franchise protectionism.

The questions involved here go to the heart of American culture. A participatory democratic culture requires that all members be able to involve themselves fully in the means of communication without permissions or claims of exclusivity. That means that they should be able to use whatever they need to make their current statements or expressions. No matter how hard people try to keep them separate, the political and the commercial intertwine; limits on the commercial necessarily impinge on the necessarily unlimited political. These aspects of American culture—the need to be able to participate and to control one's own belongings—run so deep that corporate efforts to limit them will ultimately fail. Americans will do what they want, especially with what they believe they own, even if it means illegally using copyrighted material for their own purposes.

As the DVD began to dominate home viewing, web sites dedicated to DVDs started to appear and develop followers. These sites allow fans to catalogue their own collections, read reviews (and post them), find technical details of new releases, and exchange views with others. This is a different aspect of fan culture, one of discussion and evaluation, not of creation.

Sometimes, discussions in the forums get so focused on aspects of the DVDs themselves that participants seem to forget that it is films that are the heart of their passion. One participant (Adrian A. Pinzon, writing as "Nova") in one of film-talk.com's DVD Aficionado forums started a thread entitled "Why Aren't We Talking About Movies" with a comment that tries to both move other participants back to the main purpose and away from a private obsession with the things themselves. Nova's post provides a clear description of why such boards have become so important to so many movie and DVD fans:

> Don't get me wrong, I LOVE Film Talk, yet I rarely see any threads about a single movie with any sort of opinions on it or anything, just misc threads (which are very entertaining to say the least). I love reading other's opinions on certain movies but, like I said before, rarely see any movies being discussed here at Film Talk. I just wanted to get this out there and off my chest before I [icon of explosion]. If it wasn't for reading reviews and people's opinions of movies, I would have NEVER gotten into being such a film fan as I am now. I would have NEVER gone out and bought a Criterion, I would have NEVER watched a Kurosawa or Hitchcock film (I used to HATE old movies). I would have NEVER watched a foreign film, especially one without an English language track. Now I feel that I can hold my own as an educated film buff because people like you and me took the time to express our feelings about movies.[1]

For a fan like Pinzon, the Internet has become the wider world, a place for expanding one's knowledge, and for giving back, providing the hints and help that can lead others to the same sort of pleasures one has discovered in the past. He also wants to keep the personal viewing experience of the DVD distinct from discussion of films, which is where he locates the Internet's value.

That sense of discovery, the feeling of ownership that comes from "discovering" Kurosawa, say, or Hitchcock, even through the Internet, gives an empowerment and a feeling of participating in a special group at least as much as creation of fan art does. Given the often arcane collections that some in the DVD culture focus on, it might seem that the interest is really in kitsch, not in serious consideration of film. A reading of posts on the various

DVD sites, though, provides convincing evidence that the collectors are much more interested in film as cinema than as kitsch. There is a great deal of frivolous discussion, certainly, but there are also serious amateur reviews, as well as the discussion topics such as "Must See Foreign Movies," "Underrated Filmmakers," and "Silents on DVD: How Are They Doing?" that are common (these examples are all from film-talk.com).

Among the Web sites devoted to the DVD are DVDAficionado.com, Guzzlefish.com, and DVDTalk.com. On DVDAficionado.com, a member can catalogue Owned, On Order, Wish, and Have Seen DVDs, selecting the specific DVD editions from a search function that is constantly improved by member participation. There are also reference lists and a function for rating films and their DVD incarnations. It's associated film-talk.com discussion boards allow for discussions of particular movies, packaging of DVDs, technical aspects, size of collection, how choices are made, cultural issues, and viewing habits. Guzzlefish.com contains in-house reviews, release dates, editorials, a wide variety of forums, and a catalogue function. DVDTalk.com provides reviews, forums, and even a DVD Collector Series of DVDs deemed to be of particular interest or importance.

Early in 2004, *The New York Times* profiled a number of DVD collectors, including "Ed," one of DVD Aficionado's founders (who wants to keep his identity private), and Todd Robertson, who goes by the handle "Gutwrencher" on DVDAficionado.com.[2] "Gut," as he signs himself, has become something more than simply a collector, but is an active promoter of the DVD and DVD culture on the Web. He contributes at least a couple of posts daily to film-talk.com (and that is just one board he participates in) and, given the comments on others, he has proven to be a guide not just to movies and DVDs, but to Web sites dedicated to both. The attitudes of both Ed and Gut toward their collections as well as to the Web DVD culture are, if not representative, at least reflective.

In response to a question about why he collects DVDs, Ed wrote, "Well there are the merits of the medium and then there is our innate and very human need to accumulate things."[3] This is the crucial point to any understanding of why the DVD will likely last as a discrete entity. One often hears that the DVD is merely a temporary phenomenon, that it will be replaced, eventually, by complete reliance on the Web, once broadband is ubiquitous and an effective method for legitimate download has been instituted and accepted. Possibly, home viewers could pay for permanent access to certain movies, viewing them through a personal catalogue on the Internet, much like the catalogues collectors keep now of their physical DVDs.

Asked whether he would be willing to keep his collection on the Web, Gut responded, "I would . . . but as mainly a backup. I prefer having a physical library, on hand and in the original packaging. There's nothing quite like looking at a wall full of DVDs/films."[4] Gut's feeling about his DVD collection is quite similar to that of a bibliophile about his or her library and even to what director David Cronenberg dreamt of as far back as the 1970s: "I've always had my eye on personal movie use, on the idea that films could be like books, that you would have a library of movies that you take down and watch at your leisure."[5]

Sure, it may be possible to download a book, but there's something important in the tactile item. A DVD, like a book, is more than its contents. It carries a history with it, memories of where it was bought and when, and of specific reading or viewing experiences. Ed writes:

Then there is a significant amount of gratification in owning something. As I mention in this unpublished part of my *NYT* interview: "People like owning things: It is not a matter of economics, it is just a question of whether you can afford it. We feel different when we say, 'this is mine' than when we say, 'I rented this.' One is an affirmation of our tastes and perhaps it tells a bit about ourselves. The other sounds more like an excuse or a justification—'Nah, that is just a rental.' I do not know anyone that feels proud of renting a car (although I might, if I got 'the company' to pay for it). We all know the feeling of driving around in that shiny car we just had washed and polished. It is very much like that."

I have always rented a lot of tapes, and now I could actually buy the stuff—stuff that would never make it to a rental store—not worrying about it being eaten up by the VHS player or its quality degenerating with every show. The image and sound were reasonably good and the prices were not too bad. It was also supposed not to take too much space, or so you think until he reaches 1,000 titles, then you start to wonder where you are going to put all of that stuff.[6]

Like any collection, DVDs can get out of hand.

Asked why he had become so devoted to DVDs, Ed continued:

DVDs are very accessible. They are much easier to enjoy than a book. Books can be much more rewarding, but they require a much larger investment of time and effort. . . . It is also an experience that you can share in "real-time" with your family. It can be a way to control what your kids see, but it can also be a family bonding exercise; perhaps not as traditional as board games, but certainly much easier.

For me all these factors were combined in a natural evolution. I liked watching movies at home. The idea of owning these joyful little pieces was very attractive. DVDs put everything together just in the right package.[7]

At the moment, it is difficult to personalize a DVD the way one can a book, with marginalia, dog-earing, or notes inside the cover, but that will likely change. The companies issuing DVDs are trying to make it as difficult as possible to alter them, but people will manage to do it, and to add to them in ways yet to be seen. Ed's pairing of the DVD and the book in terms of the family, however, is appropriate. In the literary culture of the past, reading aloud was a common family activity in the American middle class, just as DVD watching can be for a wider spectrum of families in today's "virtual" culture.

The parallel between books and DVDs can be taken further: For all the ballyhoo, ebooks have not been much of a success, and the possibility of downloading a book has not really hurt traditional book sales. The availability of *City of Bits: Space, Place, and the InfoBahn* by William J. Mitchell on the web enhances his project, in Mitchell's view.[8] Lawrence Lessig has actively promoted the downloading of his book *Free Culture: How Media Uses Technology and the Law to Lock Down Culture and Control Creativity,*[9] even providing a link on amazon.com to the free download, so confident is he (and his publisher—and even Amazon) that downloading will not hurt sales of the physical book but will, in fact help it. The same will likely prove true for movie downloads vis-à-vis DVD sales, though physical rental outlets may disappear (just as fee-based lending libraries have).

For many DVD collectors, the advent of the technology was immediately and clearly the opening up of a whole new way of experiencing film. As Gut says, "the first time I bought a DVD player, I knew what it meant. I would discover a whole new world of film! Italian horror, for example. Prior to DVD not many of those films were released here in the United States. Now they are the norm. The best thing to happen to film . . . was DVD!!"[10] Suddenly, having films available in a medium that allows the viewer to pick modes—such as language and subtitles, that retain the Original Aspect Ratio (OAR), that were obviously cheap to manufacture and easy to distribute—

was much like seeing a feast dropped in front of them to the millions of film fans who had been making do with videotapes with their poor cuts, sloppy pan-and-scan, and slap-dash dubbings.

Ed listed the points about the DVD that he finds most important:

> Films are presented in their original aspect ratio, in the format they were intended to be viewed by its creators without a technician figuring out which pieces to remove so that it would fit your TV. A very large amount of work, that you would otherwise never have the opportunity to see, is available to anyone with an Internet connection and a credit card. Cults, classics, artsy stuff, imported editions, you can have it all delivered to your home in a matter of days. Access to directors, actors, and crew in the form of commentary tracks. That is the final icing on the cake for anyone that at one point or another dreamed to be involved in cinema.[11]

Because of all of its "behind the scenes" extras, the DVD, in addition to everything else, makes the fan feel closer to the actual making of the film than was even possible before with earlier technology.

One of the reasons that the Internet discussions and Web sites devoted to the DVD developed was that the quality of transfer to DVD—to say nothing of the extras—varies to such an extensive degree. Early on, collectors banded together to swap information, warning each other when DVDs appeared that are simply transfers from videotape (a common practice) or when DVDs advertised as anamorphic are not. Gut claims that what led him first to DVDs was "preservation. Aside from a few delamination (rot) problems . . . these can last you forever, if taken care of properly. No degrading, no sound drops or tape lines. . . . It's the same every time."[12] Collectors, who had never seen their videotape collections as permanent, now wanted to know as much about their DVDs as possible. They look to owning them far into the future.

The joy of discovery itself is probably a large part of what led to the beginning of the DVD Web culture. Over the past decade, the Internet has become the medium of choice for enthusiasts of all sorts, not just for creators of fan art. With a simple search, it is possible to find aficionados of just about anything, to communicate with them, secure in the knowledge that no one would be mocking the passion. Some people, like Gut, make it their business to make the "newbies" feel at home. According to Gut, he does this because "the excitement comes from 'turning someone on' to something they never heard of before. It's a great feeling to influence someone into a certain direction. Besides, anybody with a hobby . . . loves talking about it!!"[13]

A short 35 years ago, it was possible for Stanley Cavell to write that the "events associated with movies are those of companionship or lack of companionship: the audience of a book is essentially solitary, one soul at a time; the audience of music and theater is essentially larger than your immediate acquaintance."[14] The theater experience was considered critical to the movies; Alfred Hitchcock's *Psycho* (1960) was seen as having been successful because of the audience's shared suspense and surprise while viewing it in the theater. There's something to be said for this view, though the book was never quite the solitary experience that Cavell claims. As mentioned earlier, reading aloud, for much of the time since the book first appeared, has been an important experience of it, at least in family situations—and solitary viewing, going to that empty earliest or latest show of the day, has always had an attraction to film buffs.

If the DVD is the book of virtual culture, then the Web DVD culture is playing the role of the book clubs that have existed for much more than a century, introducing millions to writers they might never have otherwise experienced. If anything, if the analogy holds, while services such as NetFlix and Blockbuster continue to rent DVDs (or while movies become easily available through download) and serve as commercial libraries, people will always want to have their own DVDs, as well, just as they own a few books, at the very least. Imagine the future American study: one wall covered with books, another with DVDs. At one end, a widescreen television, at the other, a desk with a reading lamp on it and an Internet connection built into it.

Like the spines in a case full of books, it takes mere seconds to run ones eyes over the backs of a rack of DVDs. And, like a room full of books, there is something comforting about a wall of DVDs. Gut says, "I just love the feeling of being surrounded by my films. It adds an atmosphere that identifies me, whether it's to myself . . . or other people who just visit. And if I have a question about a DVD, film, or any film-related subject or question . . . I just take a few steps and there they all are."[15]

One of the things that the DVD and the rest of the new home-viewing technologies unquestionably do is diffuse control of cinema from the theater chains to the home viewer. Businesses fear this lack of control, so they are trying to use copyright to regain some measure of it even in the home (just as they are trying to control fan art). Most Americans, on the other hand, are used to being able to manipulate their belongings in any way they see fit, so they resist attempts to regulate that usage. Government intrusion, even in the guise of protecting corporate property, will only be accepted for so long by the American population. Eventually, the home viewer will wrestle control of the individual DVD away from the corporate producers, and DVD culture, though perhaps only on a small, personal basis, will explode. This cannot be helped. Costs are already low and will only get lower—and lowering the costs of reproduction lowers the costs of innovation and encourages more and more people to experiment.

One of the most intriguing aspects of the DVD is its malleability, which is also (in the eyes of the film industry) one of its greatest dangers. If it has its way, the film industry will limit DVD possibilities, making commercial DVDs of films unchangeable items for viewing (though sometimes interactive viewing) and nothing more. Fortunately, though the industry has managed to get the law, for the moment, on its side, technology will ultimately give the end user a great deal more latitude than the filmmakers may like.

The central question around the possible establishment of the DVD fan movement is this: Is DVD culture going to be allowed to be a creative one, leading to many different, unknown artistic and intellectual results; or, is it going to be merely a controlled consumer grouping (simply a reactive activity)? The likely answer is that it will be a creative one. The profits from the DVD culture are going to be great (in fact, they already are), even as copyrights are undermined. Eventually the movie companies will understand that it is in their interest to not hamper, at least, manipulation of DVDs, just as they finally learned that the "record" button on the Betamax and VHS (which they had tried to ban) was in their best interest. In some respects, it doesn't even matter if they do understand this or not. As Henry Jenkins, an expert on electronic culture at the Massachusetts Institute of Technology, writes:

> [P]articipatory culture is running ahead of the technological developments necessary to sustain industrial visions of media convergence and thus making demands on popular culture that the studios are not yet, and perhaps never will be, able to satisfy. The first and foremost demand consumers make is the right to participate in the creation and distribution of media narratives. Media consumers want to become media producers, while media producers want to maintain their traditional dominance over media content.[16]

Though the media producers, right now, are unleashing impressive weapons in their own defense, it is the media consumers who will most likely win. The genie of easily accessible and mutable technology cannot be put back in the bottle. Sometime during the early years of the VCR, someone, somewhere discovered that the *Dark Side of the Moon* (Pink Floyd, 1973) album could be played while one was watching *The Wizard of Oz* (Victor Fleming, 1939) with the sound down—and that the music and visuals have an eerie correspondence. Someone will soon combine the two on DVD—someone probably already has. Others will create their own soundtracks, matching either original music or older material to their favorite movies. The possibilities are myriad.

Among the first things appearing as DVD fan activities are amateur voice-over commentaries. These are a natural extension of the discussions on bulletin boards and in chat rooms of the Internet—and some fans already create them for download. One of the most noticeable points of these discussions is the degree of knowledge of many of the participants. These are not casual posters, but people who have spent time watching, discussing, and reading. They bring extensive knowledge to their postings and to their commentaries. They want to be taken as seriously as the commercial, mass-market commentators and often are just as able as those commentators. Within the milieu of fan culture, these amateur commentaries are likely to be treated as seriously as any commercial ones by those they are shared with. The technology for creating the commentaries is simple, and only requires being able to alter commercial movie DVDs for completion.

Right now, to listen to fan commentaries, one has to use a computer or other MP3 player. Web sites like www.hurricaneandy.com, www.DVDTalks.com, and www.renegadecommentaries.co.uk are already providing downloadable commentaries that can be listened to on computer while the film is being watched. These commentators take themselves a lot less seriously than do the ones whose words come with the commercial releases, but that makes them no less interesting. Hurricane Andy, however, tends to be more analytic than Renegade Commentaries, where the attitude is more like that of *Mystery Science Theater 3000* presentations of movies throughout the 1990s. After all, they owe nothing to the creators and copyright holders and so can treat the films any way they wish.

According to information on the DVD Talks Web site, Patrick Stein founded that site after reading an article by Roger Ebert, "You, Too, Can Be a DVD Movie Critic" in the now-defunct *Yahoo! Internet Life* for February

2002.[17] The article galvanized a number of would-be commentators, giving confidence to a movement just beginning to find its way. Chris Freestone and The Q, the creators/commentators of Renegade Commentaries, say that they began their commentaries before the Ebert article, but that it certainly spurred them on. Talking about what got them started, The Q writes:

> I've always been a big fan of movies, but not just the films, the processes behind the scenes. What people did and how things got done. With the advent of the DVD and extras such as documentaries and behind the scenes clips this became more interesting. Commentaries were the next step, an opportunity to hear first hand from directors, actors, and producers. . . . But it seemed many were dull and lifeless and done as chore, so we thought we could do better ourselves.[18]

Of course, the Internet has been empowering users in numerous ways, not the least being that almost anyone can take it upon themselves to do what Freestone and The Q have done:

> At first we hadn't planned to put the commentaries on the web, we were just doing it for ourselves and friends. The original idea was to make a copy of the film and put our commentary on it so we could watch the film properly with our own track, for friends to watch. And in fact we did this with our first few. But the more we thought about it the more we wanted to share this stuff with other people, after all we had, what we considered at least, some good material. We thought there must be at least one person out there who will get what we're doing so we decided to put them on the web. So the web site was created.[19]

The importance of the distinction between home viewing and the Internet is quite clear in The Q's comments. Freestone talks about what he sees as the future of the amateur commentary:

> The non-official commentary will be with us in one form or another for years to come. Whether the DVD producers decide that it could be something they could use to add extra value to a DVD, or whether larger alternate DVD commentary sites appear with larger and larger collections of commentaries for people to try (maybe even commentaries by more than one set of people for the same film, so you could choose the style of commentary you like).

Even with the advent of digital and satellite TV, where the same film is shown over and over again in the same run, as well as the official commentary, having non-official commentaries created for the same film could again give more value for the run of a film. . . . DVDs have put the commentary track into the mainstream, whether they remain purely within DVDs or whether they move out into cable and satellite TV, as well as the Internet, we will have to wait and see.[20]

One alternate soundtrack for *Harry Potter and the Sorcerer's Stone* (Chris Columbus, 2001) was played with the film at the 2004 New York Underground Film Festival as *Wizard People, Dear Reader*. Its creator, Brad Neely, does more than merely comment on the film, but replaces the dialogue and reworks the story (though not visually). Like most alternate commentaries, it first came to notice through the Internet, when it was provided for download on www.illegal-art.org.

One of the questions submitted to Gut via e-mail was, "Are you interested in the possibility of altering your own DVDs? Would you make commentary tracks, or compilations of scenes from a variety of movies?" He answered, "a collection of fave scenes and 'moments' would be a fun project. a kind of 'best of'. . . . that I would like. I doubt doing my own commentaries would happen. I'd rather listen to the experts and the ones who created the film."[21] The alternative commentaries, however, are becoming more and more insightful—and probably will soon begin to include ones by creators who have since fallen out with the copyright holders.

Gut's creativity comes out more in guiding people to films. Chris Freestone, The Q, and Andrew Fisher (Hurricane Andy) like to guide people through films. Others will like to comment on these commentators and on the commercial experts, leading to a sub-genre of commentaries on commentaries. At first, most of these will likely be commentaries offered as corrections to the ones that come with the DVDs, or parodies of them, mixing the new commentary with the old. Later, it can be imagined that people will offer their own commentaries to others, so that they can be added to, then passed on again until one commentary track is full and a second needs adding to the DVD.

Much of the sort of information that may be found on these commentaries is already available on the Internet, but it is currently difficult to use this information in immediate conjunction with the movies. Adding it directly to the medium containing the movie itself will make the information more accessible and more utilitarian for other users.

Just as new commentaries begin to appear, underground edits of the movies will show up, too. They already have, but not yet on DVD (where they can be hidden from the prying eyes of film studios), at least, not in numbers large enough to be noticeable. These will probably be divisible into several categories. One will be serious edits by students who are trying to learn the craft, taking films that failed and trying to see if they could be tightened. A film like *The Postman* (Kevin Costner, 1997), which runs 177 minutes in its theatrical release, could certainly become the clay for crafting shorter versions that might even be improvements on the originals.

Such editing of failed films (especially long ones) could create an underground of new cinema out of the old, a whole new aspect of the art—one that has been reserved, at least until now, for the originators of the films. Charlie Chaplin, for example, re-edited his *The Gold Rush* (Charles Chaplin, 1925) for a 1942 re-release, not only editing out at least one scene (a kiss at the end) but also adding a score and voice-over. The director's cut releases of the last few years are something of the same thing. In these cases, those doing the new edits may have a great deal more material at hand, but there are many cases where movies could certainly stand cutting even further by careful hands.

There are lawsuits currently under consideration in federal court in Colorado that concern, in part, companies that buy videotapes and DVDs and then alter them so that they will not be offensive to specific audiences, editing out scenes of nudity, for example, or changing "offensive" language. The Directors Guild is part of a suit claiming that the integrity of their creations is violated and that the reputation of each director can be impaired when people associate such unauthorized edits with them. The Guild will be no happier with fan aesthetic edits.

Even if the studios and the directors successfully manage to shut down the companies offering altered versions of their movies, technological innovations are likely to keep ahead of any protection programs on DVDs themselves. It is going to be extremely difficult to stop someone from making a private edit of a film on DVD, for it will not necessitate use of the Internet and will not be a commercial product. It will pass from hand to hand with its provenance ambiguous. It will be extremely difficult for the Motion Picture Association of America (MPAA), for example, to find anyone responsible for a discrete DVD—the traces of transferral and transmittal that remain on the Internet do not exist on the hard copy.

In the music world, DJs *sample* many different works, bringing them into new formation or including them even as parts of entirely new works—

works that rarely go beyond the specific club performance, thus avoiding copyright problems. Compilation DVDs created out of scenes from many movies, passed hand to hand for the same reason, will likely serve the same function, if software guards are finally broken. It is this sort of DVD that people like Gut may soon be creating.

Sound styles change. New types of music come into fashion and there are new vocabularies for listening. On the other hand, sounds that seem quaint and old-fashioned can be made new again, using contemporary sound-editing techniques. This is already being done (for sound recordings at least) in an authorized fashion. Working with the estate of Alan Lomax, Christopher Orman has produced *The Alan Lomax Remix Project—Tangle Eye*, taking recordings that Lomax made early in the last century and adding instrumental tracks to the vocals. A DJ named Danger Mouse combined aspects of The Beatles' *The White Album* with Jay-Z's *The Black Album*, creating what he calls *The Grey Album*. Similar things can happen in a DVD underground, taking out the musical soundtrack of a film and replacing it (while even keeping the dialogue) or adding to it. People will soon be doing much more than merely playing *Dark Side of the Moon* while *The Wizard of Oz* is on.

Given the power of the Internet and the speed of access today, it is possible for anyone to download a huge amount of information about any one topic—with videos and sound. This information can be organized on almost any computer into new *featurettes* on any topic imaginable. Films are particularly apt topics for this. Actors, after all, lead public, often photographed, often taped lives. Finding sound and image for a featurette is extraordinarily easy—especially if one is not concerned about copyright considerations, as DVD fan art creators will not be. Such things are certainly being created today by film aficionados with computer skills.

Another avenue of information for featurettes or addition to a DVD is scannable material—books, magazine articles, photographs. These can be added as part of a new creation or simply as additional information for the DVD. A fan of a film might want to collect information of all sorts on DVD, including pieces from a variety of media, which can now be collected conveniently on one DVD.

The difference between seeing a movie in the theater and experiencing it alone is often the sense of ownership that comes from that discovery and, if the film was discovered through Internet discussion, from the delight in finding a small community of the like-minded. But there is also a delight in showing the film to others at home, in leading friends to appreciation of the discovery one has made. For this reason, if nothing more, people will soon be preparing their own DVDs for home group viewing.

In fact, sharing films has always been an important aspect of viewer interaction with cinema. If art is defined as that which demands a response from its spectator and cinema is art, then there is definitely a need to consider responses to films and not to merely consider viewers as a passive audience. DVD viewing is far removed from television viewing (the type of viewing most often accused of promoting passivity), and the DVD viewer is active in a way a television viewer really isn't—the remote control serves a much more proactive function for the DVD.

In Japan, beginning at least as far back as the 1960s, a type of derivative fan art, an off-copyright movement called *doujinshi* (fan-club magazine) has developed, allowing followers of certain *manga* (comic books), to create their own stories and art out of the characters, plots, and narratives of the originals. There are doujinshis springing from many other art forms, too—and from almost anything else a person might develop a passion for. There are doujinshis on everything from history to poetry, travel to fairies, heavy metal to gardening. To keep away the hounds of the copyright lawyers, doujinshi are printed in extremely small runs. Though doujinshis do appear on the Internet, their main medium is print. American fan fiction (though now primarily an Internet creature) could certainly be classified as a type of doujinshi.

The importance of all fan art, including the doujinshi, is threefold: first, it allows for a new bonding between fans of the original, deepening and strengthening their connection to each other. Second, it promotes creativity after an initial creative event, a creativity sparked from, and based on, the initial item. And, third, it provides for a release of the pressure that can build up between producer and end user.

Doujinshi is expanding beyond Japan and manga, now including books and movies from other cultures, with J.K. Rowling's Harry Potter and J.R.R. Tolkien's Middle Earth being two of the most notable original sources. It is possible that it will expand beyond print (and reproduction on the Internet) as well. In fact, doujinshi could well describe that part of the growing DVD culture sparking whole new areas of creative endeavor—if, of course, holders of copyright are willing to recognize doujinshi value as it grows without dousing the sparks.

Though laws and attitudes toward copyright are somewhat different in the United States (witness, again, those RIAA lawsuits against college students for downloading MP3s), the popularity of the doujinshi is bound to be replicated in American fan art. In a culture where comics are not a central feature as they are in Japan, films are likely to become the inspirations for American doujinshi because of their distinct narrative, character, and visual aspects. In the meantime, most of the focus of DVD fans is on collecting and commentary, though the other is certainly developing.

Certainly, the possibilities associated with DVD technology are many—especially when the DVD is complemented by the Internet. It's impossible to predict what the future holds for the DVD. There are too many ways its use can be stifled in addition to the ways it can expand.

Chapter 4

THE SPECIAL
EDITION DVD

Going to the movies has never simply been the experience of sitting in a theater and letting a film wash over you. It involves experiencing the film as a public event and as part of the collective cultural consciousness. In the theater, it is also connected with the personal, physical experience: the company, the seating, and even the snacks. Packagers of the best film DVDs recognize this and some try hard to replace what is lost from the theater when the film is viewed at home. They strive to bring back what may be (for some) a remembered public event, returning the viewer to the vanished experience, even in the privacy of home.

Some DVD producers have also learned lessons from the videotape culture that arose over the twenty years before the introduction of the DVD—though it took some doing. One of these is the recognition that, to many, a film is not something to be watched once and then abandoned. There are many films that consumers prefer to own rather than rent and they know that the films will be watched by members of their families over and over again. There's a comfort in this, a fact sometimes unrecognized in the film industry. Quentin Tarantino remembers:

> When I worked in a video store, I heard parents complain about that, and they'd get mad at their children in the store: "You've seen that already! Try something new!" And I would take on the psychology of the kid. Where the children are coming from, they're not *blasé* about the movie experience. . . . "Well, why should I try something that I might not like? I *know* I'm gonna like *that*!" And it actually makes me wish I could be them in a way, that you could watch a movie 14, 15 times in a row—and they laugh through it every time![1]

Familiarity is an important part of film (it is even the basis of the high concept strategy of film creation). This is especially so since the advent of the
videotape, although film always has had a comforting aspect—witness Loudon Wainwright's 1970 song "The Movies Are a Mother to Me." But the
videotape quite literally brought that aspect home to observant moviemakers
as much as it did to the viewing public.

There had long been television movie favorites—and television executives have always operated on the knowledge that familiarity breeds dollars
(look at the lucrative nature of reruns). However, the film industry was slow
to take up its own growing understanding of this aspect of viewing for its
own financial reward outside of acceptance of that high concept, with its
rehash of the familiar, as motivation for new movies. When *That's Entertainment!* (Jack Haley, Jr., 1974) was released its success was seen in terms of a
passing nostalgia for a type of film that had fallen out of popularity. It took
the studios quite a while to realize that another part of its success was due to
genuine interest in the older films that people had seen but that had become
generally unavailable—even though people wanted to see them again. The
first of these to break out and achieve renewed success was *Singin' in the Rain*
(Gene Kelly and Stanley Donen, 1952).

Critical to the changing popular attitudes toward both home viewing
and older films—but noticed at the time of its founding only by serious film
fans—was the establishment in 1984 of the Criterion Collection by The
Voyager Company. Using laserdisc technology that allowed more flexible
access than was possible on a videotape and a wider variety of viewing con-
figurations, Criterion found that it could offer a number of sound options,
including dubbed or original language and commentary tracks. Just as
important, Criterion decided to present its films in a form that was as close
as possible to that of their theatrical releases, using letterboxing rather than
pan-and-scan and paying close attention both to the state of the original and
to the quality of the transfer to laser disc. It was the Criterion laserdisc, of
course, that became the model for the packaging of the DVD when it came
on the market more than a decade later.

Auteur-driven in its philosophy, Criterion focuses on presenting authoritative versions of the films with the directors' wishes as the final arbiter. Criterion immediately embraced the new DVD technology as a better means of
presenting films for home viewing and it still produces the most careful versions of movies on DVD that can be found anywhere, with the broadest, most
eclectic catalogue of any DVD packager. As Criterion's mission statement says:

Each film is presented uncut, in its original aspect ratio, as its maker intended it to be seen. For every disc, we track down the best available film elements in the world . . . to create the most pristine possible image and sound. Whenever possible, we work with directors and cinematographers to assure that the look of our releases does justice to their intentions.[2]

Perhaps because it was first envisioned during the days of the laserdisc and before the advent of the DVD or perhaps because its focus remains clearly on film itself, Criterion has never taken advantage of DVD possibilities the way other producers are beginning to do. Criterion sees the medium simply as a vehicle for film and film simply as the physical object created by a group of people (operating under a director's vision) at a particular time. The films on Criterion are presented as serious works of art deserving such reverential treatment that it makes it hard to imagine taking a Criterion DVD, slapping it into the player, flopping onto a couch with one's feet over the end, and watching a bit of a movie. The Criterion DVDs, in their presentation, demand a serious approach to viewing—even when the film is something like the absurdist, comedic, and none-too-successful *Fear and Loathing in Las Vegas* (Terry Gilliam, 1998) or the hilarious *This Is Spinal Tap* (Rob Reiner, 1984). In their reverence, they reflect an older film culture—not the newer DVD culture that is now growing, where the films are seen as less remote and more the possessions of the fans.

Another significant aspect of Criterion that keeps it from taking full advantage of DVD possibilities is their focus on directors as the nexus of film creation. This neo-*auteur* stance leads to concentration on the film itself as the significant event, especially when the director has been invited to take part in the creation of the DVD (seen not as a separate event in itself, but simply as a conveyance for the movie). A new type of viewing experience is rarely promoted at Criterion, though the company does sometimes move in this direction—witness the presentation of the original press book on the 1999 DVD release of Alfred Hitchcock's 1935 film *The 39 Steps*. Generally, the emphasis is on preservation of the film as originally envisioned by the director rather than creation of a new way of interacting with movies.

Perhaps an analogy between books and DVDs may clarify the important (if limited) role Criterion is playing in contemporary DVD virtual culture. What Criterion is doing is much the same as the work of a publisher of scholarly, authoritative editions of classic works. These are more than simply facsimile editions, for the attempt to restore the work to what the creators intended may change them from what was the first release. Analogously, a new edition of *The Adventures of Huckleberry Finn*, through utilization of scholarly research, may show an attempt to bring the text more in line with what Samuel Clemens may have intended. Like the academic editions, Criterion attempts to provide a serious apparatus promoting further study of the film while keeping the extras accessible to the average viewer. Unlike popular editions, these are meant to be cherished and studied and not simply used.

Though it still sets the standard, Criterion is (fortunately) not the only source for classic films. By the early 1990s, Hollywood had finally learned (partly from the Criterion laserdisc example) that film fans wanted more than a look back at clips from earlier films; they wanted the films themselves and to know more about their creation. A first wave of featurettes and documentaries made specifically for new videotape releases of movies began to appear. Film companies had also begun responding to a demand for restored and respected home versions of older films. Letterboxing began to be accepted—even preferred by a certain segment of the buying public—even before the advent of the DVD. There was a pent-up desire to view unadulterated films at home.

The best producers of DVDs today are constantly trying to find new ways of utilizing the medium for presenting movies. They are not merely putting film on DVD or repackaging videotapes; they are creating new objects that utilize the possibilities of the new medium. The extended editions of *The Lord of the Rings* (Peter Jackson, 2001, 2002, 2003), each with more than a half an hour of extra footage inserted in the movie itself, are setting the standard for DVD releases of contemporary movies. Each of these is actually a *second* release on DVD, the shorter (theatrical) versions having been released a few months earlier. They come in matching, color-differentiated slipcovers and (in addition to the movies themselves) contain quite a number of extra features, all created and presented with a great deal of care. The main documentaries, for example, are indexed together, allowing access to specific topics. Also, creative attribution is given for each documentary or featurette, showing that they are taken seriously as works in their own right. Such a level of respect is not yet found on all DVDs.

There are a variety of possibilities for presentation on the DVD, and not merely for the end users who find new ways of altering them and personalizing them for their own collections. Because they work so well with text, image (still or moving), and sound (as well as having avenues for crossing all of these with each other), it will be years before any catalogue of DVD features will begin to be able to approach completion—and that's just talking about DVDs for film. The medium, of course, also carries games, music (including concert videos), and television shows. At some point it will also deliver books and magazines, with the remote control becoming a page-turner. This is still a new medium, after all, with a great deal of untapped potential.

Today, most new issue DVDs do contain a number of common features, a developing "standard" for DVD release, including 5.1 Dolby sound, anamorphic aspect ratio reflecting the movie's Original Aspect Ratio (OAR), subtitles in English and at least one other language, and a dubbed soundtrack. Certain other features are becoming definable for inclusion as part of the special edition DVD. Though these have not yet gelled into an expected apparatus for the authoritative DVD version of a film, viewers are beginning to demand more than merely a film, a commentary, and a trailer.

The DVD today fits smoothly into what Annette Kuhn, a professor of Film Studies at Lancaster University, identifies from interviews with filmgoers as five types of topographical memory: "memory maps; the guided tour; discursive distance/immersion in the past; shared remembering; and associations and detours."[3] Kuhn is speaking specifically of the ways we remember film, but the DVD works well with our ways of remembering films, and is certainly becoming the physical repository, in a sense, of those memories. Not surprisingly, each one of Kuhn's five types can be shown to have an analogy in a specific type of the extras commonly found on DVDs, especially those for older movies.

The *Commentary Tracks* that began as a feature of Criterion laserdiscs soon became almost a necessary part of the DVD issue of a movie—certainly of a special edition. For older movies, film critics and historians are recruited to present the commentary, focusing on the personalities of the actors and filmmakers, anecdotes about the making, and trivia concerning the films. The commentaries range from inane to interesting, but not much else outside these parameters, leaving open the possibility of commentaries that interact more vigorously with the viewing experience. Perhaps the off-the-cuff commentaries (as many are) could best be seen as what Kuhn refers to as "associations and detours." Others serve the purpose of "shared remembering."

The most prestigious commentaries are those by the directors of the films, sparked by the Criterion example. The best of these are serious discussions of the problems and background of the filming, such as Terry Gilliam's for the Criterion DVD of *Brazil* (1985). The worst are off-the-cuff reminiscences, such as that by director Jean-Pierre Jeunet and star Ron Perlman for the DVD of *The City of the Lost Children* (Jean-Pierre Jeunet and Marc Caro, 1998), who hardly seem to have been able to remember the movie as they recorded their comments.

Technical Information. This comes in all sorts of guises on DVD. Sometimes it's a simple listing of everything from OAR to sound presentation to color processing. In other cases, short documentaries detail the processes behind the movie. The DVD of *Oh! Brother, Where Art Thou?* (Ethan Coën and Joel Coën, 2000), for example, presents an interesting featurette about the way color is manipulated in the lab for the purposes of a contemporary film.

Historical Information. Most of the featurettes in this category were filmed as entertainment, not as serious attempts to present history. Often manufactured by the subjects themselves, these are clearly not meant as objective analyses of the films or their contexts. Still, if their natural biases are discounted, these featurettes can provide a great deal of useful information or can at least point the viewer toward avenues of fruitful exploration. In the future, as the lucrative nature of re-releases with extensive apparatus becomes even more apparent, documentarians may begin to focus on providing stronger material for DVD releases. Peter Fitzgerald already specializes in DVD documentaries; others will no doubt take up what he has been doing and go further. Most of these serve the purposes of the memory maps described by Kuhn.

Interviews. Like most things related to the DVD, these range from the serious and detailed to fluff. Unfortunately, reflecting a business that is to a large degree personality driven, the interviews on DVDs tend toward self-promotion, not serious examination. They also tend to be nostalgic, what Kuhn calls "immersions in the past." The best interviews are those recorded for other purposes, where the interviewer is not beholden to the interviewee or the project. Both Quentin Tarantino and Michael Moore, for example, have included interviews from *The Charlie Rose Show* on their DVDs, in part because these interviews carry more weight than the ones staged for the DVDs do.

"The Making of... " Documentaries. Some of these are merely tours of sets, with smiles from cast and crew. Others are detailed examinations of the various aspects of the production. The most interesting of these are the newest, where the filmmakers have deliberately set out to make a record of their activities for inclusion on the inevitable DVD. The absolute best of these (outside of the meticulous featurettes supervised by Peter Jackson and for *The Lord of the Rings*) are also the most independent. Keith Fulton and Louis

Pepe, for example, were given permission by Terry Gilliam to film the movie-making process of *Twelve Monkeys* (Terry Gilliam, 1995). The result was the documentary *The Hamster Factor and Other Tales of the Twelve Monkeys* (1996), which is also included on the *Twelve Monkeys* DVD. These really become the guided tours described by Kuhn.

Documents. Like the two-disc special edition DVD of *Casablanca* (Michael Curtiz, 1942), which contains a slide show of old Warner Brothers documents, some DVDs actually reproduce documents related to the production. These can range from shooting scripts to internal memoranda and even private letters from involved parties.

Games and Quizzes. Some of these are connected to the Internet, and so require DVD-ROM; others need no more than the DVD and a television. Many of them center on what has come to be called the "easter egg" of the DVD. These are hidden internal links to game clues, special information, or a special feature. There are also a number of trivia quizzes, usually dealing with information internal to the particular movies.

Deleted Scenes. The problem with these is that they are rarely cut back into the movie. There are, of course, numerous reasons for not including deleted scenes within the movies themselves on the DVDs. Clearly, adding them back in alters the movies. Sometimes, the deletions had improved the films and were made by the directors themselves to enhance the overall impact of their work. However, deletions have too often been made in order to meet external demands, such as ensuring a running time that allows a maximum number of daily showings. Adding scenes back in that were cut for this or a similar reason does make some sense.

Unfortunately, adding the scenes back in is no simple matter. There can be any number of editing considerations, not the least being the soundtrack. Often, the deleted scenes were not scored or the music was not recorded. Therefore, they cannot be easily reinserted into the films. Some more recent films were made by people who foresaw that they could use the DVD to present a larger version of their films than would be possible for theater release, taking a cue from the director's cut releases on videotape that began to appear in the early 1990s. One of these filmmakers, of course, was Peter Jackson of *The Lord of the Rings*. In most cases, however, reinsertion of deleted scenes disrupts the flow of the movie.

One temporary solution has been to include the deleted scenes, but separately. Another is to provide an easter egg link from the movie to the deleted scene. In either case, the transition is awkward. The only real solution to this problem is movement into the digital future, in which films will always be made with an eye toward eventual DVD release, and all work will be completed with the possibility of authorized alternate versions in mind.

Alternate Versions. The most notorious unauthorized alternate version now on DVD is that of *Brazil* (Terry Gilliam, 1985). The Criterion DVD contains two complete versions of the film, though only the director's cut is treated with much care. In other cases, it is alternative endings, as with *Bandits* (Barry Lewison, 2001) or, in the case of *The Adventures of Buckaroo Banzai Across the Eighth Dimension* (W.D. Richter, 1984), an alternate beginning. As with deleted scenes, there are problems with how to present these. With *Buckaroo Banzai*, because the two versions dovetail, the problem is not so great: just choose one and watch the movie. When it is the ending that provides alternatives, should a choice be provided in the film itself, or should one ending (that of the theatrical release, generally) be given precedence and the other provided merely as an extra? This last was the choice made for *Bandits*.

Music and Soundtracks. The DVDs of *Pulp Fiction* (Quentin Tarantino, 1994) and *Jackie Brown* (Quentin Tarantino, 1997), which rely heavily on popular music for their soundtracks, provide indexes of songs so that viewers can go right to the scene where a particular song appears. Sometimes the soundtrack is presented separately so that it is possible to listen to it without watching the movie or hearing the dialogue. Other DVDs present scoring sessions (the actual recording of the music for the film). Some DVDs, especially of foreign films, provide a variety of soundtracks. Not only does this provide greater viewing options, but it allows the viewer to make comparisons between soundtracks. Switching back and forth between the English dubbing and the original soundtrack of *Hong Kong 1941* (Po-Chih Leong, 1984), for example, shows the weakness not only of the English dialogue but of the music chosen in place of the original.

Cartoons, Shorts, Trailers, and Newsreels. These are added for a variety of reasons, from simple use as filler to presentation of what might have been a complete bill when the film was first released. Sometimes, trailers for other movies are inserted at the start of the DVD, making viewers watch or skip through them in order to get to the menu or the movie itself. The Walt Disney Company is notorious for doing this, especially on DVDs of its animated features. In other cases, a special feature (called suggested viewing) is presented, generally of other films produced on DVD by the same production company.

Additional Movies. Rarely—but often enough to deserve mention—an entire second feature is included on a DVD. One of these is a film starring James Mason called *Charade* (Roy Kellino, 1953) that is included on the DVD of the Cary Grant/Audrey Hepburn vehicle *Charade* (Stanley Donen, 1963). Oddly enough, another DVD, the one of the *Charade* remake *The Truth About Charlie* (Jonathan Demme, 2002) also contains the Grant/Hepburn *Charade*. These are different from collection DVDs, such as those presenting up to four early Westerns on one DVD. Here, the second film is not advertised as a primary feature, but is considered an adjunct to the main movie.

There are, of course, many other extras possible on a DVD, but these are the most common so far and are the ones most likely found on a random contemporary DVD release. Over time, new ones will appear, and some of the older ones will probably go out of style. Generally, the extras are found through a menu that appears once the DVD is loaded, a menu that also allows the viewer to pick from audio options, commentaries, and presents the possibility of skipping to a specific chapter or section of the film. DVD designers are constantly experimenting with the menus, and these, too, will likely change dramatically over the next few years.

Sometimes the attempts at providing extras become amusing, if not downright bizarre, though most of these do not show up on the DVDs themselves. A "VIP" edition of *Showgirls* (Paul Verhoeven, 1995), for example, includes pasties, shot glasses, games, and a lap-dance tutorial. A special edition of *Scarface* (Brian De Palma, 1983) has a velvet-lined case and comes with a money clip. Extras such as these add little to the movies and become, ultimately, little more than collectibles.

In part because the information explosion of the digital age allows it, interaction with the movies is no longer just with issues raised in them, but with issues around them. DVD extras allow examination of such controversies, especially when used in conjunction with the Internet. Certainly, as in the past, film fans are learning about movies from books, too, but books can't convey film quite as accurately or dramatically as video or film itself.

One significance of the DVD special edition, especially for older films, is that these editions really are bringing the films back to life. Yes, this is sometimes due to restorations that also show up in the cinemas, but it is DVD and videotape sales that make the restorations economically feasible. The DVDs, thanks to the extras, also often place the movies in context, both that of the making and of reaction after the fact. In the 1990s, young people often thought of films from the 1970s as the classics, rarely looking further back or watching black-and-white films, for example. After all, even the few black-and-white films available on videotape (in comparison with the number of color films) were generally poor transfers to boot, almost unwatchable to those born long after their day. Now that these new viewers can see the old films as they were meant to be seen, resistance to black-and-white among the young is diminishing, just as is resistance to letterboxing.

The best way to present the extent and variety of DVD extras is to examine a number of DVD special editions, some of classic films, others of recent ones—and just such an examination follows here. The choices have been made not simply because of the quality of the films or their importance (in some cases, this has not been a consideration at all), but because they demonstrate one aspect or another of what the DVD as a medium offers:

The Adventures of Antoine Doinel: Five Films by François Truffaut (Criterion, 2003). Includes *The 400 Blows* (1959), *Antoine and Colette* (1962), *Stolen Kisses* (1968), *Bed and Board* (1970), and *Love on the Run* (1979): Only once has a director had the privilege of working with one actor playing one character over 20 years, from childhood to established adulthood. Through five films—four features and a short—François Truffaut was able to do just that. This pales, however, next to the importance of the first film in the series, *The 400 Blows*. Not only was the film the first major achievement of the Nouvelle Vague, but it energized hundreds of new filmmakers in France, and then thousands worldwide. Though it rests at #160 of the top 250 films as voted by users on imdb.com[4] (as of 7/19/04; all of the listings that follow reflect ranking as of this date) that's probably only because most of the voters are native English speakers, many of whom maintain a hostility to subtitled or dubbed movies, and few of whom like to watch movies in black-and-white. Only a handful of movies have had anything like the impact of *The 400 Blows*.

One of the features of boxed set releases that has become almost standard is an extra disc packaged in a case separate from the movie DVDs (which are themselves often in pairs, one for the film, the other for the extras). Rather than focusing on the particular film, these generally present a broader perspective. For *The Adventures of Antoine Doinel*, included are excerpts from an interview with Truffaut that focuses on Jean-Pierre Léaud, who plays Antoine in all the movies. There is also an extended excerpt from *Portrait of François Truffaut*, a documentary made early in the director's career. Unfortunately, these act merely as teasers for the serious film fan or scholar, who would want the entirety of each one available. Only one of the documentaries is complete, *Working with François Truffaut*, made after the director's death, featuring interviews with several of his collaborators.

Though it is frustrating for the serious film student to find the offerings on such a set limited, the features that *are* offered would never be easily available otherwise. One of these is an early (1957) Truffaut short, *Les Mitons* (*The Mischief Makers*), which is introduced by Truffaut scholar Serge Toubiana and includes a commentary track.

The small book that comes with the set is filled with articles, reviews, and interviews, all of which could easily have been included on a second extra DVD, perhaps making room for complete (rather than excerpted) documentaries. Given that the book is probably more expensive to produce than a DVD would be, this is a surprising use of an older technology by a group as concerned as Criterion is with using technology to preserve film.

Another notable thing about Criterion is that the company does often not consider the DVD as anything more than a vehicle for carrying film and information about film. To Criterion, the DVD is not used as a radically new medium, encompassing many older media and allowing interactions not possible elsewhere. As a vehicle for a group of films and information about those films, this set of DVDs serves its purpose very well; as a set that embraces the full possibilities of the DVD, it isn't quite so interesting.

The Adventures of Buckaroo Banzai Across the Eighth Dimension (W.D. Richter, 1984; DVD, 20th Century Fox, 2001): This film grossed a miserable $6 million[5] in its theatrical release but it found new life on videotape and, now, on DVD. The movie was aimed toward becoming a cult film by presenting a fictional cult around the main character, providing a tongue-in-cheekiness that, it was hoped, could give it something of the cachet of *The Rocky Horror Picture Show* (Jim Sharman, 1975). It *has* become a cult favorite, but not quite in the way the filmmakers intended: it's not the satire that makes the movie popular, but its unintentional self-parody—oh, and the zany villainy of John Lithgow, Christopher Lloyd and their cohorts.

The DVD is constructed on the conceit that the movie tells a true story. This allows for a playfulness in the extras and menus that might be difficult to attain otherwise. The creators of the DVD must have had a great deal of fun: There is more information about the film's fictional universe here than one can imagine for anything smaller than a franchise the size of a *Harry Potter, Star Trek,* or even *Star Wars.* Yet there was only one Buckaroo Banzai film ever made, with very few spin-offs. The text profiles of the Hong Kong Cavaliers (Buckaroo Banzai's rock band and "associates") and the *Banzai Institute*

Archives (which even includes a radio interview and reviews of the movie from *The New York Times* and *Hollywood Reporter*) can lead the viewer to imagine that there is more going on here than there actually is. "Pinky Carruther's Unknown Facts" (Pinky is a minor character in the film), a subtitle trivia track, serves something of the same function during the viewing of the movie, bringing texture to a universe that exists only on the DVD.

Here, the deleted scenes, unfortunately, are taken from a videotape retained by the director; the originals having disappeared. They are not as crisp as the film, so they could never be reinserted in it. They do, however, make a little more sense of a plot that is, for the most part, impossible to untangle. It is too bad that these cannot be inserted, for (unlike many deleted scenes) they would actually strengthen the film.

To keep up the fiction of this being a "true" film, there is no room for biographies of the actors or of much discussion of the development of the film, though there is a featurette on the making of the film, *Buckaroo Banzai Declassified* (Michael Arick, 2002) which carries on the conceit of "reality" by treating the film itself as a documentary. What remains most interesting about the DVD, however, is that it clearly became the final resting place of information and ideas that Buckaroo Banzai's creators at one point must have felt would be the underpinnings of a franchise. A franchise that, fortunately or unfortunately, never came into existence.

By providing an overarching conceit for the DVD presentation, the creators of the *Buckaroo Banzai* DVD have pointed out the direction in which much DVD structure will go (in fact, is already going). Instead of simply taking things from the movies—bits of dialogue, striking visual images, or sounds—and using them to create menus, packagers are going outside of the film for some of the pieces of their constructs and creating new frameworks for the movies. The context of the film, whether fictional or real, becomes an ever more important part of its DVD presentation.

Bowling for Columbine (Michael Moore, 2002; DVD, MGM Home Entertainment, 2003): Michael Moore doesn't make films for art. He is a crusader who has embraced the movies as a means toward his political ends. *Bowling for Columbine* is a pro-gun-control film that uses examination of the surroundings of the tragedy at Columbine High School in Littleton, Colorado in 1999 as an anchor for exploration of the place of guns in American society. A film like this, with a clear, unapologetic political stance, automatically becomes part of a dialogue reaching far beyond the theater or the kitchen table, becoming part of the discourse of newspapers, news magazines, and the growing discussions on the Internet. The DVD, then, becomes something more than a vehicle for the film itself, it is both part of an ongoing debate and a corrective.

Given the firestorm surrounding *Bowling for Columbine*, it's surprising (and impressive) that Michael Moore has only identified and corrected one error in moving the film from reel to DVD:

> I have found one typo in the theatrical release of the film. It was a caption that read, "Willie Horton released by Dukakis and kills again." In fact, Willie Horton was a convicted murderer who, after escaping from furlough, *raped* a woman and *stabbed* her fiancé, but didn't *kill* him. The caption has been permanently corrected on the DVD and home video version of the film and replaced with, "Willie Horton released. Then rapes a woman."[6]

Many movies make changes for the DVD releases, but Moore makes the insignificance of the only one he needed a political statement in itself, owning up to it on his website as part of a rebuttal to some of the numerous accusations of inaccuracy that have been leveled against him.

In a way, Moore is one of the most honest filmmakers around. After all, it is impossible to keep political attitudes out of movies. Every film, when one digs deeply enough, reveals underlying assumptions and a worldview of both the director and (when the film's relative success is taken into account) the viewer. David Blakesley, a specialist in visual rhetoric, writes that

> As cultural expression, films not only reveal the predispositions of filmmakers but also serve ideological functions in the broader culture (as critique, as hegemonic force, as symptomatic) that can be analyzed as having a rhetorical function, especially to the extent that rhetoric serves as the means of initiating cultural critique and stabilizing cultural pieties.[7]

Moore keeps his attitudes at the forefront of all his work, never pretending to an "objectivity" that he sees as giving false weight to opposing, but often incorrect or even ludicrous, opinions.

Moore sees the confluence of books, the Internet, DVDs, and movies as one conversation that he is a part of, not differentiating between the specifics of the medium. All of them are changeable and all convey error. Moore writes:

[L]ately I've begun to see so many things about me or my work that aren't true. It's become so easy to spread these fictions through the Internet (thanks mostly to lazy reporters or web junkies who do all their research by typing in "key words" and then just repeat the same mistakes). And so I wonder that if I don't correct the record, then all of the people who don't know better may just end up being filled with a bunch of stuff that isn't true.[8]

The DVD and the Web site come to work in tandem, providing a documentarian and activist like Moore the chance to constantly keep on top of the controversies he is part of.

With the story of his Academy Awards speech and a speech he gave at the University of Denver, Moore makes it clear that his purpose is political. Their very inclusion on the DVD emphasizes the point. In his discussion of the Academy Award, Moore, seated in a backyard at a picnic table, addresses the camera (and his audience) in an extremely personal manner, making the talk seem as one-on-one as possible. That this segment is followed by the excerpts from his Denver speech is no accident; Moore is mixing the personal with the public in order to further his political agenda. Just so, he uses the DVD, which is personal in a way that the Internet is not, making his appeal both to the crowd and to the individual.

The assumption behind this DVD is that the DVD is preaching to the converted. That is, given the large amount of publicity around *Bowling for Columbine*, especially since the Academy Awards speech, few people antagonistic to Moore's political stance would likely buy the DVD. Thus, there is little outside of the film itself that is proselytizing on the DVD. The teacher's guide, which requires Internet connection, doesn't try to convince teachers, but to give teachers already converted ways of approaching the issues raised in the film in the classroom.

Moore, of course, tries to extend his egalitarian political philosophy to his DVD, but with mixed success. Quick to recognize the implications of the audio commentaries on DVDs, Moore provides a "Receptionists' and Interns' Audio Commentary" instead of one by the director, emphasizing that filmmaking is a collaborative process, not a simply hierarchical one. Still, Michael Moore remains at the center of the DVD, just as he is in the film. Playing with what are becoming the conventions of the DVD, Moore also includes a music video, Marilyn Manson's "Fight Song," reflecting the controversy over motivation for the Columbine killings that included fingers pointed at Marilyn Manson.

Because the DVD in general can attack its subject from so many aspects of virtual culture (even more, when used in conjunction with the Internet), it will likely soon become the propaganda vehicle of choice for political movements outside of the mainstream. Because of its discrete existence, it offers more privacy than does the Internet, so some might find it more comfortable to learn from a DVD rather than across the Internet. Movies associated with movements that are unorthodox or outspokenly critical of the status quo often have a hard time getting extensive theater distribution (*Bowling for Columbine* is somewhat the exception), as was the case with Moore's 2004 film *Fahrenheit 9/11*. Therefore, activists, be they for religions or political movements, will probably use DVDs and the mails more and more as their means of distribution. Also, it is likely that these DVDs will be anchored by movies, for they provide a focus for the political discussion that a series of shorter pieces would not be able to do so effectively. Imagine the *Bowling for Columbine* DVD without the movie, merely with the political message of the extras; it could never have the same impact.

Brazil (Terry Gilliam, 1985; DVD, Criterion, 1999): Perhaps because of his background as an illustrator and animator—or because of the nonlinear nature of *Monty Python's Flying Circus*, of which Gilliam was an important part—Terry Gilliam has never pushed narrative (or narrative consistency) to the forefront of his filmmaking. Maybe this is part of the reason that Universal Studios felt they could take this movie from him, truncate it, and change the ending. The resulting public stand-off before theatrical release was big industry news, and it led to bigger box-office receipts for *Brazil* than it could have reasonably expected. Still, its devoted fan base has grown, if anything, in the decades since its release—leading it to a spot as #182 on the imdb.com top 250 list. Even so, it is only natural that the controversy would have a central place on this extensive DVD release.

There are two complete versions of *Brazil* in this set, one a director's cut that is treated with all the respect one expects from Criterion, the other a sloppy transfer treated with all the disdain that Gilliam feels for it, for it is the "love conquers all" version cobbled together by the studio without his permission. As it was the version first shown on television, it is appropriate that it is a pan-and-scan movie, but Criterion seems to have gone out of its way to make it as unwatchable as possible, especially in comparison to the other version. Significantly, Gilliam provides the audio commentary for his version, leaving the other to Monty Python expert David Morgan, who focuses on the differences between the two versions.

Gilliam's commentary is one of the few where the director really takes the job seriously. Though there is humor in it, and trivia (Gilliam tells us that he hates baseball caps), the commentary gives a serious look at a director's artistic vision.

Also included are a number of documentaries on the making of *Brazil* and a sequence of storyboards. When this DVD came out in 1999 it set an early standard for boxed set DVDs. More importantly, however, it shows how a careful DVD release can be used to settle scores or to set the record straight (depending on one's point of view). The *Brazil* DVD certainly adds to the debate over who should control a movie—the director or the studio—even though it skews its argument to one side in petty ways (the poor quality of the "love conquers all" version, for example). This set certainly makes a strong case for directorial control; still, it will be interesting to see if anyone comes up with a DVD showing how a studio "saved" a film from the director's "excesses."

The very existence of the two versions of *Brazil* shows just how much has changed in the film industry since its early days. MGM actually destroyed most of Erich von Stroheim's *Greed* (1926); Irving Thalberg himself made sure that the full (or director's cut, as it would now be called) version of the film (some 10 hours long) would never be seen. The same thing happened to Orson Welles, who lost control of *The Magnificent Ambersons* (1942) and whose own version was subsequently destroyed by the studio.

Casablanca (Michael Curtiz, 1942; DVD, Warner Bros. Home Video, 2003): Maybe the first film to attract a cult following outside of television, *Casablanca* attracted audiences in the 1960s who were so passionate about it that many could recite the film verbatim—and this before the advent of the videotape and repeat home viewing. Lines from the film became cultural touchstones, even to the point where a deliberate misquote could become a movie title, *Play It Again, Sam* (Herbert Ross, 1972), from a play by Woody Allen (who also stars in the movie). A special edition DVD of *Casablanca*, therefore, had to be carefully prepared.

The new digital transfer, for those used to seeing the movie on television or in theaters showing much-abused elderly prints, comes as quite a revelation and shows how important the DVD can be in reinvigorating popular film culture. But it is the extras that make this a particularly interesting and significant DVD release (this two-disc set is not the first, or even the second, release of *Casablanca* on DVD, but it is the first prepared specifically for the new medium). Some of the extras have been around for years, prepared for special-edition videotapes in the 1990s, but much of the material here is new, including commentaries by Roger Ebert and Rudy Behlmer. Both are more popular than academic, but each commentator clearly knows the film well and takes the task seriously. Ebert concentrates on the movie itself, for the most part, while Behlmer puts it into its milieu. There is also a Lauren Bacall Introduction; *You Must Remember This: A Tribute to* Casablanca (1992). Again with Lauren Bacall, there is a short look at the making of the film that was created for a 50th anniversary special-edition videotape. There is a backstage tour; *Bacall on Bogart* (David Heeley, 1988), a 90 minute, adoring retrospective on Humphrey Bogart that, like *That's Entertainment!*, does little more than whet the appetite, as it is long on nostalgia but short on substance; additional scenes and outtakes; and a number of other items.

Of interest as a DVD feature is the radio production of *Casablanca* with the three main stars, presented with no attempt to add a visual aspect. Also included is a scoring session that, again, concentrates on the sound without emphasis on picture, for the most part. There is also a slideshow that reproduces original memos concerning the picture, often showing the printed message "Verbal Messages Cause Misunderstanding and Delays (Please Put Them in Writing)."[9] This fascinating feature would be a little more useful if it were set up as separate screens. As it is, it plays right through unless the viewer uses the pause button. The only problem with a feature like this is that it provides merely a selection of relevant documents. It would probably be asking too much, however, to expect to see *all* of them.

The special edition DVD of *Casablanca*, along with that of *Singin' in the Rain* (Gene Kelly and Stanley Donen, 1952), has set the bar for the non-Criterion special edition DVDs. A sadness in watching *Casablanca* over the past 20 years or more has been the loss of luster of the film itself: Ingrid Bergman's eyes had not sparkled for a long, long time. The restoration behind the DVD transfer here has brought the light back into them.

The Chaplin Collection, Volume 1 & Volume 2 (Warner Home Video and MK2, 2003 & 2004). Includes *The Gold Rush* (Charles Chaplin, 1925, 1942), *The Great Dictator* (Charles Chaplin, 1940), *Modern Times* (Charles Chaplin, 1936), and *Limelight* (Charles Chaplin, 1952); and *The Kid* (1921), *A Woman in Paris* (1923), *The Circus* (1928), *City Lights* (1931), *Monsieur Verdoux* (1947), and *A King in New York* (1957): It is odd that the first volume of the Chaplin collection doesn't concentrate on Chaplin's "little fellow," or even on Chaplin's silent films, the bulk of his work. Two of the main features do present the tramp, but the unity of this volume is sound, not Chaplin's iconographic character. Volume 2, however, which presents shorts going back as far as 1918 as well as one film more recent than any-thing on Volume 1, bookends the earlier volume and does contain a substan-tial number of movies featuring the little tramp.

The longer, silent version of *The Gold Rush* is present only on the second disc for the movie, the primary offering being the 1942 version, re-edited, scored, and narrated by Chaplin. *Modern Times*, the last of the tramp films made, is distinct in that it is also the only one where the character speaks (though in song, and in nonsense verse at that). The other two films on Vol-ume 1 are talkies and lack the Tramp. Still, *The Gold Rush*, *Modern Times*, and *The Great Dictator* are arguably Chaplin's greatest films, and so are fit for a first volume of his collected work. Volume 2 contains a number of the Tramp films as well as two later, relatively unsuccessful movies.

Most of the disc sets of both volumes follow a similar pattern, including an Introduction (directed by Philippe Truffault, 2003) by David Robinson, a Chaplin biographer, each of which opens with the camera looking over Rob-inson's shoulder as he readers from a manuscript (an interesting emphasis on the importance of text). From that point on, images primarily from each film are shown behind the narration, with occasional shots of photographs and scripts, posters and production schedules, and so forth. For the most part, the Introductions are on the second discs and not with the movies, which can be a bit inconvenient and belies their designation as the Introduction.

Monsieur Verdoux, *A King in New York,* and *A Woman of Paris* are not given 2-disc status, so Robinson's Introduction for each is actually on the same disc as the movie, as is the Introduction on each disc of the collection of short films. Though interesting, these Introductions are all too short to have much weight, and do contain errors, some glaringly obvious, as when Robinson describes a shot as showing "workers streaming out of a factory"[10] in *Modern Times* while the footage shows them coming from what is clearly labeled a subway. (This type of error, insignificant though it may be, will be less and less likely as writers like Robinson are able to see the actual film on a computer while writing about it in another window on the same screen— another small advantage of the DVD). Though each Introduction is well-meant and interesting as far as it goes, neither they nor their placement show an understanding of the possibilities in the medium conveying them, the DVD.

The *Chaplin Today* (2003) series with chapters accompanying most of the movies and created by Serge Toubiana uses old footage and interviews with contemporary directors as well as home movies and interviews with Chaplin's sons. These clearly show just how the DVD is starting to be used for more than just reminiscences. This series puts Chaplin in the middle of world cinema, where he belongs, showing the influence he has had on film-makers everywhere. Again, there is no hesitation in bringing in text as props.

On the *Modern Times* second disc is a silent Department of Labor film called *Behind the Scenes in the Machine Age* (1931) that focuses on women in the workplace. Also included is a Ford Motor Company film showing the processes of the auto industry to music called *Symphony in F* (1940), a Liber-ace short from his 1956 television show called *Smile* and the short Cuban film *Por Primera Vez* (Octavio Cortazar, 1967), a good background to the issues surrounding the film and its influence. *Por Primera Vez*, for example, shows the arrival of cinema for the first time to a Cuban mountain village. The movie shown is, of course, *Modern Times*, #71 on the imdb.com top 250 films list.

The music of *Limelight* is presented separately over stills from the movie, allowing it to be experienced alone, taking advantage of the fact that a DVD doesn't have to be watched only, but can easily carry quality recordings. Chaplin composed his own scores, so this is a most appropriate addition. Like sound, text can stand alone on a DVD, or can just work with sound. Also included on the *Limelight* DVD are two short readings by Chaplin from *Footlights*, the novel Chaplin wrote as background for *Limelight*. One shows a still from the movie, the other reproduces the page from the novel.

Unlike the Warner Legends discs, these discs are not set up as entertain-ment products in themselves. That is, the discs are not set up to be shows. Like Criterion discs, it doesn't seem that the designers of this collection were cognizant of all the possibilities inherent in the new conveyance medium. The focus is on Chaplin and the Chaplin films, not on how they (and under-standing of them) can be enhanced through utilization of the new medium.

The decision to put the 1942 version of *The Gold Rush* on the first of the two discs devoted to the film is a bit perplexing, as it gives this shorter ver-sion a primacy it should not have, though the later version was reworked by Chaplin himself, with a soundtrack including his own narration. It is the ear-lier version that most associate with the name *The Gold Rush*, later authorial desire notwithstanding. It is the 1925 version that is recognized as the more important of the two, and that is ranked #152 of imdb.com's top 250 films.

Included on *The Great Dictator,* the one film with no Robinson Intro-duction or Toubiano chapter, is the made-for-TV movie *The Tramp and the*

Dictator (Kevin Brownlow and Michael Kloft, 2002). It uses footage from Sydney Chaplin home movies, which are also included in their entirety. Using the profession of the main character as reason for inclusion, there's also an older scene, deleted from another Chaplin movie, of Chaplin as a barber. Like *Modern Times* and *The Gold Rush*, *The Great Dictator* is on imdb.com's top 250 list, coming in at #97.

The seven short films made for First National during the years just after World War I bring the Tramp back to his position as an enthusiastic and vibrant film presence, replacing the vague ghost he had become. These, perhaps even more than his great feature-length films of the next decades, are what cemented Chaplin's reputation throughout the world. The extras for *The Kid*, *A Woman in Paris*, *The Circus*, and *City Lights* are similar to those on the volume of shorts (indeed, a few are repeated). It is surprising that a movie as important as *City Lights*, and as popular (it lies at #91 on the imdb.com fan list), gets so little special attention.

Because of the skill and care shown in the transfers, and the use of restored or well-preserved originals, this set has already shown itself to be part of a movement to reestablish the silent film as a serious, effective art form, not merely as practice art awaiting sound for fulfillment. Over the next few years, other restorations and presentations of work from the silent era may well manage to completely resuscitate the genre.

Classic Movies Collection: The Cole Porter Gift Set (DVD, Warner Home Video, 2003) includes *High Society* (Charles Walters, 1956), *Les Girls* (George Cukor, 1957), *Silk Stockings* (Rouben Mamoulian, 1957), *Broadway Melody of 1940* (Norman Taurog, 1940), and *Kiss Me Kate* (George Sidney, 1953): In the entry on Eleanor Powell in his *The New Biographical Dictionary of Film*, David Thomson writes:

> You are in solitary confinement for the rest of your life. There is a screen built into the cell wall, and it is a condition of your sentence that you may have just one sequence from a movie to play on that screen. This is my choice: black and white and a hard reflective floor, a set that recedes into darkness. Fred all in white with a black bowtie. Eleanor Powell . . . wears short sleeves and puff shoulders; the skirt is magnificently light and fluid, moving to the sway of the profound, yet casual, tap masterpiece, "Begin the Beguine," from *Broadway Melody of 1940*.[11]

This set of musicals (all based on Cole Porter songs) contains no really memorable movies, but the memorable scenes are astonishing. Not only is there the one that Thomson describes, but *Kiss Me Kate* contains the first sample of Bob Fosse's unique choreography and *Silk Stockings* has a dance in it (if it can be called that) by Peter Lorre.

Boxed sets like this one, presenting movies that as a whole are not particularly well regarded or even remembered fondly, will still be an important part of the growing possibilities with DVDs. In some cases, they can provide access to a genre that changing tastes have left behind for those who want a look, but don't want everything. When they are organized, as this one is, around a particular personality, they provide the opportunity to at least keep movies that might otherwise disappear in print.

The five-part documentary *Cole Porter in Hollywood* (Peter Fitzgerald, 2003) is associated with this set and broken down to a chapter on each disc. Two of these are narrated by dancer Ann Miller, the others by performers important to the particular films. Though they provide a nice introduction to each film, they don't add up to a serious look at an abundant subject, leaving out any real background on Cole Porter and providing only hints at his biography during the years covered by the films. Nor do they really place Porter's work within the milieu of the Hollywood musical.

Each movie provides a Behind the Scenes extra, a series of text slides providing information that is basically trivial. There is also a supply of shorts and cartoons that is nice to have, ranging from an *Our Gang* episode to *Paree, Paree* (Roy Mack, 1934), a musical short staring Bob Hope, to an MGM orchestra rendition of Franz von Suppé's "The Poet and Peasant Overture" to a patriotic short called *Mighty Manhattan: New York's Wonder City* (James H. Smith, 1949), a fun look back, but probably added because of 9/11 more than as any real addition to understanding of the movie. These are the sorts of things that are becoming standard for releases from Hollywood's classic years, utilization of material that has been languishing in studio vaults since the death of the short subject as part of the theatrical film event, but there is no real attempt to bring more than the most distant cohesion to the material.

One of the special features of *Kiss Me Kate* allows watching the movie with the dialogue and sound effects removed, leaving only the music. The problem is that this leaves long stretches of silence—and it even cuts out the sound of the taps during the dance sequences. None of the other movies presents anything similar.

Dark City (Alex Proyas, 1998; DVD New Line Home Entertainment, 2001): More than any film before it, *Dark City* reflects the nature of the video game without an explicit internal connection to such games. The way that John Murdoch (Rufus Sewell) finds his wallet at the beginning of the film, for example, is copied exactly from how players progress through role-playing games. Fortunately for filmgoers, the movie does have more to offer than game spectatorship. Its sets are among the movie's most important characters, and the ways they change during the movie show Computer-Generated Imagery (CGI) at its best.

As it has grown and it has responded to its fans, the DVD has become more and more of a widescreen medium. That is, the demand for authorita-tive reproduction has led many viewers to the point where they will reject a fullscreen DVD out of hand. There are, of course, still many people who bri-dle at letterboxing's bands, but these are growing fewer, especially as HDTV begins to take over the market. The DVD packagers for *Dark City*, however, approached the widescreen/fullscreen problem by refusing to take sides. Or, perhaps, by using two sides, for they included both the widescreen and the fullscreen edition on the DVD, one on each side. At the time *Dark City* was released on DVD, it looked as though this might become a standard proce-dure. After all, it costs little more to burn a second side; much less than pre-paring and marketing two versions of the same movie would cost. Since then, the pressure for concentration on only the movie as theatrically released (except when enhanced by deleted scenes, etc.) has led to a dropping off of this method of presentation. In fact, more and more movies are being released on DVD only anamorphically and in widescreen aspect.

Dark City offers two audio commentaries. One is by the nearly ubiqui-tous Roger Ebert, the other featuring Alex Proyas, his writers, cinematogra-pher, and production designer. Ebert makes a case for the importance of the film while Proyas and his associates simply talk about it.

Given the film's clear relation to video games, it is only appropriate that a game of some sort is included on the DVD. Because it is meant to be played with a remote control, the *Find Shell Beach* game is extremely simple, especially compared to contemporary PlayStation and Xbox games, but it does emphasize the point that the movie is related to game playing.

One of the more interesting features of *Dark City* is the influence of *Metropolis,* the 1927 Fritz Lang silent film that also makes its sets characters. Included in the DVD are excerpts from two reviews of *Metropolis,* one by H.G. Wells—which is fascinating not for its having anything to do with either *Metropolis* or *Dark City* but because of the predictions Wells makes, predictions completely off the mark—and *Daily Variety.* There is also a text comparison of the two movies that includes a description of *Metropolis* with some background on Lang, a short discussion of expressionism and of the political context of the movie. This is unfortunately short, only a few screens long, and the comparison to *Dark City* is quite slight—mainly that both opened to tepid reviews and poor audience reception. Still, this feature is a herald of what might appear one day, as more and more of an apparatus on DVD becomes of interest to fans as well as scholars.

The *Dark City* DVD contains reproductions of some of the original artwork for the sets of the movie and a short essay by Neil Gaiman, author and creator of *The Sandman* comic. The artwork, however, is presented without commentary and the Gaiman essay, though again a portent of the type of extra one will see more and more on DVDs, is too short to be of much significance.

The menus of the *Dark City* DVD attempt to recreate the feel of the city changing in the movie, but they slow movement from one menu to another. It has recently been popular to have a cute bit like this on DVDs, generally clipped from the film itself, as part of the menus, but it does get to be distracting when one is trying to move about quickly within the DVD or has just seen these things too often. The most notable thing about this DVD is that it attempts to provide a little for everyone. That is, even the serious film fan can find something of interest. The creators of the DVD care about the film, and want it taken seriously—but they do not forget that film viewing is supposed to be fun.

The Godfather DVD Collection (Paramount, 2001). Includes *The Godfather* (Francis Ford Coppola, 1972), *The Godfather, Part II* (Francis Ford Coppola, 1974), and *The Godfather, Part III* (Francis Ford Coppola, 1990): Francis Ford Coppola did not have the possibility of holding his cast and characters over five films and 20 years, but he came close, time-wise, making the third *Godfather* film 18 years after the first. In terms of fictional time, even more is covered, almost a century. The sweep of the series has rarely been attempted and arguably never equaled. Even though the third film was a failure in relation to the first two, the trilogy as a whole has established itself as part of what many Americans see as their cultural heritage. So popular is it that *Part I* and *Part II* come in at #1 and #4, respectively, on the imdb.com top 250 films list (*Part III* doesn't make the list).

In an unusual opening, each of the discs takes the viewer straight into the movie, bypassing its menu screen. Or screens. Each of the movies has three different menus, providing a rotation of stills from the movies themselves. The fact of going right to the movies and not the menus may be a statement by the packagers on the relative importance of the DVD and the movies. If the movies come first, the reasoning may have gone, they should appear first, menus, commentaries, and the like are there if wanted, but not intrusive.

The Godfather Family: A Look Inside (Jeff Werner, 1991), a made for TV documentary (a promotion for the third movie) is but one of the features on the extras disc. Most interesting, however, are the deleted scenes and Francis Ford Coppola's discussion of the notebook he created by tearing apart a copy of Mario Puzo's novel *The Godfather* and inserting its pages into larger pages he could keep notes on. This provides a fascinating look at the relationship between a book and a movie, with the notebook acting as a bridge.

The extras include storyboards, a look at New York City locations, and bits on the music, the screenwriting, and the cinematography. Another feature takes advantage of the DVD possibility of a map with hot spots providing links to further material. This one is a family tree of the Corleones, providing information about each member, mainly from the movies, but occasionally from Puzo's novel. This sort of hypertext feature is becoming more and more common as a way of negotiating DVDs.

Grand Illusion (Le Grande Illusion) (Jean Renoir, 1938; DVD, Criterion, 1999): Not only was the original negative of *Grand Illusion* lost for decades, but the film, as reconstructed in the late 1950s, was made from worn prints and bowdlerized copies (the post-war French, it was thought, wouldn't stand for sympathetic portrayals of Germans). Still, *Grand Illusion* has been idolized by film aficionados for generations. *Grand Illusion* was to have been Criterion's first DVD release, but it was delayed when, unexpectedly, a negative was found that became the basis for this transfer.

Though the film really should be titled *The Grand Illusion* in English, Criterion decided to keep the title as it has been, a nod to its history within American filmgoing (and its place as #161 on imdb.com's top 250 films list). Because of the importance of the film itself, and due to Criterion's self-described mission, this is the sort of DVD that will be picked apart for years and that, one hopes, will appear in continuing revised editions as time progresses and problems—however minor they may be—are exposed.

In fact, most of the errors on the DVD are small and do not involve the film itself. In the commentary, for example, in speaking of the prison-show scene, where the prisoners break into the French national anthem on news of the retaking of Douaumont, Peter Cowie says, "Michael Curtiz must have had this in mind when he set up the similar scene in *Casablanca*, when the French drown out 'The Horst Wessel Song' with the ringing strains of 'The Marseillaise.'"[12] But it isn't "The Horst Wessel Song," it is "Watch on the Rhine" that the German officers are singing in *Casablanca*—just as it is the song being sung in the German guardhouse just moments before the scene of "La Marseillaise" in the earlier film. Curtiz certainly was aware of the juxtaposition of the two songs in *Grand Illusion*, and this probably influenced his choice, although the story is that "Watch on the Rhine" was used only because permission for "The Horst Wessel Song" could not be obtained.

One of the real advantages of the DVD for film fans is how easy it is to check something like this, once a reasonable collection has been established. Because of the possibility of jumping instantly to scenes, a fan, on hearing Cowie's comment, can slip *Casablanca* into the player and check, something that would take much more time with a videotape and that was all but impossible before that. The trivia of film scholarship will surely get much more accurate, thanks to the DVD.

Because of the influence of a film such as *Grand Illusion*, its DVD incarnation will be used by film fans as a constant reference, checking and cataloging its many descendants. Not only do many films set in wartime, including *Casablanca*, owe something to *Grand Illusion*, but almost every prison war film takes something directly from it, including *Stalag 17* (Billy Wilder, 1953), *The Bridge on the River Kwai* (David Lean, 1957), *The Great Escape* (John Sturges, 1963) and, more recently, *Hart's War* (Gregory Hoblit, 2002). And its influence goes far beyond even these. It is appropriate that the company that wants to be "the DVD producer of record" would have wanted to start its DVD series with *Grand Illusion*, one of the most influential films ever made.

The Lord of the Rings: The Two Towers Special Extended DVD Edition (Peter Jackson, 2002; DVD, New Line Home Entertainment, 2003): Three huge films in three years, one story, using modern filmmaking possibilities to their fullest—Peter Jackson's achievement is unequalled in the history of film. This is merely the middle segment. Even those who are left cold by fantasy/adventure pictures can appreciate the magnitude of this project, the most expensive ever embarked upon. The project, from conception to conclusion, took more than six years.

Because the three films in this series were made at one time, it is difficult to break down the cost of each with any accuracy, but it cost nearly $100 million dollars to make *The Two Towers*, $300 million for the whole series.

This was quite a risk, making the movie with a relatively untried director and well away from Hollywood. But it has proven worth it: *The Two Towers* alone has grossed more than three times what it cost to make the three movies. According to the Internet Movie Database, the three movies rank as #2, #4, and #8 of all-time leaders in world-wide gross (as of 7/19/04) bringing in a combined total of close to $3 billion. A *Lord of the Rings* movie was either first or second in US gross for 2001, 2002, and 2003. They also rank as #3, #8, and #9 on imdb.com's list of 250 top fan-favorite films on the same date. Whether or not one likes fantasy movies or this series in particular, it's indisputable that the series has become the most successful of its time.

The impact of *The Lord of the Rings* is just as great on the world of the DVD as it is on the world of the movie theater. The diligence and care in planning that made the series possible has also been extended to the DVD versions. In fact, DVDs were planned for from the very beginning and seen as part of the process of making and distributing the films. So important was the intersection of theater release and DVD that it even spawned a rather unusual film showing: on Tuesday, December 16th, 2003, at the Loews 42nd Street E-Walk Theater (one of 125 North American theaters where this was done),[13] a synergistic DVD/film event occurred that may speak to how DVDs and movies will relate to each other in the future. The extended versions of *The Fellowship of the Ring* and *The Two Towers* (versions developed for DVD release, not for theatrical release) were shown back to back—followed by the final film in the trilogy, *The Return of the King*—though not in its extended version, of course. That will wait until after an initial DVD release identical to the theatrical release, but with added extras, has been available for several months.

The Special Extended DVD Edition versions of the *Lord of the Rings* trilogy come in slip covers textured like old leather with embossed titles and spines reminiscent of those of old books, keeping connection both with the original Tolkien trilogy and with the literary culture it grew out of in addition to the oral cultures Tolkien used as models for much of his creation (the books are obsessed with the importance of spoken words and also with written language). The trilogy, which starts on screen with two verbal narratives—the second in the process of being transferred to text as Bilbo Baggins sets down his memories—never tries to divorce itself from the oral culture of its subjects or the literary culture of its source. Instead, with implicit understanding of the growing virtual culture of which it is a part, it gladly embraces both.

Peter Jackson and his cohorts, in constructing the project that would lead to *The Lord of the Rings*, assessed the relation of what they were doing to the extant fan base for the books. This base was so strong, they realized, that it could make or break the film. Not only did the needs and desires of the fans have to be respected, but the story at the center of their passion did, too. They could not play too freely with Tolkien's narrative if they were going to keep this base as their starting point. To further ensure that the movies would meet the approval of established Tolkien fans, Jackson hired artists who had illustrated popular editions of the books, to keep the connection between his movies and the fan base as strong as possible. So, the look also reflects what most fans knew of the books, but with a sweep and majesty reflecting more on the epic films of the 1950s than on anything seen since.

The DVD of *The Two Towers* contains four audio commentaries, not just one by the director and writers but one by people from the special-effects workshop that was so important to the movie, another by a number of the executives involved in the production, and a final one with members of the cast. One example of the care taken with these DVDs is that there is no assumption that viewers can recognize the different voices on the audio com-mentaries—and here there are a great number of them. Subtitles, therefore, are included with the commentaries, making it clear who is speaking.

Just as there is an extensive variety of commentaries, the discs of extras include featurettes on just about every aspect of the project, starting with looks back at J.R.R. Tolkien himself. Among the early topics explored are the community of writers Tolkien was among and the reasons for the trilogy's publication as three volumes instead of one. The extraordinary breadth of the featurettes can only be shown through a list, and an incomplete one at that: *From Book to Script: Finding the Story, Designing Middle Earth, The Taming of Smeagol, Warriors of the Third Age, Visual Effects: Miniatures: Flooding of Isengard, Visual Effects: Abandoned Concepts, Editorial: Refining the Story; Music and Sound: Music For Middle Earth*. There are also a number of text-based extras, including maps of Middle Earth and New Zealand, where the epic was filmed.

The impact on film and home viewing of *The Lord of the Rings* is already as great as that of the *Star Wars* series a generation earlier. Though they were aware of the importance of ancillaries—indeed, these are what made George Lucas extraordinarily rich, much moreso than the movie itself did—Lucas did not foresee the importance of the videotape, certainly not to the extent that Jackson did with the DVD. Jackson has been part of the DVD revolution, showing how it can add to film revenues, even increasing demand for the films in theaters. His staggered release of the DVDs has been a marketing coup, for many fans of the films have ended up buying the theatrical version of each movie on DVD, only to buy the extended version several months later. He has also shown that the DVD can help ensure the success of multipart movies, making it possible for other directors to follow his lead. Quentin Tarantino, for example, split his *Kill Bill* (2003, 2004) in two, scheduling the release of *Part I* on DVD for the weeks before *Part II* appeared in theaters, effectively using each medium to promote the other. If he continues to follow the model of *The Lord of the Rings*, Tarantino will release *Part II* alone on DVD, followed by a set of the two films, polished off after a year or two by a special edition. Like *The Lord of the Rings*, Tarantino's movies will provide an income stream for years after they have disappeared from theaters.

National Lampoon's Animal House: Double Secret Probation Edition (John Landis, 1978; DVD, Universal, 2003): Although *Animal House* is generally classified as a gross-out movie, it really doesn't fit within the genre. It contains little of what made *Porky's* (Bob Clark, 1982) notorious just a few years later, and seems distantly related, at best, to Kevin Smith's 1990s gross-out comedies. *Animal House* is much more of a satire than it is often given credit for being, for it is now most often seen through the films it did, indeed, influence rather than as the distinct film that it is.

The Double Secret Probation DVD sets itself up as being a special edition of the movie, something that will bring an extra dimension to the movie. Unfortunately, it does not. Instead, this is an example of an attempt to cash in on the special edition DVDs that have been appearing over the last few years, but by offering little more than new packaging. The only extras of note are *The Yearbook: An Animal House Reunion* (J.M. Kenny, 1998) and a newer work, made particularly for the DVD, *Where Are They Now? A Delta Alumni Update* (2003) The first of these does shed some light on the making of the movie, but there is little else on the DVD that will interest the serious fan.

Like "restored" versions of movies that aren't real restorations, "special editions" that contain little that is special actually hurt the movies involved. Later restorers and packagers might well ignore these movies, believing that they have already been done—though the work has been shoddy, at best. They also will not see the project as financially viable, sales having been siphoned off by the cheap versions. The production of cheap and sloppy special editions is bound to continue to happen, however, as demand for DVDs, especially special edition DVDs, continues to grow.

Once Upon a Time in the West (C'era una volta il West) (Sergio Leone, 1969; DVD Paramount, 2003): Perhaps the pinnacle of Leone's career, *Once Upon a Time in the West* saw the Spaghetti Western sub-genre move squarely into the wider Western tradition. The claim can even be made that this film, coming on top of his Man With No Name trilogy, allowed American directors to look at the Western in new ways, seeing possibilities in a genre that was beginning to seem tapped out. The users of imdb.com have voted the movie to #32 on their top-250 list.

Though Sir Christopher Frayling can be faulted for telling a little bit too much of what is being shown in the audio commentary for the movie (perhaps he has not yet developed a real comfort with the concept of the audio commentary), this commentary is one of the most interesting and slickest put together so far. That's because it is more than merely one person talking about the movie; it is cut from a number of commentaries, all related to the specific scenes. This commentary was edited for the movie, unlike many that merely pick up a commentary made while the movie was running. The difference is startling: There are pauses only where the commentators want viewers to concentrate on the screen—not while a commentator is taking a drink of water, for example. It is moving toward a standard that will utilize audio quotation (as this one does) to construct a cohesive essay about the film, a standard that will soon come to dominate audio commentaries.

Pulp Fiction (Quentin Tarantino, 1994; DVD, Miramax Home Entertainment, 2002): Though his first film, *Reservoir Dogs* (1992), established his reputation as a master of gore and snappy dialogue, it was *Pulp Fiction* that brought Quentin Tarantino to the center of public attention. For all the aura of violence that surrounds his films, Tarantino's body counts are surprisingly low. It's the idea of violence—almost always present in his films—that provides the edginess Tarantino achieves and that places this film at #16 on the imdb.com list.

Like *Buckaroo Banzai*, *Pulp Fiction* has an option for a trivia subtitle track, although it does not provide an audio commentary—which is not surprising, given the importance of the music and dialogue to this picture. One of the extra features is a series of reviews of the movies. These are not reproductions but are transcriptions that are easily read off of a television screen.

Because it is a recent film of a working director, there's little current need for the sorts of extras one finds on DVDs of films from Hollywood's classic era or for foreign films. Also, Tarantino's continued popularity makes it unnecessary to "sell" his older films through new packaging (though this is itself a repackaged DVD). It is probably for these reasons that the DVD extras of this movie don't seem to be taken particularly seriously. That, the packagers seem to be saying, will come in its own good time.

Singin' in the Rain (Gene Kelly and Stanley Donen, 1952; DVD, Turner Entertainment and Warner Home Video, 2002): It may be that *That's Entertainment!* revived interest in *Singin' in the Rain*, but videotape had something to do with its continuing strength. *Singin' in the Rain* has proven to be one of those movies that can be watched again and again, either seriously or just playing in the background. That it also deals with the most earth-shaking time in the history of Hollywood, the switch to sound (and that it was made by people who could remember that switch) hasn't hurt either—nor does the dancing, which exhibits every side of Gene Kelly's inexhaustible enthusiasm.

Like *Casablanca*, *Singin' in the Rain* had to be approached with care when a special edition DVD was being planned. After all, *Singin' in the Rain* ranks as the top musical on the Internet Movie Database fan list for the genre. On imdb.com's list of 250 greatest films, it ranks #47, well behind *Casablanca* at #7 and *The Godfather* at #1, but a significant placement, nonetheless.

This DVD is close to being a history of the MGM musical, with a look (though not a particularly good one) at the coming of sound. Because the movie uses songs by the team of Arthur Freed and Nacio Herb Brown that date back to the beginnings of the musical on film, the extras do not seem out of place, but work to enhance the film. Though the DVD includes a commentary by Debbie Reynolds and others, it is the history of the musical provided that makes this DVD such a fascinating release.

One of the extras, Reel Sound, provides links to scenes from movies of the earlier era. The scenes are long enough not to frustrate the viewer, but they will make movie fans hope that the movies that are clipped from will soon come out—whole—on DVD themselves. One of these is *Don Juan* (Alan Crosland, 1926) with John Barrymore. Text is used to describe these movies, along with poster reproductions that serve as links to these sample scenes from the films. Other movies described this way are *The Jazz Singer* (Alan Crosland, 1927) with Al Jolson, *Lights of New York* (Bryan Foy, 1928), and Academy Award winner *The Broadway Melody of 1929* (Harry Beaumont, 1929). A similar feature is Singin' Inspirations, with links appearing in the movie allowing viewers to see footage from movies that inspired it. These bring up screens like those for Reel Sounds, including one for *Show Girl in Hollywood* (Mervyn LeRoy, 1930) with a scene much like the one at the start of *Singin' in the Rain*.

One of the documentaries provided, *What a Glorious Feeling: The Making of* Singin' in the Rain (Peter Fitzgerald, 2002), was made specifically for this DVD, and is hosted by Debbie Reynolds. Another, on the Freed unit at MGM that made the movie, *Musicals Great Musicals* (David Thomson, 1996), was added because of its relation to the musical itself, to Arthur Freed (who produced the movie and co-wrote the songs), and to the history of the MGM musical, all of which are critical to an understanding of the film.

A most fascinating feature of the DVD is *Song Cuts—Excerpts from Features Where the Songs Originated* which provides the original film versions for almost all of the songs in *Singin' in the Rain* along with a short print introduction to each song. Not only to they make for interesting comparisons with the versions in *Singin' in the Rain* but, taken together, they provide as strong a visual and aural introduction to the development of the MGM musical as can be found. As with all excerpts, it is a little frustrating to have the songs taken out of context, but eventual DVD release of each of the movies should take care of that.

Sunset Boulevard (Billy Wilder, 1950; DVD, Paramount, 2002): Though *Sunset Boulevard* is another of the films that has shown incredible staying power—it ranks #31 on the imdb.com list and has spawned a Broadway musical re-creation—it is not presented here with the same sort of hullabaloo that accompanies some special edition releases. Still, what it presents shows more understanding of the possibilities of a DVD than do many splashier releases.

Of particular interest is the way the packagers dealt with the problem of a second opening to the movie, what could be called the *morgue prologue*, for the opening scene of *Sunset Boulevard* was not the original one shot or shown. That first one was cut after the first preview, when audiences reacted poorly to it, even laughing. The film of this opening remains, but the soundtrack has been lost, so alternate openings dovetailing into the film were not really considered as feasible for the DVD—especially since that soundtrack contains the voice-over necessary for making sense of the sequence. Instead, two versions of the script for that opening are presented, with links to the appropriate footage.

Also provided is a Hollywood location map. This combination of fact and fantasy uses an actual map of Hollywood as a menu for discussions of locations important to the movie. The links are to selections from the film with voice-over. Items are Norma Desmond's car (linked to a spot shown in a driving scene), Schwab's Drug Store, the real apartment building where the character Joe Gillis supposedly lived, and the Getty Mansion that was used for exteriors of Norma Desmond's house.

Vertigo (Alfred Hitchcock, 1958; DVD, Universal, 1999): Hitchcock's most adored film suffered for years from its fans. That is, because of its popularity (#33 on the imdb.com top 250 list), hundreds of prints were made from the negative, stripping it of its own elements, leading to a faded, scarred movie. The film restoration was completed and released to the theaters before the DVD came into existence, but it is home viewers who benefit from it most. One of the first major classic films released in a restored version on DVD, *Vertigo* has few of the features that later DVDs sport, but it helped set the standard for presentation quality that has continued to be part of the best of DVDs—and that DVD fans are now insisting upon. Included with the movie is *Obsessed with Vertigo: New Life for Hitchcock's Masterpiece* (Harrison Engle, 1997), a documentary that focuses on the work of Robert Harris and James Katz, the restorers who are responsible for bringing the film back from the brink of ruin.

Warner Legends Collection: Flynn, Cagney, Bogart (Turner Entertainment and Warner Bros. Entertainment, 2003). Includes *The Adventures of Robin Hood* (Michael Curtiz and William Keighley, 1938), *Yankee Doodle Dandy* (Michael Curtiz, 1942), and *The Treasure of the Sierra Madre* (John Huston, 1947): This odd assortment of Warner Brothers Films seems simply an excuse for release of *Here's Looking At You, Warner Bros.: The History of the Warner Bros. Studio* (Robert Guenette, 1991), a fun but frilly documentary. The three films certainly have little in common aside from their packaging in this set, which is of a piece. Still, they do provide a glimpse at the world of the Hollywood film from the late 1930s to the late 1940s, a decade that saw the studios at their height.

One of the best ideas on the package is a *Night at the Movies* feature on each disc hosted by Leonard Maltin. The idea is to recreate a bill that someone might have actually seen when the movies were in first release, down to cartoon, short, trailer, and newsreel. Not only is this a nice way for Warner to use some of its idle shorts, but it gives current filmgoers a sense of what the changes have been in the theater experience over the past 50 years. All three movies also come with radio broadcasts, labeled as audio-only. These are a nice added touch.

A big, splashy Technicolor movie, *The Adventures of Robin Hood* has remained popular through the years, maintaining a place at #154 on the imdb.com top 250. Fittingly, one of the extras with it is *Glorious Technicolor*

(Peter Jones, 1998) a look at the history of the Technicolor process. Most of the other extras seem to have been added merely because they had at least a little relation to the movie, not really to bring much additional understanding to it. There's a short about a sailing trip that Errol Flynn made, for example, and one on archery by Howard Hill, who was the expert for the film itself. Perhaps the most interesting of the features is also the most frustrating, a look at the Douglas Fairbanks *Robin Hood* (Allan Dwan, 1922) hosted by Rudy Behlmer. Behlmer provides a guided tour through parts of the film, but leaves the viewer wanting to see the film itself—and to see it in a restored version (the clips used here are not in very good shape).

Yankee Doodle Dandy shows James Cagney attempting a type of dance that was outdated by the time of the movie, replaced by the more fluid styles of Fred Astaire and Gene Kelly. Though it might have been appropriate for the heyday of George M. Cohan, Cagney doesn't show it in a very good light, though he certainly does exhibit a certain skill. It is grace that he lacks. Still, this is a good example of the sort of bio-pic that Hollywood sometimes still makes. Its relation to reality is tangential at best (there's only a fictional wife, for example, because Cohan didn't want either of his real wives represented). The biography featurette on Cagney that is included is a little light on analysis; the only really interesting extra is a World War II short Cagney starred in that shows the way Hollywood tried to contribute to the war effort, especially in the realm of selling bonds.

Given the essentially lightweight fare on the rest of this set, *The Treasure of the Sierra Madre* (#68 on the imdb.com top 250) would come as something of a surprise—if it weren't so well known for its director and leading man. Two documentaries make up the bulk of the extras, one on the life of John Huston the other on the making of the movie.

8½ (Federico Fellini, 1963; DVD, Criterion, 2001): Movies become classics because they draw viewers back to them again and again. Whatever the reason for enjoyment, and there are many, they can produce new pleasure at each watching. The film *8½*, though it confuses viewers both new to the movie and old, continually provides reasons to watch it. On the bulletin board at film-talk.com, complaints are rarely that it is a bad film, only that the viewers are struggling to make sense of it. Sure, it is possible to explain much of what happens as daydreams and fantasy—but is that really explanation? Or does it simply move the discussion to another realm? None of these question has answers, but the movie remains as high as #210 on imdb.com's fan-favorite list.

The film is given one of Criterion's more scholarly treatments, which is to be expected but is also slightly ironic, given the film's definite anti-interpretation bent. Perhaps to offset this, *Fellini: A Director's Notebook* (Federico Fellini, 1969) is included. This TV film pretends to be a documentary, but it becomes a Fellini fiction as well, telling the viewer not to trust anything. There is also a long featurette on the composer Nino Rota and interviews with actress Sandra Milo, cinematographer Vittorio Storaro, and director Lina Wertmuller.

As this sampling shows, the range of possibilities for special edition movie presentation on DVD is quite extensive. Not only that, but some of the packagers take their tasks seriously, putting together impressive packages that not even the most dedicated *cineaste* can complain about. Others, however, are simply attempts to take advantage of this new technological phenomenon.

Certainly, much more can be done with the DVD than is presented through this particular selection of movies, but this is meant to be simply a cross-section of what is being packaged now on some of the DVDs claiming quality transfers and consideration for the collector and film fan. As can be seen, some of the features are already on their way to becoming standards. Others will fall aside as new ways of utilizing the DVD are presented.

Clearly, though, the ways of presenting the DVD are changing the way movies are viewed at home, increasing viewer options and, ultimately, viewer knowledge of the movies.

Chapter 5

THE DVD AUDIO COMMENTARY

Toward the beginning of the audio commentary for *The Magnificent Seven* (John Sturges, 1960), producer Walter Mirisch quotes Sturges, "I thought we were making movies, not history."[1] Many directors, and even actors and producers, feel much the same way about their work. When it is done, they want to go on to the next project, not reminisce about the last. Some, for other reasons, feel they cannot afford to pay more attention to the last project. "I never feel happy with anything," explains director Anthony Harvey on the audio commentary for his *The Lion in Winter* (1968), "I didn't feel happy with anything as an editor. I never felt the film was ever finished. I could have gone into those cutting rooms for years. I could go on cutting this film for years. I don't think you ever feel at peace."[2] Going back, even just to make an audio commentary, can be extremely uncomfortable for someone with an attitude like Harvey's. Others don't like making commentaries for other reasons, because it makes them feel pompous or somehow places them "above" others who contributed to the project. Films, however, have become history—not simply as artifacts on their own, but as emblems of their times. They are part of the vast cultural web supporting what we are and do today. Audiences, as a result, are demanding more from their movies, especially for home viewing, and even people with attitudes like Sturges' or Harvey's are feeling pressure to meet that demand.

The audio commentaries on today's DVDs make up one of the most important new strands reinforcing that cultural web. And they do more. Not only do they place films in context, but they often provide a great deal of technical information about everything from acting to animation, film to frame. A standard format for the audio commentary has yet to emerge, but they are becoming a part of the filmmaking process; they are often in preparation even as the film is being made. For older films, they can now provide the missing element that can make accessible a sensibility long ago outstripped by changing tastes and technologies.

Clearly, the audio commentary is one of the most revolutionary aspects of the DVD—but it actually first appeared more than a decade before the DVD even existed, as a feature of the laserdisc. Yet, it is with the DVD that the audio commentary as an important popular feature accompanying the home viewing of a movie has come into its own, expanding from a fairly academic feature to one that can be anything from inane to sublime. Though DVD packagers are still experimenting with methods for presenting commentaries effectively, the fact remains: The DVD audio commentary has become the sign of class in a DVD presentation.

Not surprisingly, it was Criterion that created the first audio commentary, doing so long before the advent of the DVD, with an added track on its laserdisc release of *King Kong* (Merian Cooper and Ernest Schoedsack, 1933) in 1984. Ronald Haver, a curator at the Los Angeles County Museum of Art who had recently come to attention for his work on the restoration of *A Star Is Born* (George Cukor, 1954), was asked to provide a commentary for *King Kong* that could be accessed while watching the laserdisc. He did, providing a detailed analysis to go with each scene of the movie. Haver started the audio commentary movement on a high note, and it is likely that Criterion only expected that the commentaries would be of interest to serious film students. That they are now changing the way viewers interact with film, to say nothing of the knowledge provided that a viewer can easily soak up, is probably as surprising to Criterion as to anyone else. Given the favorable reaction to that first commentary (though unnoticed by the general public), Haver continued to provide commentaries for Criterion for the rest of his life.

Though there is no formula for an audio commentary as of yet, certain patterns are starting to become evident. The most basic results from someone connected with the film sitting down, watching the movie with the sound lowered, and recording whatever comments happen to come to mind. There can be a certain charm to this style, for the spontaneity and ramble can take the speaker to all sorts of unusual and amusing places, but these, for the most part, fail to illuminate much about the movie. This can also be a little disingenuous: someone not wanting to take too much credit themselves might feel that side-stepping serious analysis for playfulness makes them appear less responsible.

At the other end of the spectrum is the academic analysis of each scene. Though these can show care and real attention to detail, they can also contradict the very spirit of the movie, sometimes even making it seem more of a deliberate crafting than might be the case. In the audio commentary for *The Day the Earth Stood Still* (Robert Wise, 1951), Nicolas Meyer gently quizzes Wise about Biblical parallels to the events in the movie. Though he is clearly not satisfied that Wise's memory that he had not thought at all about such parallels during the shooting is accurate, Meyer notes, "This really bears out my theory that oftentimes artists have very little idea, or very imperfect or very incomplete notions of what it is they've done."[3] Many academic audio commentaries assume the contrary—that is, the filmmakers knew exactly what they were doing. Or, at least, that someone, somewhere in the process, recognized the implications and decided to keep it in. Of course, that's true in many cases, and in others every aspect of the film is planned out carefully in advance. As director of photography Roberto Schaefer says on the audio commentary for *Monster's Ball* (Marc Forster, 2001), "the way we designed to shoot the film, every frame pretty much has a meaning."[4]

One problem with the academic audio commentary—opposite of the problem of the off-the-cuff audio commentary—is that it can be boring to most viewers, many of whom are interested only in the anecdotal, in the types of comments that might arise during a TV talk-show interview. For this reason, some DVDs are now appearing with more than one commentary, each aimed at a specific audience. Audio commentaries take up relatively little storage space on a DVD; it is possible to include quite a few of them without giving up other features.

Between the slapped-together ramble and the carefully researched and written commentary rests a developing range of possibilities. The most common, and most important, is the director's commentary, which can itself be broken down into several types. Generally, directors are interested in more than a nostalgic look back, so try to provide justification for the decisions that they made in creating the film. Some prefer to do this solo and without preparation, making the commentary an informal discussion of a work they might have completed as long as 50 years ago, but completely controlled by the speaker. In his commentary for *M*A*S*H* (Robert Altman, 1970) Altman provides interesting background comments on production and on the script and the way it was used (or misused) in the ensemble production. Altman isn't scared of silence, allowing long pauses, watching the movie "with" the home audience, rather than blathering just to fill time. He also spends a great deal of time on problems with the studio, especially in relation to the connection with the Vietnam War.

Mel Brooks is understandably proud of his *Young Frankenstein* (1974), a movie that, according to his comments, was turned down by Columbia because its $2 million budget was too high. The film, of course, has grossed 50 times that since its release. Brooks' extensive knowledge of film history makes this an interesting connective, especially for viewers who may not know the history of Frankenstein in movies. Brooks points out the homages, and explains the use of black-and-white, placing his parody firmly within the tradition it gently mocks. Brooks also has enough sense to talk with the movie, to pause at times to let the viewer see—rather than always telling—though he can fall into unnecessary description. Outside of a few unintelligible mumbles, this commentary is, as Brooks says of the movie itself, "nothing to be ashamed of."[5]

Oliver Stone is another director who can look back on his work alone and provide a wealth of information in an interesting presentation. For his *Wall Street* (1987; DVD, 20th Century Fox Home Entertainment, 2000), Stone does not limit himself to talking directly about the movie or technical details (though he does address these, albeit more briefly), but speaks, for example, of the influence of his own family on the making of the film. When he talks about the actors, he speaks candidly, never attacking anyone, but laying out gentle criticism (particularly for Charlie Sheen) when he feels it is needed. Stone allows his audience to learn something about the personalities involved with the film, even if (like his father, the model for Hal Holbrook's character) they are only tangential to the film itself.

In her commentary for her *Monsoon Wedding* (2002), Mira Nair attempts a number of different tasks. Unlike Stone, she doesn't feel she can limit herself to the personalities ⌐ provide a background for the film. She knows she addresses American viewers, primarily, and has to try to give them a bit of information about Bollywood films, about Delhi, and about middle-class Punjabi life—as well as about filmmaking. She isn't pedantic, however, nor proselytizing or patronizing. "The great thing about cinema is you can incorporate all these things you love, the music, the view, the photograph that you've seen and make it a scene, make it come alive."[6] Though she is trying to bring to American audiences lives that can seem quite alien, she manages to make connections, too, both in the film and in her commentary.

In other cases, the director's commentary includes another person, someone (often another director knowledgeable about the film) guiding the director in discussion of a work that the director may not have seen or thought about for years. For the commentary on *Catch-22* (Mike Nichols, 1970), director Steven Soderbergh and Nichols do the commentary together, making it an informal conversation/interview. Soderbergh takes the lead, clearly having prepped for the commentary, letting Nichols respond—at times even prompting him. Similarly, for the commentary on *The Day the Earth Stood Still* (Robert Wise, 1951), Nicolas Meyer conducts it as an interview.

For *Shattered Glass* (Billy Ray, 2003), the director is joined on the commentary by former *New Republic* editor Chuck Long, who might be seen as the hero of the true story the movie depicts. This adds an aspect to the commentary that is impossible to achieve, of course, for most films—one of the very subjects of the film giving his views on it. It allows for a discussion on the differences between the film and the actual events and the reasons for the changes—everything from lack of permission to lack of money. Because Long's role is one of uncovering fraud, not of perpetuating fraud itself (the center of the movie), he is not vested with protection of the central character, or even with further discrediting him (for blame is well established).

One of the other aspects of the *Shattered Glass* commentary that makes it a little unusual is Billy Ray's admission of his own lack of experience. This was his first directing experience, and he had to rely heavily on more experienced members of his production team. He admits this with a grace that a more experienced director might not be willing to convey. Because of his candor, listeners to Ray can learn more about the actual interactions between members of a filmmaking team than they might from a commentary by a director who wants to take the credit for the entire production.

In a third type, the director presides over a group discussion including members of the cast and the crew. It can be difficult to make this sort of discussion work, for there are generally a number of strong egos involved. In the commentary for *12 Monkeys* (Terry Gilliam, 1995), Gilliam's overlarge character and enthusiasm completely eclipses the contribution of producer Chuck Roven. Gilliam, as usual, is worth listening to, but one wonders why he felt the presence of Roven was needed. In other cases, the commentary can turn into a dismal failure, with no one taking charge. An example of this is the commentary for *Clerks* (Kevin Smith, 1994). Perhaps Smith and his cast and crew intentionally recorded only an extremely informal commentary, spending part of a day talking over a showing of their film for an additional piece of DVD profits, yet the Miramax Collector's Series 1999 release of *Clerks* deserves more. The commentary was made during the filming of

Mallrats (Kevin Smith, 1995), so it may be that no one was willing to concentrate on an earlier film, feeling that it might be at the expense of the current effort. Certainly, the sound is uneven—it appears a microphone was being passed around the room—and the comments are unfocused and often pointless. Still, Smith does manage to provide an interesting description of making a film on a budget.

Because *Clerks* was the first movie (and one made on a shoestring) by a director who has since proven quite successful with bigger-budget movies, a better commentary certainly was warranted. Even in 1999, when Smith's career had progressed a great deal from *Mallrats* and *Clerks* (but not as far as it has since), the Miramax packagers should have realized that a stronger effort than this was warranted by both the reputation of the director and the continuing regard for the film. After all, Smith had made two successful films after the failure of *Mallrats*—*Chasing Amy* (1997) and *Dogma* (1999)— and had certainly matured as a filmmaker in the intervening years.

Fortunately, a 2004 3-DVD edition of *Clerks* has now replaced the 1999 release. It does contain the older commentary—but it plays a smaller role within the extensive new release. The weakness of the commentary is further alleviated by a subtitle trivia option also on the first disc that, when played in tandem with the commentary, can keep the viewer from becoming too annoyed with the speakers. The second disc contains a longer, earlier cut of the movie—and a commentary is provided for this, as well. Many of the same group are involved, but here they seem to take what they are doing a bit more seriously and Kevin Smith seems more assured and in control. Still, they do manage to veer off target from time to time. Certainly, the inclusion of this one does make up for the weakness of the earlier commentary.

Another movie with a Special Edition commentary that makes one wonder why the packagers bothered is *The City of Lost Children* (*La Cité des Enfants Perdue*) (Jean-Pierre Jeunet and Marc Caro, 1995) which was released by Columbia TriStar Home Video in 1999. The commentary, by Jeunet and star Ron Perlman, is a ramble that centers more on complaints about members of the cast, at times, than on the movie itself. In comments on the first scene, Jeunet says "So this is the first scene" and then "This is a strange scene,"[7] giving no explanation. It certainly is fair not to want to explain what one has created, but to provide a commentary without comment goes a little far. From evidence in the commentary, it seems that neither Jeunet nor Perlman had seen the film for years before making the recording—nor, apparently, had they seen each other or talked about what they would do.

No matter how one feels about the *auteur*, the director remains best positioned of anyone connected with a movie to provide an audio commentary on it. Having had to coordinate the disparate elements of a film's production, the director can discuss the relations of shot to sound to narrative and so on. Ron Shelton, in his commentary for his *Bull Durham* (1988) says, "I obviously look through the lens on every shot but I also like it to feel like the life is slightly spilling off of the frame."[8] Like many directors, he is involved in every aspect of the movie—even those parts that have to be imagined are occurring off screen—and this is why the director will always be at the heart of the audio commentary.

Billy Morrisette's *auteur*-like project (he both wrote and directed the movie), *Scotland, PA* (2002), which is based on Shakespeare's *Macbeth*, includes a Morrisette commentary, which, like the movie, is his first. Morrisette clearly had some experience listening to DVD audio commentaries when he made this one. Not only does he speak comfortably and directly to the audience, but he is able to make jokes about previous commentaries: "This scene, I was inspired by the wedding scene in *Godfather*. [Laughs.] That's not true, but I've been waiting to say that."[9] Certainly, the audio commentary has already accumulated its own share of cliches.

As interest in commentaries continues to grow, and as they develop more and more into a *de rigueur* extra for the DVD, new ways of presenting them will certainly continue to be developed but they will continue to center on the director—at least for new films. DVD releases without a director's audio commentary will likely be considered of the second rank. In fact, the type of commentary provided will start giving clues as to the importance the packagers give to the film.

At first glance, one might think that a film's writer would be able to provide a close reading of the film for a commentary, but there are few of these. After a little thought, the reason appears: the writer's task is completed (for the most part) going into the production of the film. What comes out may have little relation to what the writer envisioned, so that writer could easily be at sea trying to explain it. Ernest Lehman, screenwriter for *North by Northwest* (Alfred Hitchcock, 1959), provides comments that probably for this reason rarely go further than "this was shot as written." He tells a story of his attempting to climb up Mount Rushmore, only to give up halfway to the top; his commentary gives up, too—probably because he was not directly involved enough in the actual making of the film. Lehman relies only on memory and has clearly not prepared for the commentary—nor have the packagers provided him with background information that could augment his own experience.

Another of the problems with Lehman's commentary is that he clearly doesn't know just who his audience is. Though the commentary had been around for more than a decade when this one was recorded, the DVD was still new and the earlier commentaries, primarily for Criterion, had been limited to laserdiscs and their small distribution. It's not surprising, then, that Lehman is a bit tentative, even stating that he assumes those listening have seen the picture before—as though anyone might view a commentary before seeing the film as a whole!

Lehman does try to work with the movie, rather than merely talking over it, but he even loses the opportunity to illuminate one of the greatest scenes in movie history, the confrontation between Cary Grant's Roger Thornhill character and a crop duster. He drops hints that there is much more to tell, including saying that he concocted the scene after hearing Hitchcock comment that he had always wanted to film a scene of a man in the middle of nowhere, with a clear horizon all around him. But we get no insight as to why. What we get instead are comments on the gunshots with Lehman wondering why they are there if the intent of the assassins is to make the death look like an accident. This is interesting, but not illuminating.

Actors are often no better equipped than writers to provide a commentary on a movie as a whole (though they can be excellent, of course, on acting). Their involvement with the film is generally too close all of the time, with a concentration on one role and only the specific scenes relevant to that part. The difference between the two commentaries for *Monster's Ball* points this out clearly. Director Marc Forster is involved in both commentaries, doing the first with his director of photography and the second with his two principal actors, Billy Bob Thornton and Halle Berry. Close to the beginning of the commentary, when Forster is trying to make a connection between his opening credits and an earlier film, Thornton states "I don't see many movies," following that with, "Generally, I don't like credits at the beginning of a movie because I think it makes you realize you are watching a movie so much."[10] The former of these statements, at first glance, seems appalling for someone involved in filmmaking; the latter seems to show a naïveté that is unexpected in someone who has both successfully directed and acted (no one watching a movie ever needs to be reminded they are watching a movie). Some of Thornton's later comments, however, show that this is a deliberate attitude that he uses to bring as much power as possible to his performances.

He mentions that he prefers to actually sleep when a shot of him asleep is needed, and one line in the script, where he refuses to let a condemned man make a last phone call, bothered him a great deal, he says, in performing it. Thornton, clearly, wants to be inside the film he is making, to the point where he convinces himself that the actions and their consequences are real—he even extends this to his own waking up. So, to him, credits get in the way of a deliberate fantasy he creates for his work.

Interesting as this might be, it has little relevance to the film as a whole—one reason we should be thankful that the decision was made to provide two commentaries for *Monster's Ball*.

For many older films especially, there is no possibility of a director's commentary, or even one involving other people directly responsible for the creation of the film. In these cases, the families of the principals can be brought in to provide a flavor to the commentary that an anonymous academic cannot. This necessarily tints the commentary with nostalgia but, given how important personality is to filmmaking (especially on the part of the actors), such commentators can shed light on the film in ways that no other commentary possibly can. For *High Noon* (Fred Zinnemann, 1952; DVD, Republic Entertainment, 2002), the commentators even include actor John Ritter, whose father sang the movie's theme song. The other commentators are also children of people important to the movie: the daughter of Gary Cooper and sons of Fred Zinnemann and writer Carl Foreman. In this case, the commentary does succeed, but because of preparation and editing, not the personalities used. Rather than sitting the commentators in a screening room, starting the movie and a tape recorder, and then slapping the result on a DVD, the packagers of *High Noon* made sure that this group was prepared for their task. A shooting script, for example, was available as the commentary was made. And the final product is the result of editing together a number of different sessions and interviews. This technique does move the commentary away from direct interaction with the film, but this group is not one that can provide the scene-by-scene analysis that a director or film scholar can give. The purpose, here, is contextualization of the film.

Although there is a bit of technical detail, most of the discussion of *High Noon* centers on the characters and on the politics that surrounded the film. *High Noon* was made during the time of the Red Scare that resulted in the blacklisting of many Hollywood writers, actors, and directors, including some associated with this film. Much of the discussion, not surprisingly, centers on the relation of the movie to the politics of the personalities involved and the impact their beliefs had on their lives afterwards.

Perhaps the most intriguing ensemble commentary comes with the 2004 HBO Home Video DVD release of *American Splendor* (Shari Springer Berman and Robert Pulcini, 2003). In part, this is due to the very nature of the film. *American Splendor* combines *Underground Comix* art, a narration by Harvey Pekar (the subject of the film), footage of the real Pekar, and dramatization (with Paul Giamatti playing Pekar). Other characters, including Pekar's wife Joyce Brabner, stepdaughter Danielle Batone and fellow worker Toby Radloff, also appear both as themselves and as dramatized versions. Pekar, Batone, and Radloff all participate with the directors in the audio commentary as well, making the commentary yet another level of this multi-faceted project, rather than an unnecessary add-on. Though Berman and Pulcini do try to insert some technical information, most of the commentary is taken up with discussion of the characters—appropriate for a film that is completely character driven.

In terms of the average home viewer, the impact of the audio commentary is, and will likely continue to be, one of connection, of expanding horizons. Most commentaries mention other films, providing something of a viewing list for fans of the film being commented on. They can also help viewers inexperienced in specific genres learn the hallmarks of the genre, providing a means of access that has never before been so easily available. In addition, they can inform the viewer of the meanings of cultural allusions that have slipped away in intervening years or that assume a different cultural basis. From a marketing viewpoint, the commentaries also encourage home viewers to buy their DVDs, not to simply rent them, for the audio commentaries are not something that one wants to watch the first time through a film—and few people want to watch a movie then watch it *again* for the commentary in the space a of a day or two (as one must with a rental). Even if a viewer is switching back and forth from the commentary to the film's soundtrack, the commentary is probably an item for concentrated viewing, not simply for an evening's leisure.

The audio commentary represents a happy confluence of marketing and home viewing. Cheap to create, they not only entice viewers to purchase DVDs, but they can encourage the purchase of further DVDs. In fact, they may be the single largest impetus (though there are, admittedly, many others) moving home viewing away from a rental-based economy to one centered on purchase. They may also prove to be one reason that downloading movies may not replace the DVD as the vehicle of choice for home viewing in the near future. The single, simple package, rather inexpensive but containing everything one wants, will be hard to beat.

The impact of the audio commentary on film studies should be immediately apparent, including, as it does, a *de facto* revival of the *auteur* theory of cinema. Directors, of course, have always been celebrities, but their importance in the popular perception of film has grown even as the *auteur* theory has fallen out of favor. Francis Ford Coppola, for example, actually titled his *The Godfather* (1972) *Mario Puzo's* The Godfather—but no one remembers it that way. If anything, the movie is now referred to as Coppola's *The Godfather.* Yet scholars are, with reason, steadfast in their insistence that films be viewed as much more than the result of a singular vision. With very few exceptions, filmmaking remains a group activity, with the final product resulting from the combined visions of a number of people in a variety of roles.

Too many commentaries by more than one person devolve into nostalgia for the filming or into a mutual admiration match. One that does not, making for a most interesting commentary, is that by director Steven Soderbergh and writer Lem Dobbs for *The Limey* (1999). Their visions for the movie are distinct, and sometimes at odds. Soderbergh, of course, was the final decision maker so Dobbs has to spend his time pointing out what should have been, with Soderbergh defending his decisions. The heart of the disagreement is character. Dobbs feels that Soderbergh presented the characters too thinly, never making them really believable. Soderbergh agrees, to an extent, but argues that he needed to work within the constraints of a 90-minute film. The two have clearly heard each other's views before, but they are patient, hearing each other out once again.

Few commentaries contain much that is negative about the film or the filmmaking. Everyone involved was wonderful and talented; problems, when they are recounted, generally revolve around nameless "suits," the studio executives not directly involved in the project. In the commentary for *La Cite des Enfants Perdue*, however, Jeunet repeatedly disparages one of the actors. Likewise, in the commentary on *The Day the Earth Stood Still*, both Meyer and Wise put down the actor Hugh Marlowe, Meyer wondering why he was cast and if a better actor could have brought more depth to the role. In both of these cases, there seems something mean spirited in the criticism, unlike that offered by Oliver Stone (who never attacks the person; he only analyzes the performance).

Though the unwillingness to criticize is natural, it is too bad that more of the commentators don't feel that they can let the viewers in on a little more of the reality of the situations. In a few commentaries, they do, but generally only obliquely. In the commentary for *The Magnificent Seven* (John Surges, 1960), the gathered actors and producer talk gingerly about the late Yul Brynner, all on the edge of criticizing his haughty and demanding nature, but none willing to go further than making slight jokes about it. For the actor/director commentary on *Monster's Ball*, the participants agreed before the start that they would not "slander" anyone.

One impact of the commentary on film studies is, quite simply, the wealth of information brought forward by them. They make it hard for the scholar to examine the work in itself as an independent entity, for its very presentation (after the theatrical release) is now tied up with the commentaries, not to mention all the other DVD extras. This is especially true of a film that did not do particularly well in the theater, but that has found much more of a life on DVD. Matthew Bright's 1996 film *Freeway*, for example, relies on the DVD audio commentary for the very connection Bright returns to again and again, between what the film promotes and what he loves in his own life. Bright even says, at one point, "I want to be the Roger Vadim of psychopaths."[11] By comparing himself with Vadim, as famous for his wild sexual lifestyle as for his wild sexual films, Bright, of course, is commenting with tongue in cheek, but the point remains: Bright does not want to dissociate himself from the attitudes expressed in his film—and understanding of this changes any reading of the film.

By providing a new and ubiquitous context for film, the commentary changes more than the way a scholar may look at an individual film or may consider as responsible for a film. It also changes the relation between the average home viewer and the film—and with films in general. When it is the director or another person involved in the production end of filmmaking who creates the commentary, a certain amount of technical detail is presented. Part of this becomes actual lessons in the vocabulary of filmmaking. Frequent reference by directors to a *two shot* eventually makes it clear to any viewer what the meaning is, a single shot showing little more than two actors in conversation or, sometimes (used rather incorrectly), a series of two-camera back-and-forth shots of the actors. The concept of forced perspective— where sets are made to provide a sense of equal size, though one is well behind the other so that, for example, one actor can appear to be quite a bit larger than another—is another that without audio commentaries might be of only passing interest to most film viewers. Prior to the introduction of the audio commentary, in fact, there had been little reason for the average home viewer to know or care about the meaning of such terms. With it, the terms are becoming commonplace. It is possible, now, even to speak informally of the relative advantages of a tracking shot or a zoom without being accused of resorting to technical jargon.

One reason the commentaries are so attractive is that they can appeal both to the enthusiasm for trivia that has always accompanied film fandom and the serious student who wants to understand the decisions behind the actual making of the film. In the commentary for his *Catch-22*, Nichols points out that a large photograph on a backdrop wall changes twice in one shot as the camera pans away from it then back to it, from Roosevelt to Churchill to Stalin. He then says, "It's just a little way to amuse ourselves."[12] It was, and recognition of it amuses contemporary viewers, as well. At other points, Nichols and Soderbergh discuss the details of the lighting of the movie in ways that many viewers won't have the background to be able to understand, but that they will learn as they watch more commentaries—and that scholars examining the film might find quite useful.

One of the most common—and most important—of the audio commentaries for older films is that created by the popularizing historian. These are not scholars speaking to other scholars—in fact, some are not scholars at all in the sense of having academic affiliation or training. They are, nonetheless, people with outstanding knowledge of film (particularly of the history of film), some as directors themselves or as film critics. The commentaries these people create are meant as entertainment themselves as much as they are scholarly exercises, things for home viewers to enjoy in the same way they might a retrospective on television. Because film is a popular art—and because some of these commentaries are extraordinarily good—it is likely that, for older films at least, these will be the most common commentaries.

In packaging releases of older films on DVD, the Hollywood studios have been turning to what has become a cottage industry of commentators like Ronald Haver, with predictably uneven results. For earlier films, a few of the older, more well-known figures in film popularization seem to have cornered the market in audio commentaries—for the moment. Rudy Behlmer, Roger Ebert, and Leonard Maltin, between the three of them, seem to be doing more commentaries of classic films than any other 30 commentators. They provide bright, entertaining comments, fun in their own right—for these are knowledgeable and skillful writers. Their lock on the commentary will change, however, as viewers (and scholars) begin to demand more specific and detailed analysis along the lines of that provided by Criterion and also by the best commentaries made by contemporary directors. Film scholars like Stephen Prince have already been lured into the business by Criterion, with Prince writing and narrating commentaries for a number of Akira Kurosawa films, among others. Outside of Criterion, there seems a disinclination to use film scholars as commentators, using instead, as we have seen, people with some connection (no matter how tangential) to the film.

Until recent years, the history of film, both on a scholarly and popular level, has been primarily anecdotal and a little bit slipshod—much as is the work of the most popular of the audio commentators. For a variety of reasons, many academic film scholars were more interested in film theory rather than in the history of film (though this has now changed). The few popularizers of real quality, such as Maltin and Behlmer, have had to try to cover much more ground than is possible with any precision. The very existence of the audio commentary will ultimately make their work easier, providing a ready source for information that, as commentaries progress, will be more and more accurate, more frequently vetted.

Maltin, for example, now relies too heavily on Hollywood legend in his commentaries, though the breadth of his knowledge is impressive. In his commentary for *A Night at the Opera* (Sam Wood, 1935), for example, Maltin speaks of Harpo Marx's harp playing, stating that Harpo was self-taught, that his fingering and tuning were idiosyncratic to the degree that one harp teacher advised him, when he did try to take lessons, to keep doing things his way. This is not completely true—at least, it is not accurate. Harpo, a serious harpist, took lessons as an adult, even over the phone when he had to. He studied with Mildred Dilling, one of the top performers and teachers of her time. "He was . . . exceptionally eager . . . , though he already knew how to play the harp with a zany kind of virtuousity."[13] His fingering technique, clearly visible in his movies, isn't perfect (probably reflecting his early self-taught playing), but it is quite good and standard, and his harmonics technique is exactly what would be expected from a well-trained professional. It is also clear to anyone familiar with the harp, from watching and listening, that his tuning is that expected for the instrument.

Maltin, however, is not attempting a scholarly rigor and, again, he is trying to cover a huge amount of ground—both in commentaries on specific movies and in the breadth of movies he provides commentaries on. Still, his work would last a little bit longer if it were vetted a little more carefully. After all, Maltin, a film enthusiast if nothing else, brings charm and joy to his commentaries, wanting to bring his viewers the same pleasure that he, himself, feels on watching a film. Perhaps it would have been possible for Maltin's commentary to be but one for *A Night at the Opera*. In the boxed set that contains both it and *A Day at the Races* (Sam Wood, 1937), Glenn Mitchell, a Marx Brothers expert, provides a more detailed commentary on the other film. Perhaps both could have commented on both movies.

What Maltin is best at is bringing information to the viewer in a manner that is neither condescending nor simplistic. Rather than simply and pompously explaining the correct pronunciation of Chico Marx's name (properly pronounced 'chick-o'), Maltin admits that he, himself, had mispronounced the name most of his life. He draws the viewer into his own excitement and exploration, addressing the viewer directly and bringing him or her into exactly the sort of exploration that Maltin revels in. At one point in his commentary on *A Night at the Opera* he says, "There's a famous story about the shooting of this sequence that I'm not able to document too well, but maybe you'll have a better chance at it than I now that we have DVD technology at our disposal."[14] By this, Maltin is inviting his audience into the same sort of careful observation of film that he likes to do, in this case looking to see if the father of the Marx Brothers can be seen twice, once on shipboard as the ship departs and once on the dock, watching the ship depart, in the same scene. Peter Jackson similarly brings the viewer into close examination with him in his commentary on *The Fellowship of the Ring* (2001), trying to spot if there is a label on an apple tossed at one point in the film.

Maltin can explain the details of filmmaking without reverting to the technical or pedantic. Without the viewer really even noticing, he goes over basic filmmaking vocabulary and biography, making his comments seem like natural parts of discussion of the film. His work is carefully written and structured and only lacks the detailed research to match. The anecdotal nature of much of his information needs confirmation of a sort that has rarely before been desired, but that now, thanks to the DVD and the audio commentary, is necessary. Behlmer and Ebert are almost as good, the former taking a more historical approach and the latter making constant connections to other movies.

The commentary on *Sunset Boulevard* (Billy Wilder, 1950) by Ed Sikov, who wrote *On Sunset Boulevard: The Life and Times of Billy Wilder*, is so heavily scripted that a viewer might wonder if the movie was actually playing while it was read. Sikov does provide a great deal of interesting information and points out aspects of Wilder's filmmaking that a viewer might miss, but he also describes a number of the scenes in a way that is not necessary when they are being seen. One of the most disconcerting tics of this commentary is Sikov's habit of quoting lines from the film right before they are actually spoken in the film. A specialist on Wilder, certainly, Sikov does not have the experience or breadth of a Maltin, who has long since developed his breezy delivery through constant talks about film.

The Criterion release of *Citizen Kane* (Orson Welles, 1941) offers two commentary tracks, one from Roger Ebert and one from Peter Bogdanovich, who spent a great deal of time with Welles and has written about him. Bogdanovich tends to be overly descriptive. It is as if he has lectured about the movie so often he forgets that his audience is actually viewing the scenes. Ebert, on the other hand, while also quite descriptive in the other commentary, understands a little more clearly that he is watching the movie "with" his audience, and makes it his business to point out things that might otherwise be missed.

Since the introduction of the DVD the most significant and (arguably) influential uses of the audio commentary have been those incorporated into the DVD releases of the *Lord of the Rings* (Peter Jackson, 2001, 2002, 2003) movies. Part of the reason for this may be an attitude of Peter Jackson's, one quite distinct from that of John Sturges, who could move from film to film without looking either back or forward. In the audio commentary for *The Fellowship of the Ring*, Jackson comments, "As [director] Bob Zemeckis used to say to me, 'Pain is temporary; film is forever.'"[15] Jackson wasn't just making a movie, he was creating something that he hoped would be watched forever, and something he knew would last best in the public imagination in its DVD incarnation.

The Fellowship of the Ring presents four distinct audio commentaries. The first commentary features Jackson and his two writers, with all three of them commenting on the entire movie. In the other three commentaries there are so many people involved that they are often brought in to comment only on parts relevant to their own activities. The second of these focuses on the design team and has "only" six commentators, ranging from the production designer to the set decorator. The third, with 13 commentators, provides insight from the producers and the post-production team, including composer Howard Shore. The fourth features 10 of the principal actors.

The division of commentaries works well in several ways. First, it gives viewers a chance to decide just what sort of commentary they are interested in, if any. In this case, the distinctions between the commentaries are clear. The director/writers one concentrates on problems of translating from J.R.R. Tolkien's books to the screen, on pacing, and on other decisions relating to storytelling. The second focuses on the WETA Workshop, the source of all the CGI (Computer-Generated Imagery), miniatures, props, and more for the film. The people providing the third commentary worked on the film (for the most part—and with the exception of the producers) after principal photography had been completed. The final commentary was made by members of the cast, the people associated with the film who have the highest public profiles.

For many viewers, the most interesting commentaries might be those of the director/writers and the cast. The inspiration for this movie, after all, is arguably the most popular fantasy saga ever, and many viewers come to the movie already familiar with the story and the characters. Listening to comments on why Jackson, who provides the bulk of the commentary, and his writers made the choices they did will allow fans of the trilogy to make their own judgments on the film with a greater understanding of just why certain changes were made.

The actors present the most light-hearted commentary of the four. They had clearly bonded during the filming and were now able to look back on what they had done with nostalgia and satisfaction—and with little desire to explain how or why each scene was performed. Ian McKellan does provide a little bit of gravitas, and Christopher Lee adds his extensive knowledge of Tolkien, but this is not a group trying to defend its work. Perhaps that is due to the enthusiastic critical reaction to the film, but it may also be because this is definitely an ensemble piece: no single actor holds this film together, so none feels a need to defend it.

Serious film fans will probably be most interested in the design team commentary, for this is the area of the greatest advances over the last decade, technological innovations that have made movies like *The Fellowship of the Ring* possible. The group of commentators includes two artist/illustrators who Jackson brought in because of their past experience with Tolkien as well as the people who took their concept drawings and made them into the pieces of the movie. These are the people who took the look envisioned by Jackson (in part due to his familiarity with the work of the artist/illustrators) and transformed it into the movie itself.

The other commentary may seem a bit more specialized or even dry, but it includes comment on sound design and score as well as editing. This one may be a little more of interest to people actually involved in the film industry, or who want to become involved. It is likely that Jackson formed this group so that he could not be accused of leaving anything out.

Jackson's foresight and planning have placed him in a position that is likely to be as influential as Criterion's in terms of the audio commentary. He was the first filmmaker to make sure that the commentary was prepared for as the film was made, thereby offering something to home viewers that they had never had before: an extensive discussion of a film by a wide variety of the people actually involved in the making.

In the future, the audio commentary on a movie DVD will evolve in directions yet unimagined. It will likely split into three distinct (and clearly identified forms). First will be the "popular" commentary, meant for the fan of the specific film, its cast, and director. These will probably be anecdotal in nature, breezy, and fun. The last will be the "academic" commentary, a vetted, significant contribution to scholarship surrounding the film. Between these will be the more careful director's commentaries and those by film critics and historians outside of academia. These will have a great deal more depth than the popular commentaries and will likely be more accessible than the academic ones. Each will play a significant role in furthering film as an important component of American culture.

Chapter 6

THE DVD,
THE FILM
SCHOLAR, AND
THE CLASSROOM

In 1971, Stanley Cavell wrote in reference to his own film scholarship, "I am often referring to films I have seen only once, some as long as 30 year ago. In a few instances I have seen a film three times, but in no case enough times to feel I possess it the way it deserves."[1] He goes on to say that he has not hesitated to watch films on television, but that "I have in no case given a reading of a film that I have not seen in the flesh,"[2] placing even an ancient viewing ahead of home viewing in the hierarchy of film experience. Later in that decade, Raymond Bellour commented on "the vertigo of not being sure of my text, and with it, hidden by the relative impossibility of doing so, a different kind of profound vertigo determined by what the implications would be if I were someday able to be sure of it."[3]

Two aspects of these comments are important to film studies of the early twenty-first century. First, we can now see films at home (or in the office) when we use DVD technology in a form akin to Cavell's "in the flesh"—that is, with an integrity that was not previously possible. Second, the very idea of writing from memory about a film one has seen but once now seems quaint and archaic. Today, Bellour's "vertigo" would stem from knowledge that one had stepped beyond the bounds of what has come to be seen as academic rigor. In fact, Cavell's further statement on his methodology would horrify many contemporary scholars: "my way of studying films has been mostly through remembering them, like dreams."[4]

Over the past 20 years, for a number of different reasons, scholars have rationalized film studies, establishing a rigor beyond the ken or interest of early practitioners. No longer can scholars simply speculate or mull over possibilities. Precision and detail are demanded of them—and by them. A generalization not backed by a number of specific examples no longer has a place in the field. Because of the ease of access it brings to film, among other reasons, the DVD will likely further this rationalization, heightening the precision that scholars have already been bringing to the field.

This new rigor brings with it its own problems, for it does seem to ignore the more ethereal elements of filmmaking and film viewing, sidestepping considerations of such concepts as *photogénie*, that indefinable element of film subject resonating with viewers in ways beyond filmmaker control. The magic of the movies, in other words, gets left behind. The DVD may allow us to bring this back, to immerse ourselves in the films with a privacy and absorption rarely before possible. It allows us to write *with* the films, taking directly from the viewing experience and landing it into our prose.

No longer should the field feel the need to impose limits on itself, as David Bordwell believed it should when writing his "Lowering the Stakes: Prospects for a Historical Poetics of Cinema" in 1983: "At this point in film study, we are best served by framing limited questions."[5] Now, thanks in part to the DVD, we are at a new point in film study and can certainly afford to expand our questions. Film, after all, is entertainment. Shouldn't study of it be fun, too?

Bordwell, to give him credit, was reacting to those earlier critics who, like Cavell, were removed both from the text of the film and, usually, from the film's original milieu. They had no anchor in the "text" of the film or in the "texts" surrounding its making. As Robert Ray explains, in "Bordwell's view, 'truth' diminishes as we move away from the text itself: thus, while 'primary' sources contemporary with a particular filmmaking mode (e.g., Hollywood's trade, technical, and union journals) are relatively trustworthy, later historical interpretations are not."[6] Because, today, we can more easily stay close to the original film through the DVD, we no longer have to be tied so closely to those other primary sources. The fact of being able to work more easily and more integrally with the original movies makes those primary sources secondary (though still important) considerations. We can now return to our flights of fancy secure in the knowledge that they are powered by several decades of careful research (resulting, in part, from Bordwell's leadership) and by utilization of the possibilities inherent in DVD technology.

Before the 1970s, the small film studies field was dominated by a tiny number of scholars with remarkably strong visions of cinema and the cinematic. For the most part, they did not see themselves as involved in a particular academic field, much less in defining it. Their emphasis was really on film, not film studies. They felt no constraints from the academic community, and so joined their battles and espoused their passions with a *joie de vivre* that later scholars must have found, on looking back, quite embarrassing.

During the 1970s, a self-conscious and serious academic film studies movement did begin to gain momentum, and scholars began casting about for a theoretical framework that could unite what was still a disparate and iconoclastic field. This was also the decade of the growth of interest in theory in literature departments, of attempts to place close textual examination within a milieu of careful consideration of the philosophical, political, and linguistic factors influencing the varying approaches to works of art—and of doing so under an overarching thesis. Film scholars, not surprisingly, began to share in this interest, applying concepts such as Structuralism, Post-Modernism, and Feminism to film.

Theory, of course, is an overly broad term for a movement of diverse opinions and approaches, each attempting to provide an all-encompassing structure for the study of arts (in this particular). Without going into detail, theory centers on the works of psychoanalyst Jacques Lacan, especially on the power of the unconscious; of linguist Ferdinand de Saussure, the father of semiotics whose *langue/parole* and sign/signifier distinctions find quick resonance in any consideration of film; and of philosopher Jacques Derrida, the father of Deconstruction. Many other thinkers—Roland Barthes comes immediately to mind—have had an impact on theory, but these are three of the most central.

Soon after the 1970s, even as the influence of theory was peaking, other critics became increasingly frustrated with the state of film criticism. These scholars had come to see the field as hijacked by this heightened emphasis on theory, taking its discussions too far away from the movies themselves. Theory might be useful for some purposes, and is often quite insightful and relevant to the world at large, but theory, in these scholars' eyes, often does little to help us become better viewers of film.

Theory, they argued, is but one tool for studying film, and should not be considered the necessary starting point for academic discussion. Theory should inform discussion rather than control it. The experience of film itself is dynamic; so should its study be. As Byron Hawkes (after Gregory Ulmer) writes:

> Theory neither constitutes the viewer and viewing process nor provides a transparent window on them. Film is neither just a forum for dominant ideology nor a site open to any interpretation. Spectatorship is neither a site for passivity nor a space for resistance. . . . All of the above elements are at play in the inventive act of active spectatorship.[7]

And so they are, too, with scholarship. Theory had closed off too much from film studies. Many scholars wanted to open it back up, moving argument from belief to object.

To counterbalance theory, the first of these academics, starting in the 1980s, began to turn their attention to historical aspects of film, exploring everything from the development of the Hollywood studio system to viewing habits and populations. The research possibilities that opened up were immense. So huge were they (and, unfortunately, often so fragile) that, in the face of them, Bordwell's desire to "lower the stakes" makes sense. Sources were disappearing at an alarming rate.

The historical approach broadened film studies to include consideration of audience backgrounds and what the audience brings to the film experience—and how the audience changes film. This developed into a loose approach called *Cognitivism*, with a centering on conscious viewer perceptual processes—rather than on film's influence on viewer subconscious perceptions (a more Lacanian approach).

The changing technological milieu today is making discussion over the place of theory lose importance. Theory had taken the forefront in large part because it was hard to concentrate on anything else: it was difficult to study film in its breadth, and concentration on just those films that were easily available to the scholar seemed unrewarding, especially since those movies had been well picked-over by the end of the 1960s. Today, thanks in part to the expanded view of historical research and in part to technological developments, there is so much to do in the realm of film study that theory, rather than dominating the field (as it once threatened to do), is becoming just one of many tools that can be used in examining film.

There are also new and urgent peripheral questions, such as defining and contrasting the significant distinctions between the various vehicles for film now available. Film studies, as a field, also needs to begin to present a formal structure of film documentation that not only takes into account these new viewing vehicles but that is able to succinctly distinguish between the various versions of films now appearing. Filmography is just as complex a field as bibliography, but it has yet to develop the rigorous form and method it now needs.

Because it is a field that owes its very existence to technology, changes in technology have a tremendous impact on film studies. In the past, film scholars had to write from notes taken in the dark about specific films. Only in rare and special circumstances was it possible to write carefully about a film while viewing that film. Today, with a laptop computer and a DVD, it is possible to write while the film is playing, stopping on particular lines or scenes as necessary. Because examination can now be detailed and accurate, there is little room for acceptance of the errors of memory that have dogged film writing since its inception.

Oddly enough, being tied to new demands for accuracy arising from technical possibilities should not make film studies increasingly pedantic. On the contrary, it may very well establish a confidence in the base material—the films themselves—that can allow scholars to extrapolate with more vigor, moving into Robert Ray's realm of "allure," the tangible giving the scholar a base for dealing with the intangible aspects of film. DVD technology allows scholars to add Ray's "spectacle" to their work, something that will be increasingly important as film studies turns to avenues of publication beyond print. Why not loop a bit of Bernard Hermann's score behind an essay on *North by Northwest* (Alfred Hitchcock, 1959) or present the prose over a still from the film? These may be an expansion of "fair use" possibilities, but should be legitimate. They are meant, after all, to enhance appreciation and understanding of the film, not to steal from it.

There are, and will be, objections to making the DVD the central viewing device for film studies. The mode of viewing, of course, is as important to film studies as to film enthusiasm. Speaking or writing about a film seen in a theater is completely different from speaking or writing about a film seen at home or, for that matter, on a viewing table or a computer. For a long time, and for many people still, the concentrated, theatrical viewing of a film was sacrosanct. Raymond Bellour even felt that doing anything at all while watching a film—besides watching—was somehow demeaning to the film, writing that even to "take notes during a projection is in fact nothing less than a denigration: it is a way of freezing the image without violating the law of continuity."[8] He goes on to describe that "law" as forbidding one "to watch a movie the way we read a book, by stopping and starting."[9] The law, he says, is enforced by "the lack of individual (or semi-collective) ownership of the means of projection (projectors and above all prints of films freely at one's disposal)."[10] Fortunately, this enforcement is no longer possible, no matter how we may long, nostalgically, for a past age of cinema "purity." There is no way that film can any longer be seen as a creature solely of the theater. The DVD has erased almost all objections to taking home viewing seriously in film studies, thereby smashing Bellour's "law" and expanding the universe of cinema studies.

It is in the presentation of scholarship, as we have seen, that DVD technology may have the most to offer, for here it can resolve one of the greatest frustrations that has faced film scholars for the past century: how does one write about film without using film? Literary scholars can work with texts in their own texts concerning them, quoting them directly in the fullness of original intention. That has not been possible with film—until now. To date, however, film scholars have not grasped the possibility before them, but the time for that is surely upon us.

Part of the problem for integrating the new technologies with presentation of film scholarship comes from the lack of integration, so far, between print media and digital media. Textbooks are now appearing with CD-ROMs or DVDs, but these, for the most part, provide a simple function of support. Not yet are they integral parts of the texts. Both the academic community and the publishing industry remain wedded to the traditional book and the print journal—academic publication online, for example, is not given the same weight in consideration for promotion as publication in print. A book is needed to attain tenure, not a DVD.

Those involved in academic publishing and in scholarship itself have an understandable bias in favor of print. After all, when they have published before, it has been in print, it is print where their expertise lies, and print is what the channels of production and distribution are set up to handle. Making a break with this is daunting: the first ones to do it may sink, just as many ebook publishers have, though the long-term prospects remain strong.

Because of frustration at the limitation of trying to convey almost anything about a film without being able to use the film itself, movement toward film scholarship on DVD will inevitably begin to build, culminating at a point where the idea of film scholarship in print alone will seem quaint. Soon, no film scholar will think of presenting a series of stills of frames from a film to make a point; clips from the films themselves will always be used instead. Given its unique position, film scholarship will likely lead the way for the academic community in this regard, other fields following suit as they discover ways that the integration of text, sound, and image on a DVD can enhance their own scholarship.

As an example of how the new possibility can affect presentation, take Seymour Chatman's 1980 article for *Critical Inquiry* "What Novels Can Do That Films Can't (and Vice Versa)." The essay might, today, be better titled "What Film Criticism on DVD Can Do That Print Can't (With No Vice Versa)." Using Guy de Maupassant's story "Une Partie de campagne" and Jean Renoir's 1936 short film based on it, Chatman sets out to compare fiction and film, doing so in a way that many scholars have, both before and since.

At one point in his essay, Chatman states parenthetically that it would be best "if you would watch the film as you read this essay."[11] He includes stills from the movie instead, clearly hoping that with his commentary the stills could stand in for the movie. Of course, they cannot, and could only be imagined to do so when no other possibility existed. In the future, when film scholarship turns to computers and the DVD, Chatman's essay will have possibilities of actual interaction with the film that could not even be imagined in 1980. Perhaps, one day, some DVD anthologist will take essays like Chatman's and packaged them on a DVD along with the pertinent clips from the films considered.

Interestingly, this new possibility for scholarship is going to require film scholars to become much more technology savvy than they may be at the moment. It won't do to ask a techie to put together picture and text; the integration will be part of the scholarship itself. How, in the particular instance, should text and film, and sound, interact? This will not simply be a question of packaging. The scholar will have to decide how the linkages will work, and why they want them to, working through hypertext or through menus—or through a combination of the two or some other means. Will a high-speed Internet connection be assumed? Or will the particular DVD be expected to stand alone? Work on these questions has already begun, with a few scholars already presenting their studies as integrations of text, sound, and image, but so far most of this is meant for the Internet or for conference presentation. Little of it is meant for discrete DVD release, certainly not as a replacement for traditional scholarship in text alone.

Film scholarship often stays away from the technical aspects of film production—partly because few film scholars have much real experience of it. What film school teaches remains quite distinct from what is found in film studies departments. As film scholars are forced to become more and more conversant with the technologies of the Internet and DVD for their own work, they will also start to deal more directly with some of the technical concerns of filmmakers, for manipulation of image will become a direct and important part of their own work. This should broaden the field of film studies, providing a new common ground between the scholar and the film-maker, Ray's "spectacle" promoting a type of discussion that has been hith-erto quite rare.

In the future, even a book like this one will benefit from a DVD aspect. The bibliography of a DVD version could link to specific online bookstores and libraries, and other links could be provided to sites, such as The Internet Movie Database (imdb.com), that can provide much more detailed informa-tion about specific films and DVDs. Samples of the various DVD extras dis-cussed could be presented, as could clips from the films mentioned, making the points about them much more vividly than is possible in print. At this point, however, such features would only be sensible as adjuncts to the print book, and as minor ones, at that. It will be some time before the book and the DVD can be seamlessly integrated.

Leading the way to that day will probably be film journals, which may find it harder and harder to resist turning to DVD publication completely. Because DVD manufacture is so inexpensive and journals are so notoriously underfunded this technology will strengthen presentation and will also be attractive because it will save money—in the long run (it will take time to train staff and set up software and design) and even in the short run (imagine the savings on postage). At first, the journals will probably provide printer-friendly versions of the articles, but these may disappear as the works become more involved in utilizing the available technology as part of their discus-sions.

Anyone who tries to predict the future fails, for the most part. So the possibilities presented here, while not outlandish, will probably prove quite different from what does finally appear. The point, however, is that film scholarship will have to change in response to new technical possibilities. It cannot continue to view film from a purely print perspective. Those in the field who do so will soon be left behind, unable to participate in the develop-ing discussion.

The new technologies are also demanding new ways of referring to specific films. These have not yet been established, but they will be, as scholars find their old means of reference failing them. Right now, primacy is held by the theatri-cally released version of a film, with title, director, and year of release considered sufficient for most discussions. In the past, it has been ponderously difficult, if not downright impossible, to catalogue all the films in even one collection, establishing the differences in versions, the dates of copying (if it was copied from a master or a negative), etc. Questions of the authority of any print have been put slightly to the side, with an imagined "authoritative" version posited (something of a Platonic *form* of the movie), though too often not existing at all. And that's not all. As William Uricchio writes:

> [S]ince the early cinema evidence record contained so many gaps . . . and deformations . . . film historians of necessity had to think through the consequences of how to account for absences. . . . The result . . . included new techniques of textual analysis, and new approaches to extra-cinematic evidence. . . . [T]he development of an elaborate series of collaborations among scholars, film archives, and film festivals helped to stimulate and guide the restoration of the cinematic evidence base (restoring films, getting them back into circulation, providing period documentation, etc.), while at the same time amplifying new perspectives on the medium's history.[12]

Because digitized films can be stored so easily and take up so little space, DVD technology can be used as a means of cataloguing and even comparing actual film prints. Certainly, some prints are too damaged to even be transferred, but most can be—if the work is done by careful technicians. These "originals" (whatever their remove from the initial negative or master of the film in its pristine state) can then be carefully stored and the digital copies used for purposes of identification and comparison. Such a process extends the possibilities of film preservation, removing the fear of damaging valuable prints through overuse.

All that is going on is not quite so rosy. What is happening in many places is that entire collections of film, especially 16mm film, are being lost as institutions convert to digital. A false assumption that the film is fully preserved in a digital form may be behind this, but it is also likely that the rarely used films are seen as merely taking up space—and that someone else has preserved a copy, anyway.

With film now having so many different vehicles for storage and for showing, it is necessary to develop a clear and distinct system of labeling for each medium. Also, a method of tracking pedigree ought to be created. A transfer to DVD from a videotape is quite different from a transfer from a new 35mm master. Film library records should begin to keep track of exactly

where a film came from, and how, for even the place and equipment of transfer can make a difference in the quality of the copy. Counterintuitively, even
the assumption that a digital copy made from another digital copy is exactly
like the first doesn't always hold true.

Of course, the question also arises of the relative importance of restored
films versus what does remain of the "original." In film, the original (in part
because it is so rare) is treated with even more respect and awe than a first-
edition book. Literary scholars have gotten away from a simple concentration on the first edition as the authoritative edition, however, while trying to
trace back and re-create exactly what the author intended. In literature, this
is much easier than in film. In literature, there is generally just one author
whose work passed through (usually) a single editor and print shop. A relatively clear line of changes exists. For a film, however, with so many different
people involved, along with factors of sound and image, and with the possibility of wildly divergent versions appearing at different points along the line
of creation, it is much harder to establish the primacy of any one version.
Verifying authority can be difficult enough, even in literature—witness the
attempts to establish an authoritative edition of James Joyce's *Ulysses*. In film,
it can be nearly impossible. Probably, the only real (though feeble) way to
start dealing with the problem is to make sure any copy of a film is clearly
labeled with its provenance.

Possibilities for close reading of films are much greater for scholars now
that the DVD is commonly and cheaply available. These must be more carefully conducted than in the past, for the scholar's audience will now share
much of the scholar's access. Though the extras showing up on DVDs are
meant primarily as marketing devices, they offer film scholars new possibilities beyond what the DVD offers in and of itself. One of the first tasks of
film scholarship in response to the DVD will be to examine new DVD
releases to see if they are, indeed, accurate portrayals of the film and its history.

Even with the videotape, it was hard to respond to a critical assertion
with the ease that one has with a book, pulling it down from the shelf and
quickly flipping to the appropriate page. This helped keep film scholarship
focused on the theoretical, for the practical was just too unwieldy. A decade
ago, a reader would likely have responded to a Stanley Cavell claim about
Tom Jones (Tony Richardson, 1963) with a shrug, not seeing it as worth the
effort to check, even if the movie were easily accessible on videotape. Now,
one can access the relevant scene in seconds, so one is more willing to engage

Cavell's assertion that the eponymous character places his cloak over the camera, in one scene, through misplaced courtesy, "leaving the woman as naked as ever, merely out of our sight."[13] A look at the DVD shows that not only is Cavell's own memory factually wrong (Tom Jones uses his hat), but that it is clearly no concern for modesty that sparks Jones's action: he wants *privacy*.

This ease of access leads to new ways the DVD can be used in the classroom. Cavell says that the cloak he mistakenly believes is thrown over the camera could have been thrown over the woman, if modesty had been desired, so sees the incident as a sly joke. It is a joke, yes, but one of different nature than Cavell imagines. In a classroom, after reading Cavell's comments then viewing the scene itself, discussion can go in a number of directions, toward consideration of sexuality in cinema, toward humor, or even toward the interactions between screen characters and the camera—and the implications of such interactions. If a film DVD library is immediately available, discussion can go directly to other films with concrete backing of discussion points and not merely speculation.

Of course, sound should not be forgotten as an aspect of film, or even as part of the way the DVD can be used in the classroom. Leaving music aside (though there are tremendous DVD possibilities there), sound effects themselves can now be studied in ways never before possible. Consider usage of the *Wilhelm*, perhaps the most famous sound effect of the last 50 years. It has appeared in at least 75 movies since it first was used in *Distant Drums* (Raoul Walsh, 1951). *Star Wars* (George Lucas, 1977) Sound Designer Ben Burtt is probably responsible for naming the scream Wilhelm, christening it after a character made to utter it in *The Charge at Feather River* (Gordon Douglas, 1952). Though it had been used more than a dozen times before *Star Wars*, its usage has skyrocketed since, appearing in upwards of 50 different movies, becoming something of a Burtt signature and a tribute to him by subsequent sound designers.

It is significant that the Wilhelm has become most popular since the advent of the VCR, for it is something that would be easy to miss in the theater, but that can be sought via a remote control. Even in the arcane world of sound design, people don't work solely for their own pleasure, but want others to notice what they are doing. The Wilhelm has become a signal to other sound designers, yes, but it is also a game played for viewers—and often against directors, many of whom don't want to see it in their films, only to discover it once someone points it out when the film is in release. Searches

The computer monitor, however, has a number of advantages, as does individual viewing, when one has the kind of control that the computer allows. Zooming in and out, changing subtitles and soundtrack, and other things can all be done individually when the student is viewing on his or her own. In nonsynchronous viewing, the student can also replay scenes at will, and pause.

The greatest advantage of the DVD in terms of the classroom, however, is portability. The videotape is many times larger than the DVD and requires a large, specific-use player. Not only can DVDs be played on most contemporary computers, but even the players have become small units that can be easily transported themselves. Because of its portability, the DVD begins to play a role similar to that of a book in classroom situations. This new role changes both the way film can be studied and the DVD can be used as a tool for film studies, particularly on individual student assignments.

The ways the DVD can be used in the classroom are fairly obvious from the possible ways of viewing them. They make it easier to look at specific scenes and even frames of individual movies, allowing for minute examination never before possible in the average classroom. Because they often come with additional material, they also provide an apparatus for analysis that has never before been packaged so comfortably with the film itself (the occasional featurette with a videotape, positioned after the film, makes access difficult while viewing the film). Because most DVDs divide the movies into chapters for easy access, the teacher or student can turn immediately to any part of the film, finding a particular bit of dialogue within seconds.

Three things became quickly apparent as my own students at Pratt Institute began their work with film in the spring of 2004. First, the DVD was concentrating their attention on formal aspects of the film. Second, their idea of each film was caught up more with the director than might have been expected, presenting a mini-*auteur* sensibility (though this might also be the result of the current star quality of Quentin Tarantino, who is by far the favorite director of these students. Tarantino is, in fact, one of their favorite stars of any kind). Third, the students who worked directly with images showed no reluctance to make text a part of their own DVD creations.

One student created a DVD containing a scene of the movie he was studying, *Fear and Loathing in Las Vegas* (Terry Gilliam, 1998) and filmed the pages—and a voice-over reading—of the relevant chapter of the original book by Hunter S. Thompson. His analysis was focused on minute detail in both film and book, and on the relation of word and image. He pointed out the differences between the two and speculated on the reasons for them. Though he wants to be a filmmaker himself, he surprisingly showed no hesitation at making text a part of his own film, something that would once have been decried as non-cinematic. He was quite comfortable moving back and forth between media, and gave precedence to neither. Perhaps this was simply because he could now manipulate the two in similar manners.

Another student created an original film illustrating the opening of Kôji Suzuki's 1989 novel *Ringu* to compare it to the first scene of *Ringu* (Hideo Nataka, 1998). He shot digitally, edited on a computer, and burned his movie onto a DVD. His analysis was between his more literal filming of the opening of the novel and the changes that were made for the movie— changes that were extensive indeed. He used all three, the novel and the two films, in his discussion, moving back and forth easily.

A third student examined presentations of Oscar Wilde's Dorian Gray in *The Picture of Dorian Grey* (Albert Lewin,1945) and in *The League of Extraordinary Gentlemen* (Stephen Norrington, 2003). He also decided that he could make his points about the movies more easily if he created his own scene from the novel, one that could be contrasted with a scene from the older of the two movies.

Most of the students lacked the time and familiarity with editing software to be able to create scenes to make their points about the movies they were studying, but many of the others expressed that they would have, if they could have. They all grasped the implications of being able to use image as more than a visual aid to a presentation or a paper, and immediately saw ways that they could put image to use. Soon, the software needed for such exercises will be even easier to use and more generally available in the classroom. The resulting student creations should be quite interesting, to say the least.

Foreign films and silent films often prove difficult viewing for contemporary audiences, especially students. With its selections of languages and subtitles, the DVD even allows the viewer to compare original and dubbed versions. Also, some DVDs of foreign films provide the viewer the possibility of stopping and viewing translations of text appearing in the film. Though some silent films were scored, many were not; DVDs sometimes provide alternate soundtracks that make access easier for contemporary audiences, particularly young people who have had very little exposure to older films.

In addition to changing film scholarship and the way films are used in classrooms, the DVD is having an immediate impact on filmmakers themselves. Questions of editing and scoring with an eye toward the DVD as well as theatrical release are becoming part of the consideration and planning for any new film. The DVD is also making filmmakers a bit more comfortable with the idea that the eventual home of their work will be that medium, and that most viewers will be introduced to their work, if it lives at all, in the home. At least, they are much more reconciled to it than they were just a few yeas ago. In 1997, for example, on the eve of the DVD explosion, Lance Lawson interviewed Quentin Tarantino:

> As far as the special features that DVD offers, I know what language *I'm* going to watch movies in, and I don't need to be offered pan-and-scan when I'm going to be watching letterboxed anyway. As far as being able to offer different-rated editions, well, I don't like that just as a filmmaker. If I make my R-rated movie, then that's the movie I want out there. Now if I sell it to television and cut it, then that's my decision as a filmmaker: I've consciously sold it to television and agreed to cut it. But, to have hotter or milder versions of it floating around—I want people seeing the movie I made.[14]

Clearly, even the savviest members of the filmmaking community were capable of underestimating the DVD. Though most directors are still leery of the altered versions of their films that are possible through DVDs, they see the other extras as adding to viewing possibilities. As DVDs are used more and more in the classroom, watch for directors and packagers paying more attention to extras directed at them.

Though the future of the DVD remains unclear, it is already having an impact of film scholarship, on film in the classroom, and on the ways filmmakers consider their new projects. Technologies continue to change, and the shape of the DVD may change as a result; even its name may soon be different. Its place in American virtuality culture, however, is more than assured. It has been embraced in too many ways, and offers too many possibilities for the future for it to disappear altogether.

Chapter 7

THE QUESTION
OF
OWNERSHIP

Because the future of the DVD may depend on evolving copyright laws, an examination of the DVD will not be complete unless it includes a look at contemporary copyright privileges and controversies. Concepts such as *fair use* and *the public domain* are running afoul of others, including *creative control*. Only time will tell the outcome of the current debates, but it is worth looking at the issues and at the current situation, unstable though it may be.

In the early days of all technologies, those technologies are expensive—especially on the production side. Companies want to keep it balanced that way: they struggle to create affordable products while keeping the means of making them too expensive for the average person. One of the results of the computer revolution, however, has been a drastic reduction in the costs of making quality products in quite a number of areas. Sound and moving-image editing, for example, were so costly before the year 2000 that only expensive high-tech studios could provide the means for a professional-quality job. Today, home computers run programs allowing users to edit nearly as well as a studio—and to do it without extensive training.

What alarms corporate owners of movie and music rights (among other things) even more than competition from amateurs is that a kid can take one of their products and alter it, making something new, something that in no way seems amateurish. Given the still-high initial cost of production for the corporate creator (who pays for the stars, publicity, and the like—in addition to production), the loss of control this represents is extremely frightening. So, control of *derivative rights* has become an important issue to corporate producers of music, video, and even text. Extension of copyright protection has become an extremely important point on media companies' political agendas.

This isn't a completely new concern, though before the advent of the printing press questions of copyright were minimal. There was little money to be made, after all, out of a hand-copied book. With that first technology of mass media, however, the printed word started to become more valuable. In England, however, it really wasn't until the end of the seventeenth century that producing the words to be printed started to become a gainful occupation. It was also the time when the unscrupulous began to take advantage of the words of others for their own gain, producing what came to be known as *pirated editions* of a variety of popular works. In 1710 a Copyright Act was instituted in Great Britain, the first copyright law in what has become the Anglo-American copyright tradition, providing exclusive rights to the author or his/her agents for fourteen years. These rights have been expanding ever since.

Questions about copyright beyond the printed word have been contentious since the introduction of the earliest of the components of virtual culture. Just as film was getting off the ground as a cultural phenomenon, American courts were addressing the question of whether or not photographers should be required to get permission to photograph—whether the contents of a photograph could be owned in the sense that reproduction of the image of the contents (as opposed to the image itself) would be protected by copyright. Except for specific exceptions, it was decided it could not be.

With the growth of film archives dedicated to the preservation of movies, questions of copyright also became important and, sometimes, quite ticklish. Though the prints were (and are) owned by the individual archives, with rights to show them (with few restrictions—unlike videotapes and DVDs which are restricted, generally, to home viewing) and even lend them, rights to duplicate them were held by the initial copyright holder. Henri Langlois at Cinémathèque Française, in large part responsible for the growth of national archives through the Fédération Internationale des Archives du Film (FIAF) that he helped found—and that served, in part, as a vehicle for the exchange of films—eventually left FIAF in part, probably (though the details are murky), because he was uncomfortable with the growing feeling in the organization that films are cultural artifacts that should not be restricted by copyright. He saw a divide between showing and duping, feeling that the former helped everyone including the copyright holder (by increasing knowledge and appreciation of the work) while the latter did deprive the *auteur*. Prints of films were expensive items (and remain so, today). Any profit from their creation and sale, Langlois believed, should go to their creators.

With the advent of the VCR, however, reproduction of film (though of a low quality) became possible, simply and inexpensively. Even with the loss of quality, movie studios were scared: Universal Studios and Disney even took Sony to court, claiming that the record button on the Betamax abetted in copyright infringement. Obviously, they lost. Just as obviously, they have benefited from that very button, for it is what led to the continuing craze for home collection of movies—now one of the film studios' biggest profit centers.

One of the most radical aspects of virtual culture is the removal of control of the work itself from its creators to those who experience it, a change that copyright conventions, among other things, have not managed to adapt to in any sort of rational manner. Instead of recognizing that electronic media have instituted a fundamental shift in the way people interact with artifacts such as books, music, and images, the copyright holders have attempted to hold to a standard that not only cannot be enforced without the use of intrusive technology but also that no longer makes sense to most end users. This has led to an ongoing tension between the rights of the user and those of the creator. The opening for possible new creation via technology, today, confronts the desire to control past creation.

The resulting tension is exacerbated by the changing relationship—again caused by technology—between art and time. The static arts aside, the timing of art was initially controlled by the performer/creator, be it a storyteller or an actor. With the introduction of the book, however, the reader began to have more control, able to read, reread, browse, or skip at will. Until the introduction of the VCR, the movie viewer was at the mercy of the filmmaker, distributor, and showing venue. Only a memory of this remains in home viewing: When there is text connected to a DVD, we are more likely to use the pause button so that we can read at our leisure than we are to slow down a motion-picture scene, or pause it to examine it. Yet we still feel we are attacking the integrity of the work in a way we never do about a book we flip through. As the timed experience of the art falls more and more under the control of the viewer, making its discreet, timed units differently viewed and utilized, respect for the original pacing will fade.

In the audio commentary of *Once Upon a Time in the West* (Sergio Leone, 1969), when commenting on a close-up of Claudia Cardinale looking into a mirror, Sir Christopher Frayling says, "Feel free to freeze frame at this particular point."[1] He is purposely drawing viewer attention to their new power over the film. This process of control makes viewers feel a greater ownership of the work as they gain control over one more aspect of it, time. This new viewer control, of course, again heightens the tension between the creator and the viewer or user.

Legislatures and courts are in the process of addressing issues of copyright, but in a variety of ways, some even in direct conflict with others. On one side are strong arguments for freedom to make use of past creations in new endeavors. On the other are the rights, just as strong, of those who created something, something that not only reflects on them and on their public image, but that provides a livelihood for them. These are core issues of free speech and ownership; issues at the very heart of the American system, and resolution of the conflicts around them will change our culture irrevocably. It is impossible to say how, for this is not a war between two conflicting items, but one engendered by and within the thing itself. The technologies that are allowing new profit possibilities for the owners of the technologies and the creations transmitted through them are also opening up new nonprofitable or pirated uses of both the technologies and the creations.

In a literary culture, the clear lines of ownership of written material allow for sale of the physical manifestation of copyrightable material but not its reproduction into another discrete physical entity for resale. This insures that financial rights to first sale of any book, record, or other copyrightable item stay with the creator or with whomever the creator has assigned the rights to. It also protects use of written material as a part of another work (not merely as reproduction) through the related fair use doctrine.

Fair use stems from realization that the past is a necessary tool for the present and the future. We cannot create from nothing, but must use extant items, changing them, developing new possibilities out of them. Henry Ford did not invent the automobile; he simply found cheaper, more efficient ways to manufacture it. If he had been forced to seek permission for use of every idea he incorporated into his production line and final product, he never would have been able to open his first plant. At that time, however, the ideas themselves were not seen as the centers of value that they have since become. Corporate worth was based on physical assets, raw material (or access to it), means of production and distribution, and income-producing property. Today, corporate worth has as much to do with the *intellectual property* it controls—and this will be more and more important as the United States continues to become more a source of creativity and less a source of created things. Fair use can now often appear to be misappropriation of someone else's property. Yet limiting this misappropriation also limits the creativity of the culture, perhaps ultimately leading to its stagnation.

In the early years of the United States, a copyright was available for 14 years (following the English model), and the holder could renew it for another 14, giving a possible total of 28 years of control of the work by the author. By the middle of the nineteenth century, the maximum time a copyright could be held had been extended to 56 years, a doubling of the earlier length of copyright. This increasing of the life of a copyright has continued, as has an expansion of just what is covered (a result of the changes in technology, but also of the natural desire to maintain economic control of one's creations, whatever they may be). The 1998 Sonny Bono Copyright Term Extension Act has added 20 more years of protection to copyrighted works. So, at the start of the twenty-first century, a copyright held by an individual could remain in effect for 70 years after that individual's death. If a corporation holds the copyright, the life of the protection is generally 95 years. Such extensions change the very nature of copyright from a negotiation between the needs of the creator and the needs of the culture to a means of nearly permanent property protection.

There are two forces at work in determining copyright law as we move further into a virtual culture. One of these wants to insure protection, even for perpetuity, of intellectual property and other copyrightable items. A corporation like Microsoft or Disney sees a future where it loses control over its most valued assets—for Microsoft, its software codes, for Disney, its animated creations and its movies—and thus worries. These corporations depend for their very existences on proprietary *goods*, things that could be easily produced by others, were there not a legal protection for the corporation. It's understandable, then, that the corporations fight tooth-and-nail to protect these resources.

On the other side of the question are those people sometimes referred to as the *copyleft*. They worry about the erosion of the public domain and the weakening of the fair use doctrine.

Mickey Mouse is more than 70 years old. In another generation, if copyright isn't once again extended, the cartoon that built a corporation will be available for anyone to use, in any way they may wish to.

Mickey wouldn't even have to be re-drawn, but merely copied. It can easily be imagined, then, that questions of electronic copies create nightmares for copyright holders. Can the very concept of copyright survive, corporations ask, in face of new electronic technologies? They often feel they need it to, if they are going to survive themselves. In fact, they feel it needs to be expanded. Thus come their attempts at Digital Rights Management (DRM), meant to protect material from digital copying. But creativity necessitates the ability to freely incorporate works of the past into present creations. If T.S. Eliot had been forced to buy the rights from Dante Alighieri's heirs to the passage from *The Inferno* that he quotes at the start of "The Love Song of J. Alfred Prufrock," the poem would inevitably be different from what it is. And the loss would be all of ours.

The copyleft argues that, eventually, every creation either disappears or is incorporated into to the culture as a whole, no longer belonging simply to one individual. Otherwise, invention and creativity are stifled and the very culture begins to deteriorate. An open field allows progress; possessiveness, no matter how seriously conceived, impedes it. Thus, the necessity of a public domain that constantly grows, providing new material for potential creators to plow through without worry that they are going to have to stop and negotiate for rights that they may find they cannot, ultimately, even afford.

The question of fair use also arises in relation to technological restrictions against copyright infringement. As it stands, students have the right to use clips of a DVD, for example, in presentations for classes. But if that presentation is over the Internet and anti-piracy devices make it impossible for the student to copy from the DVD and so utilize it, that right becomes meaningless. A right that cannot be exercised, the copyleft says, is no right at all.

The erosion of the public domain through constantly extended copyright protection (both in time and in breadth) and the limiting of the ability to exercise fair-use rights through imposed technological restraints threatens to make it impossible for the independent artist or creator to work. Only those with corporate resources (who can then afford what rights they need) will be able to be involved in cutting-edge creative endeavors. And that, says the copyleft, is dangerous, for corporations are inherently conservative, wishing to protect what they have, not to experiment in areas that may prove beyond their control.

The changes in technology of the past century have also changed the meaning of "freedom of speech." In the past, anything at hand was fair game—as long as the intent or outcome was not to reproduce an earlier work for profit. Today, when so much intellectual property—the building blocks of speech—is proprietary, it becomes more and more dangerous to utilize free-speech rights as they more and more often conflict with ownership rights.

Questions of where protection of speech ends can become particularly sticky when they are extended to viewer manipulation of copyrighted material—which is happening now. ClearPlay software that comes on certain DVD players contains filter files for hundreds of movies, making it possible to watch those movies secure in the knowledge that sexually explicit scenes and profanity will be elided. The trouble with this, from the creators' point of view, is that the resulting film viewed might make no sense—important information may be cut—and the cadences of the film are changed.

Though this technology is as vehemently opposed by the Motion Picture Association of America (MPAA) and the Directors Guild as they oppose the altering of tapes and DVDs before resale, it has more of a chance of surviving the copyright minefield. The significant point is that ClearPlay doesn't alter the product itself—it acts simply as an automated fast-forward. It will be hard to argue that skipping ahead in any way violates copyright.

If the question becomes simply one of when the alteration is done, the MPAA and the Directors Guild worry that software allowing permanent alteration of DVDs by end-users will have to be allowed also. The ultimate decision concerning this question may be what finally determines the fate of the DVD. If it is forced to remain exactly what is marketed by the industry in many respects, it will merely be a better videotape. If it can be opened up to its potential for end-user modification, it will surely become something completely new in its cultural role, perhaps even a replacement for the book.

Ultimately, the erosion of the public domain by copyright extension will mean an erosion of free speech: If one cannot speak about something because it is protected, then one cannot speak at all. If it requires use of the images of a film to talk about it—as it more and more does, especially as technology makes it simpler—then it will only be possible to talk about that film with permission of the filmmaker (especially as DRM expands). And the filmmaker, of course, may have definite ideas of what should or shouldn't be said about that film.

The most significant milestone so far in the copyright debate is the Digital Millennium Copyright Act (DMCA), which was intended as a means for the stopping of piracy of intellectual property, mainly through the Internet. The DMCA, which became law in 1998, was designed to:

- Bring US into compliance with the 1996 treaties signed at Geneva during the World Intellectual Property Organization (WIPO) conference, though it goes further than WIPO requires. Copyright protections—

and piracy—have become world issues, with the DVD being a prime example of a highly profitable object of piracy.

- Criminalize circumvention of anti-piracy measures. This, in effect, even bans someone from finding a way to access a DVD, for example, without having to watch whatever introductory material (including warnings against unauthorized use) the manufacturer has put there.

- Ban devices to help illegally copy software, except for testing and research and, in some situations, by libraries, archives, and educational institutions (it also limits the liability of scholars), specifically for distance education. This ban stops legal copying as well, for any device meant for the legal copying of software could also be used for illegal copying. A home user cannot, for example, buy software that would allow the keeping of originals in pristine condition by making copies for everyday use. This section of the act may be akin to banning copying machines because they could be used for making copies that infringe on copyright.

- Limits Internet Service Provider (ISP) liability when used as a carrier of items infringing on copyright, but makes an ISP responsible for removal of infringing material from Web sites. A fan could not create a Web site dedicated to a movie complete with clips from that movie copied without permission from a DVD and keep it on an ISP's server.

Though the intent of the DMCA is to stop piracy through making it illegal to defeat anti-piracy protections, it has the effect of limiting the sorts of things one can do even with legally purchased DVDs. The industry-established Content Scrambling System (CSS) encryption is meant to prevent DVD copying. Circumvention of CSS is effectively illegal under DMCA. Although fair use provisions remain, fair use would require utilization of proscribed devices, and so becomes illegal. The magazine *2600* was sued by Universal City Studios for publishing DVD decryption software (software it had not created) on its Web site. The magazine was forced to remove it, the First Amendment notwithstanding. Even providing the possibility for copying DVDs, then, is now against the law.

One of the things you cannot legally do with a DVD is legally stream it over a network, even a home network, though this may be changing. This is to stop people from swapping over the Internet. To insure encryption, DVD manufacturers must be licensed by the DVD Copy Control Association (DVDCCA), which requires implementation of a CSS. This puts the DVD-CCA in a position to determine what sort of devices can be used for playing DVDs. Continuing its fear of new technology, the film industry is trying as hard as it can to limit the ways DVDs can be used.

It will be a long time before the unstable copyright situation settles down, and it is impossible to tell, right now, what forms the laws and their interpretations will take. One possibility is establishment of a fee-based copyright-renewal process. This would encourage many holders of copyright to let their rights lapse, rather than continuing to pay for them. The public domain, then, would continue to grow. The most significant copyright holders, however, are now corporations. They could afford any fees across the board (protecting even unlikely future usage), so the growth would probably be limited.

Because technological and cultural situations are changing quickly, laws such as the DMCA are, at best, efforts to catch up with real-world situations and, at worst, they are attempts to stop the changes that are occurring. The legal situation of copyright remains murky, as courts attempt to interpret the new law and legislative bodies continue to refine it or even add to it. DMCA-ensuing state laws, for example, are being enacted to protect ISPs. Some of these laws, in the interests of stopping piracy, may even dictate what sorts of devices may or may not be connected to the Internet, taking control from the individual user and turning it over to the ISP.

Like the film industry when threatened by new technologies in the past, the music industry has reacted to digital copying with a reactionary and punitive stance, refusing to find ways of working with the new technology. Instead it is trying, for the most part, to protect itself from what it sees as a threat. The Recording Industry Association of America (RIAA) has tried to scare individuals away from digital copying by a series of lawsuits, but to little effect. Following this example, the Motion Picture Association of America (MPAA) wants to make DRM mandatory for DVDs, circumventing the type of file-swapping that RIAA is viewing with such horror. The idea of people downloading films held by others and burning them onto their own DVDs makes studio executives blanche.

Only recently have the recording and movie industries begun to explore alternatives to the defensive and punitive stances they have taken. One of these, the licensing of Internet music distributors, is already in effect, but what its ultimate impact will be remains to be seen. It is possible that it may be a precursor to a *pay-as-you-play* system that will keep tight rein on all usage of copyrighted material.

Such a system has been explored for DVDs, but with little success. When the technology was developing, Circuit City put a great deal of money into a system called DIVX (DIgital Video eXpress) that would require telephone connection for activation. Each time a DVD was played, a charge would be assessed. Needless to say, the system was a flop. Still, the idea of instituting some sort of system that would enforce payment for the right to use still beckons. One vision of the virtual future, in fact, shows a world where, each time someone uses a dictionary or checks in a phone book, a small amount is deducted from their bank account. That way there could never be a question of copyright infringement, for any usage of any intellectual property would be recorded and appropriate charges made. The Circuit City idea would be back—in spades.

Another approach to piracy is to lower prices to the point where the "real" thing becomes competitive with the pirated edition. The motion-picture industry is trying this in Mexico and in Russia, in an attempt to push aside the huge pirated-DVD industry that has grown up in both places. The problem is that lower prices for legitimate DVDs in Mexico could lead to something like the situation the drug industry finds itself in vis-à-vis Canada. Exported US-manufactured drugs, sold for much less in Canada, are finding their way back into the United States. The film industry does not want to see the same thing happening with DVDs and Mexico.

Ultimately, both the music and film industries may find that the only effective way to fight piracy is to reduce prices everywhere. The industries, quite naturally, feel that this would lead to reduced profits, so they are loath to do so. They do not believe that the increase in volume would make up for the decrease in per-unit profit.

Neither industry believes in what might be called "the Grateful Dead effect," the phenomenon that was partially responsible for what became the most popular live act in the United States for more than a decade in the 1970s and 1980s. Early on in the band's existence, the members of the Dead made a conscious decision to assist fans who desired to tape their shows. The band even went so far as to require specified areas be designated for taping in each venue where the sound would be best for the tapers. The Dead also encouraged the exchange of tapes; soon, fans all over the country had dozens, if not hundreds, of tapes of live shows that they then would copy and give to (or trade with) others—all with the blessing of the band.

These tapes piqued the interest of thousands of listeners, many of whom flocked to Grateful Dead concerts as soon as they could, some making tapes of their own. The development of the dedicated fan base over the years had other causes as well, but the tapes were a part of the glue that held it together—as well as providing a means for its expansion.

It may be that, rather than ultimately hurting the music industry, the downloading of songs will eventually help it. Allowing people to develop familiarity with a musician's work even before spending money on it will lead the new fans, in the end, to attend concerts and buy the music on CD or through a licensed service on the Internet.

It is not likely that quite the same problem the music industry has with downloading could happen with DVDs. They cannot be broken into discrete, small, stand-alone units the way popular albums are. Even if movies could be easily downloaded, the history of the videotape gives reason to believe that copying movies does lead to buying. Many people whose collections of movies in the 1980s were made from television showings or by copying the tapes of others eventually replaced those tapes with commercial videotapes in the 1990s. It may be that it was the very fact of their collections that made them want to upgrade, just as those same people are now upgrading to DVD, buying movies in the new format that they already own in the old.

So, it may be that both the film industry and the music industry would find that they can maintain profitability even by backing off from promotion of technological protections that make many people feel as though a corporate Big Brother were breathing down their necks. People do not respond well to being treated like potential criminals—and often decide to act like criminals when they feel they are viewed that way, arguing that they are treated like criminals, anyway.

When it was instituted, the copyright system was meant to encourage innovation while protecting prior creativity. It has become something else completely. Seen most cynically, it has simply become a device for insuring the profit stream of corporations. Earlier in the virtual age, people argued that the Internet was an example of information trying to be free. Control of intellectual property seemed to be slipping from governmental, corporate, and personal fingers. Since then, we have seen the beginnings of a backlash. Where things will go, and the impact they will have on the DVD and its place in the virtual culture and in popular acceptance remains to be seen. It is quite possible that through technological or legal changes (or a combination of the two), the DVD will disappear as completely in a couple of years as did the laserdisc just a short time ago.

On the other hand, the DVD has a number of real advantages within a virtual framework—that is, it can have them, if they are allowed to become manifest. Some of these have to do with information storage and retrieval, which is a different topic than this book is considering—and is a function of the DVD that may have an extremely short life, as new devices, such as the tiny drives that can now be connected to a computer's USB port, come into extensive usage. Most, though, revolve around the DVD's ease of access to image, sound, and text. Its flexibility and ability to deal with all three components of a virtual culture (sound, image, and text) make it well situated to become the preferred device, much as the book, and not the pamphlet or broadsheet, became the prestige focus of literary culture.

A medium that has those four aspects—accessibility, high-quality sound capability, visual flexibility (as well as superior reproduction), and the ability to incorporate text—as well as flexibility in its presentation of each, at one time or together, lends itself well to the needs of a virtual culture. Because it can also incorporate the formal as well as the informal without a clash, the DVD easily fits in even with the renewed orality of the virtuality culture.

Because of the limitations currently imposed by the manufacturers, DVDs of films cannot yet reach their potential, but it is certainly in sight. The film commentaries, for example, that often come with commercial DVDs could conceivably give way to quite individual commentaries by anyone with the desire to make one. They would be commentaries that could then be passed around hand-to-hand or, more likely, via the Internet, but commentaries designed to be heard while the films are watched and that could be copied onto the DVD (currently they must be played separately). Another possibility, one that has not yet appeared (except as trivia tracks), is a commentary in type that scrolls below the picture, allowing for commentary that does not clash with the soundtrack, as current commentaries invariably do. However they are done, such commentaries could allow fans to trade viewpoints about the movies without removal of concentration from the primary material.

Because it is a medium so ideally suited for conveyance of movies, the DVD will soon become a vehicle for fan films, opening it up further to problems vis-à-vis copyright laws. It was *Star Wars* (George Lucas, 1977) that spawned the first fan films in the 1970s, for the movie appeared just as home video systems were offered for sale at a price and with enough flexibility to attract amateur filmmakers who wanted to do more than record pool parties. This new technology extended the reach of fan art, bringing it firmly within the virtual culture itself, enfolding songs and stories into the new mix.

George Lucas and his *Star Wars* franchise have long recognized that they could easily lose control, and that *Star Wars*, with its tremendous cultural impact and penetration, could become firmly established within the public domain. They have even gone so far as to offer free web space for fan creative activity—with the single stipulation that all material posted become the intellectual property of the franchise. This way, they reasoned, fans could continue their activities without endangering the prerogatives of the franchise. In the minds of some fans, however, the franchise had already become the evil empire, and the fans who avoid its copyright restrictions had taken over the role of the valiant rebels.

Unfortunately for Lucas's attempts at control, *Star Wars* came into being just as fan media possibilities were beginning to explode, those video recorders replacing Super-8 cameras in what was to become a continuing escalation of technical innovation. The growth of cheap communications and storage tools connected to computer, digital, and Internet technology has now made it next to impossible for any franchise holder to control a phenomenon with as broad a global impact as *Star Wars* has had. Impossible, at least, without planning before the fact and careful utilization of DMCA regulations. Even the Harry Potter franchise, which has remained fairly clearly under the thumb of J.K. Rowling and her corporate associates, has become the basis for extensive fan art.

What may be the most famous example of fan film art, *The Phantom Edit* (Mike J. Nichols, 1999) is an alteration of *The Phantom Menace* (George Lucas, 1999), making a new work, one without the Computer Generated Imagery (CGI) character Jar-Jar Binks, a character universally decried upon the movie's release. LucasFilms Limited eventually put the brakes on distribution of the movie, arguing that the new movie was not a separate work of art, but one that fell within the copyright of the old one. LucasFilms couched its objections in terms of someone making money off of its copyright—but is that really the issue?

In 1919, Marcel Duchamp produced a work based on a postcard showing a reproduction of Leonardo DaVinci's "Mona Lisa"—with a moustache and slight VanDyke beard drawn upon it and the letters "L.H.O.O.Q." (which may or may not be a comment in French, if the letters are pronounced as the French would, on the subject's rear end) underneath. Though the Mona Lisa was clearly in the public domain at the time, Duchamp could probably have done the same with a contemporary painting, his action causing no more than outrage on the part of the artist of the original. In today's atmosphere of copyright protectionism, however, he might find himself burdened by a heavy lawsuit, had he chosen the work of a living artist.

One of Andy Warhol's more famous images wasn't his at all, but was a utilization of the Campbell's Soup can. In fact, Warhol used a variety of cans in a number of ways starting in 1962. At the time, the company did not feel it needed to protect its design. Today, a corporation might feel quite differently, in similar circumstances. Strangely enough, in 2004, Campbell's licensed Warhol silkscreen designs based on Campbell's early cans for a special line of its own new cans.

The movie industry strongly backs laws that make it illegal to reproduce their films for any purposes—even other art. Baltimore artist Jon Routson produces DVDs from recordings he makes with a hand-held camera in theaters. His films show, at times, the movie being projected, the audience, and even the walls. Such films may soon be criminal to make (they already are, in a few states). Routson does not sell his work: It is not commerce in the images that is being proscribed, but the actual filming.

One of the reasons for the increased concern on the part of media companies about copyright, of course, is that the concept of *original work of art* is changing radically in a virtual environment. If something is created on a computer and posted on the Internet, there isn't even an original to which one can point. No longer are there original manuscripts for most writers, for they, too, work on computers. To make matters worse, the making of a copy of something from the Internet in no way affects the artifact that was copied. No physical damage is done. The damage is ethereal but, according to corporate copyright holders, nonetheless real. It is simply to emphasize this point that the Recording Industry Association of America (RIAA) has sued student downloaders for astronomical amounts of money. The music industry is trying to make a point, not gain restitution.

In an evolving technological and legal situation, it is difficult to make claims for the future. If the past is any guide, the corporations are eventually going to have to find ways of coming to terms with consumer manipulation of copyrighted material without permissions. The weight of perceived individual prerogative is extremely high, and its pressure will be hard for the corporations to withstand—especially when technology constantly makes it easier and easier to circumvent controls. The corporations, however, are extremely powerful, and they perceive such manipulation as attacks on the basis of their very existences—so they will fight hard to protect themselves. At the very least, it will be interesting to see which side wins out, or if a compromise acceptable to all is ever worked out.

AFTERWORD

As television producer and scholar John Ellis writes, "the examination of cinema begins not with the structure of a single film, but with the conditions in which 'a film' exists as a separate entity in our current culture."[1] At some point, exploration of the DVD requires placing it within the context of communication, education, storytelling, and other forms of entertainment, and of the changes in American culture that the technological innovations of the electronic media have augmented. It also needs expansion of the discussion from films on DVD to the myriad other applications for the technology, some already enthusiastically endorsed (by video-game fans, for example).

Just as we long ago moved from an oral culture to a print culture, starting about 150 years ago (with the advent of photography) we began to progress from that literacy culture to what might be called a post-typographical, visual, virtual, or representational culture—or even, for the first time, a global mass culture or a truly democratic (in the sense of anyone, anywhere having the possibility of involvement) participatory culture. Whatever it will be called, the DVD is at its heart (at least for now—as always, technological changes may change that at any time).

One of the most important aspects of the virtual culture is the placement of the image in a centrality it hasn't had—at least, not since the development of moveable type and the ascendancy of print. This, in turn, changes the position of the reader or spectator who is no longer necessarily expected to interact with the work in a linear fashion at all, but who can change perspective in interaction with the work in a manner that concerns that reader or viewer only. One of the implications here is that our old forms of scholarship will not even be able to encompass this new "looking," for their vocabulary is centered on print. Thus, until our books are fully incorporated into whatever form appears at the center of virtuality, we can only grope toward under-standing what is happening around us, using our old *literacy* tools but all the while aware of the paradox of speaking of something that may quickly show the limitations of these very *speaking* tools.

How we imagine "reality" and our responsibilities and relations to it is determined in part through our relations with the worlds presented in the media. When we accept a film experience, when we are willing to enter into the "world" of a film, we accept the idea that there is a comprehensible thread within, that there is, generally speaking, a narrative. So inculcated in us is this concept (which at times has little relation to the "real" world) that we transfer it to the camera images we create ourselves, believing that they must contain something knowable, within discrete limits of beginning and end. Of course, the negotiation that our interaction with the film (or book, for that matter) represents has an impact on our perceptions of the greater world. It tells us that, if the world can be captured on film or tape, it can be unraveled, that its story will become knowable. This is a useful fiction that brings us great comfort—and the DVD is part of that comfort. There is security in knowing that there is a seeing beyond our eyes, a hearing outside our ears, even a feeling away from our hands. There is meaning, even media we create ourselves tell us, external to our fears.

Though it certainly has its private aspects and will be sustained by its discrete nature, the DVD can still have a public impact. The extensive and growing role of the DVD in the wider American culture is exemplified by the case of *Capturing the Friedmans* (Andrew Jarecki, 2003), a documentary con-cerning a child-molestation case brought against a father and son, Arnold and Jesse Friedman, on Long Island, New York. Both pleaded guilty and went to prison, but doubts about the case have remained. As Peter M. Nichols writes in *The New York Times*, "here the DVD has a chance to step into current developments and play a part in a continuing judicial process. On Jan. 7, citing disclosures in Mr. Jarecki's documentary, a motion was filed in Nassau County Court to vacate the conviction of Jesse Friedman."[2] It was the DVD, which contained pieces about the investigation not included in the theatrical release, that was submitted to the court. Nichols quotes Jarecki: "A lot of that didn't fit into the film, but it's interesting in a legal action."[3]

Like a growing number of DVDs, *Capturing the Friedmans* became the center of an ongoing cultural event. In the article, Jarecki is again quoted: "We heard from theater managers that there was a problem. . . . People weren't leaving after the film. They were sitting in their seats, and arguing about things, so they couldn't clean the theater."[4] Sensing an opportunity, Jarecki began to interview lingerers with an eye toward incorporating their questions and concerns into the eventual DVD release. Though there are clearly doubts about the investigation, on the DVD itself Jarecki has attempted to maintain a speculative balance about the Friedmans' actual guilt rather than to answer the questions, intending the DVD not as a place to go for answers, but as a facilitator of continuing discussion.

Most people hunger to be more than merely passive viewers. The "couch potato" cliché never really captured the whole of what was being experienced, or what was desired, as the explosion of the interactive Internet has shown. One of the most important aspects of movies is the community it engenders and discussions it furthers, as in the case of *Capturing the Friedmans*.

Even standing in line waiting for a show can be important to this community, a fact Woody Allen plays with in *Annie Hall* (1977), when his character pulls the real Marshall McLuhan onto the screen to rebut the pompous opinions of a fellow theatergoer. At the openings of *Harry Potter and the Sorcerer's Stone* and *Harry Potter and the Chamber of Secrets* (Chris Columbus, 2001 and 2002), young fans appeared in outfits inspired by the characters in the J.K. Rowling books, giving the lines outside the theaters a sense of shared excitement and a rare charm.

McLuhan, long before his *Annie Hall* appearance, posited that media could be divided into two types, hot media, and cool media.[5] Hot media requires nothing from its audience besides attention. Cool media forces its audience into some sort of interaction or reaction (generally through having to add in missing information). Though the distinction may not be as useful as it first appears (all media is, in the final analysis, cool), this hot/cool dichotomy can illustrate the difference between how corporate media producers view their products and how end-users relate to them. Film studios, dreading the loss of control that audience interaction requires, try to make their products as hot as possible, even going so far as to try to argue that "cool" interactions violate copyright.

From any standpoint, filmgoers should not be taken as inactive. Evaluation is always part of the experience, not an adjunct or mere add-on. "Film viewing is a natural pretext for sociability,"[6] writes Noel Carroll, a film scholar and professor of art. The act of viewing a movie, also, is something more than turning oneself into a receptacle for the logic of the universe of the film. The viewer becomes a predictor, even a seer, a puzzle-solver, and a moral evaluator.

Whatever the future of the DVD may be, home viewing is secure. As people get more and more involved with their collections of movies—and with the movies themselves—they will want to have them at home, physically. For music, books, and more, the DVD may soon be the vehicle of choice just as it is now for movies and games. Beyond that?

We'll see.

# NOTES

INTRODUCTION

1. "The Imposter Files," *Imposter*, 2002, DVD (Home Dimension Video, 2002).

CHAPTER 1: HOME VIEWING OF FEATURE FILMS IN AMERICA

1. Jean-Louis Baudry, "Ideological Effects of the Basic Cinematographic Apparatus," *Film Quarterly* Vol. 28, No. 2 (Winter 1974–75), rept. in Braudy, Leo and Marshall Cohen (Eds.), *Film Theory and Criticism: Introductory Readings*, 5th edition (Oxford University Press, 1999), 349.

2. Kenneth Turan, "Master of the Seas," *The Los Angeles Times*, 11/14/03.

3. Mike Nichols with Steven Soderbergh, "Audio Commentary," *Catch-22* DVD (Paramount, 2001), Chapter 2.

4. Chris Willman, "Celluloid Heroes," *The Los Angeles Times* Calendar Section, 26 March 1995, rep. in Peary, Gerald (Ed.), *Quentin Tarantino Interviews* (Jackson: University Press of Mississippi, 1998), 139.

5. Lance Lawson, "My Evening with Q, Part I," *Entertainment@Home*, Vol. 1, No. 3, May, 1997, rept. in Peary, Gerald (Ed.), *Quentin Tarantino Interviews* (Jackson: University Press of Mississippi, 1998), 186.

6. Sharon Waxman, "Studios Rush to Cash in on DVD Boom," *The New York Times*, 4/20/04:E1.

CHAPTER 2: *CINÉMATHÈQUE FRANÇAISE* AT OUR HOUSE

1. Tom Gunning, "Animated Pictures": Tales of Cinema's Forgotten Future, After 100 Years of Films," in Gledhill, Christine and Linda Williams (Eds.), *Reinventing Film Studies* (London: Arnold, 2000), 317.

2. Academy of Motion Picture Arts and Sciences inscription on the Oscar statuette presented to Langlois, http://awardsdatabase/oscars.org/ampas_awards/DisplayMain. jsp?curTime=1081712223754.

3. Eric Rohmer, *Cahiers du cinema*, No. 135 (September, 1962). Quoted in Roud, Richard, *A Passion for Films: Henri Langlois and the Cinémathèque Française* (New York: Viking, 1983), 65.

4. Francois Truffaut, interview with Richard Roud, from Roud, Richard, *A Passion for Films: Henri Langlois and the Cinémathèque Française* (New York: Viking, 1983), 67.

5. Richard Roud, *A Passion for Films: Henri Langlois and the Cinémathèque Française* (New York: Viking, 1983), 154.

6. Larissa MacFarquhar, "Profile of Quentin Tarantino," *The New Yorker* (10/20/03), 156.

7. Stanley Cavell, *The World Viewed: Reflections on the Ontology of Film* (New York: Viking, 1971), 6.

8. Quentin Tarantino, Interview with Charlie Rose, 10/14/94, http:// www.godamongdirectors.com/tarantino/faq/rose.html.

9. Roger Avary, quoted in Biskind, Peter, *Down and Dirty Pictures: Miramax, Sundance, and the Rise of Independent Film* (New York: Simon & Schuster, 2004), 127.

10. Larissa MacFarquhar, "Profile of Quentin Tarantino," *The New Yorker* (10/20/03), 150.

11. Jean-Luc Godard, *Jean-Luc Godard: A Critical Anthology*, Toby Mussman (Ed.), (New York: Dutton, 1968), 103.

12. Stanley Cavell, *The World Viewed: Reflections on the Ontology of Film* (New York: Viking, 1971), 124.

13. *His Girl Friday*, dir. Howard Hawkes, perf. Cary Grant, Rosalind Russell, 1940. DVD, DK3 Films, 1999.

14. Bernardo Bertolucci, "Commentary on *Once Upon a Time in the West*," *Once Upon a Time in the West* (1969), DVD, Paramount, 2003, chapter 17.

15. Quentin Tarantino, " Interview with Chris Willman," *The Los Angeles Times* Calendar Section, 3/26/95, reprinted in Peary, Gerald (Eds.), *Quentin Tarantino Interviews* (Jackson: University of Mississippi Press, 1998), 139.

16. Terry Flew, *New Media: An Introduction* (Oxford University Press, 2002), 110–111.

17. Richard Griffith, in a conversation with Richard Roud, quoted in Roud, Richard, *A Passion for Films: Henri Langlois and the Cinémathèque Française* (New York: Viking, 1983), 133.

CHAPTER 3:   DVD FAN CULTURE

1. http://www.film-talk.com/forums/index.php?showtopic=945. Used with permission of the poster.

2. Wilson Rothman, "DVDs? I Don't Rent. I Own," *The New York Times*, 2/26/04:E1.

3. "Ed," e-mail interview with Aaron Barlow, 4/21/04.

4. Todd Robertson, e-mail interview with Aaron Barlow, 4/20/04.

5. Thomas Arnold, "Cronenberg's Scary Movies Will Not Die," *USA Today*, 6/11/04, 5e.

6. "Ed," e-mail interview with Aaron Barlow, 4/21/04.

7. Ibid.

8. See William J. Mitchell, "Designing Digital Books" in David Thorburn and Henry Jenkins (Eds.), *Rethinking Media Change: The Aesthetics of Transition* (Cambridge: The MIT Press, 2003).

9. Lawrence Lessig, *Free Culture: How Big Media Uses Technology and the Law to Lock Down Culture and Control Creativity* (New York: The Penguin Press, 2004).

10. Todd Robertson, e-mail interview with Aaron Barlow, 4/20/04.

11. "Ed," e-mail interview with Aaron Barlow, 4/21/04.

12. Todd Robertson, e-mail interview with Aaron Barlow, 4/20/04.

13. Todd Robertson, e-mail interview with Aaron Barlow, 4/20/04.

14. Stanley Cavell, *The World Viewed: Reflections on the Ontology of Film* (New York: Viking, 1971), 10.

15. Todd Robertson, e-mail interview with Aaron Barlow, 4/20/04.

16. Henry Jenkins, "Digital Cinema, Media Convergence, and Participatory Culture," in David Thorburn and Henry Jenkins (Eds.), *Rethinking Media Change: The Aesthetics of Transition* (Cambridge: The MIT Press, 2003), 286.

17. DVD Tracks, www.dvdtracks.com. Viewed 6/06/04.

18. The Q, e-mail interview with Aaron Barlow, 6/7/04.

19. The Q, e-mail interview with Aaron Barlow, 6/7/04.

20. Chris Freestone, e-mail interview with Aaron Barlow, 6/7/04.

21. Todd Robertson, e-mail interview with Aaron Barlow, 4/20/04.

CHAPTER 4: THE SPECIAL EDITION DVD

1. Quentin Tarantino and Gerald Peary (Ed.), *Quentin Tarantino Interviews* (Jackson: University of Mississippi Press, 1998), 140.

2. "Our Mission," http://www.criterionco.com/asp/about.asp, viewed 5/11/04.

3. Annette Kuhn, *Dreaming of Fred and Ginger: Cinema and Cultural Memory* (New York University Press, 2002), 18. This and all the following ratings are from www.imdb.com, the Internet Movie DataBase, and reflect the standings as of 5/21/04.

4. This and all the following ratings are from www.imdb.com, the Internet Movie Database.

5. This and all other statistics concerning film in this chapter, come from The Internet Movie DataBase, www.imdb.com.

6. Michael Moore, "How to Deal with the Lies and the Lying Liars when They Lie about Bowling for Columbine," http://www.michaelmoore.com. Viewed 5/08/04.

7. David Blakesley, "Introduction: The Rhetoric of Film and Film Studies," in Blakesley, David (Ed.), *The Terministic Screen: Rhetorical Perspectives on Film* (Carbondale: Southern Illinois University Press, 2003), 5.

8. Michael Moore, "How to Deal."

9. "Production Research," *Casablanca* Collector's Edition DVD (Warner Bros. Home Video, 2003).

10. David Robinson, "Introduction to *Modern Times*," *The Chaplin Collection, Volume I* DVD (Warner/Mk2, 2003).

11. David Thomson, *The New Biographical Dictionary of Film* (New York: Knopf, 2002), 693.

12. Peter Cowie, "Commentary on *Grand Illusion*" (DVD, Criterion, 1999), Chapter 7.

13. "'Ring Fanatics' Long Wait Finally Ends, with an Eyeful," *The New York Times* 12/18/03, E1.

CHAPTER 5: THE DVD AUDIO COMMENTARY

1. Walter Mirisch, et al., "Commentary on *The Magnificent Seven*," *The Magnificent Seven* DVD (MGM Home Entertainment, 2001), Chapter 2.

2. Anthony Harvey, "Commentary on *The Lion in Winter*," *The Lion in Winter* DVD (MGM Home Entertainment, 2001), Chapter 10.

3. Robert Wise and Nicolas Meyer, "Commentary on *The Day the Earth Stood Still*," *The Day the Earth Stood Still* DVD (20th Century Fox Home Entertainment, 2003), Chapter 4.

4. Marc Forster and Roberto Schaefer, "Commentary on *Monster's Ball*," *Monster's Ball* DVD (Studio Home Entertainment, 2002), Chapter 2.

5. Mel Brooks, "Commentary on *Young Frankenstein*," *Young Frankenstein* DVD (20th Century Fox Home Entertainment, 1998), Chapter 28.

6. Mira Nair, "Commentary on *Monsoon Wedding*," *Monsoon Wedding* DVD (VCI Distribution, 2002), Chapter 12.

7. Jean-Pierre Jeunet and Ron Perlman, "Commentary on *The City of Lost Children*," *The City of Lost Children* DVD (Columbia TriStar Home Video, 1999), Chapter 1.

8. Ron Shelton, "Commentary on *Bull Durham*," *Bull Durham* DVD (Image Entertainment, 1998), Chapter 11.

9. Billy Morrisette, "Commentary on *Scotland, PA*," *Scotland, PA* DVD (Showtime Entertainment, 2004).

10. Marc Forster, Billy Bob Thornton, and Halle Berry, "Commentary on *Monster's Ball*," *Monster's Ball* DVD (Studio Home Entertainment, 2002), Chapter 1.

11. Matthew Bright, "Commentary on *Freeway*," *Freeway* DVD (Republic, 1997), Chapter 35.

12. Mike Nichols and Steven Soderbergh, "Commentary on *Catch-22*," *Catch-22* DVD (Paramount, 2001), Chapter 5.

13. Spencer Klaw, "The Lady and the Harp," *Harper's Bazaar*, August, 1951, rept. in *The American Harp Journal*, Vol. 18, No. 2, Winter, 2001, 39.

14. Leonard Maltin, "Commentary on *A Night at the Opera*," *A Night at the Opera* DVD (Warner Home Video, 2004), Chapter 15.

15. Peter Jackson, et al., "Director and Writers Commentary on *The Fellowship of the Ring*," *The Fellowship of the Ring: Extended Edition DVD* (Warner Home Video, 2002), Chapter 16.

CHAPTER 6: THE DVD, THE FILM SCHOLAR, AND THE CLASSROOM

1. Stanley Cavell, *The World Viewed: Reflections on the Ontology of Film* (New York: Viking, 1971), xiv.

2. Ibid.

3. Raymond Bellour, *The Analysis of Film*, Constance Penley (Ed.), (Bloomington: Indiana University Press, 2000), 3.

4. Stanley Cavell, *The World Viewed*, 12. My comments should in no way be taken as a criticism of either Cavell or Bellour, whom I see as astute and useful observers of film, however they may approach knowledge of them. I am merely pointing out changes in attitudes in film studies.

5. David Bordwell, "Lowering the Stakes: Prospects for a Historical Poetics of Cinema," *Iris* 1:1 (1983), 6.

6. Robert Ray, *How a Film Theory Got Lost and Other Mysteries in Cultural Studies* (Bloomington: Indiana University Press, 2001), 44.

7. Byron Hawk, "Hyperrhetoric and the Inventive Spectator: Remotivating *The Fifth Element*," In Blakesley, David (Ed.), *The Terministic Screen: Rhetorical Perspectives on Film* (Carbondale: Southern Illinois University Press, 2003), 71.

8. Raymond Bellour, *The Analysis*, 2.

9. Ibid.

10. Ibid.

11. Seymour Chatman, "What Novels Can Do that Films Can't (and Vice Versa)." *Critical Inquiry, Vol. 8 (1980).* Reprinted in Baudry, Leo and Marshall Cohen (Eds.), *Film Theory and Criticism: Introductory Readings*, 5th edition (Oxford University Press, 1999), 438.

12. William Uricchio, "Historicizing Media in Transition," in Thorburn, David and Henry Jenkins (Eds.), *Rethinking Media Change: The Aesthetics of Transition* (Cambridge: The MIT Press, 2003), 29–30.

13. Stanley Cavell, *The World Viewed*, 125.

14. Lance Lawson, "My Evening With Q, Part I," *Entertainment@Home*, Vol. 1, No. 3, May, 1997, rept. in Peary, Gerald (Ed.), *Quentin Tarantino Interviews* (Jackson: University of Mississippi Press, 1998), 184.

CHAPTER 7:   THE QUESTION OF OWNERSHIP

1. Christopher Frayling, "Audio Commentary," *Once Upon a Time in the West,* 1969 (DVD Paramount, 2003), Chapter 6.

AFTERWORD

1. John Ellis, *Visible Fictions: Cinema, Television, Video* (London: Routledge, 1982), 25.

2. Peter M. Nichols, "Abuse Case Revisited, Cloudier Than Ever," *The New York Times,* 1/27/04:E1.

3. Ibid.

4. Ibid.

5. Marshall McLuhan, *Understanding Media* (Cambridge: The MIT Press, 1994), 23.

6. Noel Carroll, "Introducing Film Evaluation," in Gledhill, Christian and Linda Williams (Eds.), *Reinventing Film Studies* (London: Arnold, 2000), 265.

SELECTED BIBLIOGRAPHY

Acland, Charles. *Screen Traffic: Movies, Multiplexes, and Global Culture*. Durham, North Carolina: Duke University Press, 2003.

Bazin, André. *What Is Cinema? Essays Selected and Translated by Hugh Gray*. Berkeley: University of California Press, 1967.

Bellour, Raymond. *The Analysis of Film*. Constance Penley (Ed.). Bloomington: Indiana University Press, 2000.

Biskind, Peter. *Down and Dirty Pictures: Miramax, Sundance, and the Rise of Independent Film*. New York: Simon & Schuster, 2004.

Blakesley, David (Ed.). *The Terministic Screen: Rhetorical Perspectives on Film*. Carbondale: Southern Illinois University Press, 2003.

Bordwell, David and Noël Carroll (Eds.). *Post-Theory: Reconstructing Film Studies*. Madison: University of Wisconsin Press, 1996.

Bordwell, David, Jane Staiger, and Kristin Thompson. *The Classical Hollywood Cinema: Film Style and Mode of Production to 1960*. London: Routledge, 1985.

Braudy, Leo and Marshall Cohen (Eds.). *Film Theory and Criticism: Introductory Readings*, 5th edition. Oxford: Oxford University Press, 1999.

Briggs, Asa and Peter Burke. *A Social History of the Media: From Gutenberg to the Internet*. Cambridge: Polity Press, 2002.

Brooker, Will. *Using the Force: Creativity, Community, and Star Wars Fans*. New York: Continuum, 2002.

Brooker, Will and Deborah Jermyn, (Eds.). *The Audience Studies Reader*. London: Routledge, 2003.

Carroll, Noël. *A Philosophy of Mass Art*. Oxford: Clarendon Press, 1998.

Carroll, Noël. *Theorizing the Moving Image*. Cambridge: Cambridge University Press, 1996.

Cavell, Stanley. *The World Viewed: Reflections on the Ontology of Film*. New York: Viking, 1971.

Durham, Meenakshi Gigi and Douglas M. Kellner (Eds.). *Media and Cultural Studies: KeyWorks*. Malden, Massachusetts: Blackwell, 2001.

Dyer, Richard. *The Matter of Images: Essays on Representations*. 2nd Edition. London: Routledge/Taylor & Francis, 2002.

Ellis, John. *Visible Fictions*. London: Routledge and Kegan Paul, 1982.

Flew, Terry. *New Media: An Introduction*. Oxford: Oxford University Press, 2002.

Gledhill, Christine and Linda Williams, ed. *Reinventing Film Studies*. London: Arnold Publishers, 2000.

Godard, Jean-Luc. *Jean-Luc Godard: A Critical Anthology*, Toby Mussman (Ed.). New York: Dutton, 1968.

Hallam, Julia and Margaret Marshment. *Realism and Popular Culture*. Manchester: Manchester University Press, 2000.

Hill, John and Pamela Church Gibson (Eds.). *Film Studies: Critical Approaches*. Oxford: Oxford University Press, 2000.

Jenkins, Henry. *Textual Poachers: Television Fans and Participatory Culture*. New York: Routledge, 1992.

King, Geoff. *New Hollywood Cinema: An Introduction*. New York: Columbia University Press, 2002.

Kracauer, Siegfried. *Theory of Film: The Redemption of Physical Reality*. London: Oxford University Press, 1960.

Kuhn, Annette. *Dreaming of Fred and Ginger: Cinema and Cultural Memory*. New York: New York University Press, 2002.

Lehman, Peter and William Luhr. *Thinking About Movies: Watching, Questioning, Enjoying*. Malden, Massachusetts: Blackwell, 2003.

Lessig, Lawrence. *Free Culture: How Big Media Uses Technology and the Law to Lock Down Culture and Control Creativity*. New York: Penguin, 2004.

Lewis, Jon (Ed.). *The End of Cinema As We Know It: American Film in the Nineties*. New York: New York University Press, 2001.

McLuhan, Marshall. *Understanding Media*. 1964. Cambridge: The MIT Press, 1994.

Mast, Gerald. *Film Cinema Movie: A Theory of Experience*. 1977. Chicago: The University of Chicago Press, 1983.

Mast, Gerald and Marshall Cohen (Eds.). *Film Theory and Criticism: Introductory Readings*. Oxford: Oxford University Press, 1974.

Mitchell, W.J.T., *Picture Theory*. Chicago: The University of Chicago Press, 1994.

Mitry, Jean. *Semiotics and the Analysis of Film*. Trans. by Christopher King. Bloomington: Indiana University Press, 2000.

Moores, Shaun. *Media and Everyday Life in Modern Society*. Edinburgh: Edinburgh University Press, 2000.

Myrent, Glenn and Georges P. Langlois. *Henri Langlois: First Citizen of Cinema*. Trans. by Lisa Nesselson. New York: Twayne/Simon & Schuster, 1995.

Natoli, Joseph. *Memory's Orbit: Film and Culture 1999–2000*. Albany, New York: State University of New York, Albany. 2003.

Neale, Steve. *Genre and Hollywood.* London: Routledge, 2000.

Nowell-Smith, Geoffrey. *The Oxford History of World Cinema.* Oxford: Oxford University Press, 1996.

Ong, Walter J. *Orality and Literacy: The Technologizing of the Word.* 1982. London: Routledge/Taylor & Francis Group, 2002.

Peary, Gerald (Ed.). *Quentin Tarantino Interviews.* Jackson: University of Mississippi Press, 1998.

Ray, Robert. *How a Film Theory Got Lost and Other Mysteries in Cultural Studies.* Bloomington: Indiana University Press, 2001.

Roud, Richard. *A Passion for Films: Henri Langlois and the Cinémathèque Française.* New York: Viking, 1983.

Thorburn, David and Henry Jenkins (Eds.). *Rethinking Media Change: The Aesthetics of Transition.* Cambridge: The MIT Press, 2003.

Ulmer, Gregory. *Internet Invention: From Literacy to Electracy.* New York: Longman, 2003.

Williams, Linda (Ed.). *Viewing Positions: Ways of Seeing Film.* New Brunswick, New Jersey: Rutgers University Press, 1995.

INDEX

Academy Awards, 18, 35, 88
Academy flat, 3
Adventures of Antoine Doinel: Five Films by François Truffaut (2003), 84–85
Adventures of Buckaroo Banzai Across the 8th Dimension, The (1984), xi, 48, 82, 85–86, 103
Adventures of Huckleberry Finn, The, 78
Adventures of Robin Hood, The (1938), 47, 106
Affaire Langlois, 38, 53
Air Force One (1997), 14
Alan Lomax Remix Project–Tangle Eye, The, 71
Allen, Woody, 90, 159
Altman, Robert, 111–112
Amazon.com, xi, 63
American Splendor (2003), 118
Anamorphic enhancement, 4, 29
Annie Hall (1977), 159
Antoine and Colette (1962), 84
Anxiety of Influence, The, 55

Arnheim, Rudolph, 5
Around the World in 80 Days (2004), 25
Astaire, Fred, 107
Auteur, 39, 76, 115, 140, 144
Avary, Roger, 43

Bacall on Bogart (1988), 91
Bandits, 82
Bartel, Paul, 21
Barthes, Roland, 129
Batone, Danielle, 118
Baudry, Lean-Louis, 6
Bazin, André, 6–7, 37
Beatles, The, 71
Beaumont, Harry, 33, 104
Bed and Board (1970), 84
Behind the Scenes in the Machine Age (1931), 93
Behlmer, Rudy, 91, 121–123
Bellour, Raymond, 127, 131–132
Berman, Shari Springer, 118
Berry, Halle, 116

Bertolucci, Bernardo, 38, 46–47
Betamax, 1, 17, 66
Bigelow, Kathryn, 26
Black Album, The, 71
Blade Runner, 16, 25, 56
Blair Witch Project, The (1999), 22, 23
Blakesley, David, 87
Blockbuster Video, 4, 17, 65
Bloom, Harold, 55
Bogdanovich, Peter, 124
Bordwell, David, 128, 130
Bounty, The (1984), 10
Bowling for Columbine (2002), 86–89
Brabner, Joyce, 118
Brazil (1985), 79, 82, 89–90
Bridgeman, Sharon, 25
Bridge on the River Kwai, The (1957), 99
Bright, Matthew, 120
Broadway Melody of 1929 (1929), 33, 104
Broadway Melody of 1940 (1939), 5, 94
Brooks, Louise, 40
Brooks, Mel, 112
Brown, Nacio Herb, 104
Brownlow, Kevin, 94
Bull Durham (1988), 115
Burtt, Ben, 137

Cagney, James, 107
Cahiers du cinéma, 37
Capacitance Electronic Disc, 17
Capra, Frank, 8
Capturing the Friedmans (2003), 158–159
Caro, Marc, 80, 114
Carroll, Noel, 159
Casablanca (1942), xi, 8, 44, 81, 90–91, 99, 104
Cast Away (2000), 14
Castle Films, 2
Catch-22 (1970), 11, 113, 121
Cavell, Stanley, 39, 46, 65, 127, 136–137

Chaplin, Charles, 26, 30, 33–34, 91–94
Chaplin Collection, The, Volume 1 & Volume 2 (2003, 2004), 91–94
Chaplin Today (2003), 92
Charade (1953), 83
Charade (1963), 83
Charge at Feather River, The (1952), 137
Chasing Amy (1997), 114
Chatman, Seymour, 133
Chicago (2002), 5
Ciné-club, 35
Cine-Kodak Motion Picture Camera, 2
Cine Kodograph, 2
Cinemascope, 3–4
Cinémathèque Français, 34–39, 42, 45, 53, 144
Circuit City, 151–152
Circus, The (1928), 91
Citizen Kane (1941), 6, 124
City Lights (1931), 34, 91
City of Bits: Space, Place, and the InfoBahn, 63
City of Lost Children, The (1998), 80, 114, 119
Classic Movies Collection: The Cole Porter Gift Set (2003), 94–95
ClearPlay, 149
Clemens, Samuel, 78
Clerks (1994), 113–114
Clockwork Orange, A (1971), 16
Coates, Nelson, xi
Coën, Ethan and Joel, 22, 80
Cognitivism, 130
Cohan, George, 107
Cole Porter in Hollywood (2003), 95
Columbus, Chris, 69, 159
Computer Generated Imagery (CGI), 12, 96, 125, 155
Content Scrambling System (CSS), 150
Continuity, 6
Cooper, Gary, 117
Cooper, Merian, 110

Coppola, Francis Ford, 97–98, 119
Copyleft, 147–148
Copyright Act of 1710, 57
Coraci, Frank, 25
Corman, Roger, 41
Cortazar, Octavio, 93
Costner, Kevin, 70
Cowie, Peter, 98–99
Cox, Alex, 21
Criterion Collection, The, 39, 76–78, 82, 84–85, 89, 93, 98, 108, 110, 116, 122, 124, 126
Crosland, Alan, 32–33, 104
Cukor, George, 94, 110
Curtiz, Michael, xi, 8, 44, 47, 81, 90, 98, 106

Daily Variety, 96
Danger Mouse, 71
Darabout, Frank, 48
Dark City (1998), 95–97
Dark Side of the Moon, 67, 71
Day After Tomorrow, The (2004), 25
Day at the Races, A (1937), 123
Day the Earth Stood Still, The (1951), 111, 113, 119
Demme, Jonathan, 83
De Palma, Brian, 83
Derrida, Jacques, 129
Dick, Philip, 55
Digital Millennium Copyright Act (DMCA), 149–151, 155
Digital Rights Management (DRM), 59, 148–149
Digital Video Express (DIVX), 151
Dilling, Mildred, 122
Directors Guild, The, 70, 149
Direct to video, 19
Di Sica, Vittorio, 6
Distant Drums (1951), 137
Dobbs, Lem, 119
Dogma (1999), 114
Dolby, 14, 79
Donaldson, Roger, 10

Donen, Stanley, xi, 76, 83, 91, 104
Don Juan (1926), 32–33, 104
Douglass, Gordon, 47, 137
Doujinshi, 72–73
Dreamers, The (2003), 38
DVD Aficionado, 41, 52, 60, 61
DVD Copy Control Association (DVDCCA), 150
DVD Talk, 52, 61
DVD Talks, 67
Dwan, Alan, 47, 107

Eating Raoul (1982), 21
Ebert, Roger, 67–68, 91, 96, 121, 123–124
"Ed" (pseudonym), 61–64
8½ (1963), 107
Eisenstein, Sergei, 4–6
Ellis, John, 157
Emmerich, Roland, 25
Engle, Harrison, 106
Eraserhead (1977), 21

Fahrenheit 9/11 (2004), 23, 89
Fairbanks, Douglas, 107
Fair use, 59, 144, 146
Fear and Loathing in Las Vegas (1998), 77, 140
Fédération Internationale des Archives du Film (FIAF), 144
Felix the Cat, 30
Fellini: A Director's Notebook (1969), 108
Fellini, Federico, 107–108
"Fight Song," 88
Film Movement, 24
Film Talk, 52, 60–61
Fisher, Andrew, 69
Fitzgerald, Peter, 80, 95, 105
Fleder, Gary, xi
Fleming, Victor, 8, 44, 67
Flew, Terry, 49
Flynn, Errol, 107

Ford, John, 44, 47
Foreman, Carl, 117
Formalism, 4–6
Forster, Marc, 111, 116
Fosse, Bob, 95
400 Blows, The (1959), 84
Foy, Bryan, 33, 104
Frayling, Christopher, 103, 145
*Free Culture: How Media Uses
        Technology and the Law to Lock
        Down Culture and Control
        Creativity,* 63
Freed, Arthur, 104
Freestone, Chris, 68–69
Freeway (1996), 120
Fulton, Keith, 80
Fuqua, Antoine, 25

Gaiman, Neil, 97
Gance, Abel, 30
Gasnier, Louis, 138
Giamatti, Paul, 118
Gibson, Mel, 23
Gilliam, Terry, 77, 79, 81, 82, 89–90,
        113, 140
Glorious Technicolor (1998), 106–107
Godard, Jean-Luc, 37, 45
Godfather, The, 98
Godfather, The (1972), 97, 104, 115,
        119
Godfather Collection, The (2001),
        97–98
Godfather Family: A Look Inside, The,
        (1991), 98
Godfather, Part II, The (1974), 97
Godfather, Part III, The (1990), 97
Gold Rush, The (1925), 26, 70, 91–94
Gold Rush, The (1942), 26, 70, 91–93
Gone With the Wind, 57
Gone With the Wind (1939), 44
Good, the Bad, and the Ugly, The
        (1966), 47
Grand Illusion (1938), 98–99
Grant, Cary, 46, 83, 116

Grateful Dead, The, 152
Great Dictator, The (1940), 91–94
Great Escape, The (1963), 99
Greer, Pam, 40
Grey Album, The, 71
Griffith, Richard, 53
Guenette, Robert, 106
Gunning, Tom, 30–31
Guzzlefish, 41, 52, 61

Haley, Jack Jr., 76
*Hamster Factor and Other Tales of the
        Twelve Monkeys, The* (1996),
        81
Harris, Robert, 106
Harry Potter and the Chamber of Secrets
        (2002), 159
Harry Potter and the Sorcerer's Stone
        (2001), 69, 85, 159
Hart's War (2002), 99
Harvey, Anthony, 109
Haver, Ronald, 110, 121
Hawkes, Byron, 129–130
Hawks, Howard, 46
Heeley, David, 91
Hensel, Frank, 35
Hensleigh, Jonathan, 25
Hepburn, Audrey, 83
*Here's Looking at You, Warner Bros.: The
        History of the Warner Bros. Studio*
        (1991), 106
Hermann, Bernard, 131
High concept, 19
High Noon (1952), 117–118
High Society (1956), 94
Hill, Howard, 107
His Girl Friday (1940), 45
Hitchcock, Alfred, 26, 44, 60, 65, 77,
        106, 115, 131
Hoberman, J, 43
Hoblit, Gregory, 99
Holbrook, Hal, 112
Hong Kong 1941 (1984), 82
Hope, Bob, 95

Hurricane Andy, 67
Huston, John, 106

Illegal Art, 69
Imposter (2002), xi–xii
Independence Day (1996), 25
Independent (Indie) film movement, 20–22
It's a Wonderful Life (1946), 8

Jackie Brown (1997), 82
Jackson, Peter, 12, 47, 78, 80, 81, 99–102, 123, 124–126
Jarecki, Andrew, 158
Jarmusch, Joseph, 22
Jay-Z, 71
Jazz Singer, The (1927), 33, 104
Jenkins, Henry, 66
Jeunet, Jean-Pierre, 79–80, 114, 119
Johnny Guitar (1954), 47
Jones, Peter, 107

Katz, James, 106
Keighley, William, 47, 106
Kellino, Roy, 83
Kelly, Gene, xi, 76, 91, 104, 107
Kenny, J.M., 102
Kid, The ((1921), 91
Kill Bill, Parts I & II (2003, 2004), 102
King Arthur (2004), 25
King in New York, A (1957), 91–92
King Kong (1933), 110
Kiss Me Kate (1953), 94–95
Kloft, Michael, 94
Kodak, 1–2, 30
Kodascope Projector, 1, 30
Kracauer, Siegfried, 7
Kubrick, Stanley, 16
Kuhn, Annette, 79–81
Kurosawa, Akira, 60, 122

Lacan, Jacques, 129
Landis, John, 102
Lang, Fritz, 96
Langlois, Henri, 34–41, 49–51, 53, 144
Laserdisc, ix, 16–17, 39, 76
Lawson, Lance, 142
League of Extraordinary Gentlemen, The (2003), 141
Lean, David, 99
Léaud, Jean-Pierre, 84
Lee, Christopher, 125
Lee, Spike, 22
Lehman, Ernest, 115–116
Leone, Sergio, 46–47, 103, 145
Leong, Po-Chih, 82
LeRoy, Mervyn, 104
Les Girls (1957), 94
Lesher, John, 26
Lessig, Lawrence, 63
Letterbox, 3–4, 44, 78, 84
Lewin, Albert, 141
Lewison, Barry, 82
Lights of New York (1928), 33, 104
Limelight (1952), 91, 93
Limey, The (1999), 119
Lion in Winter, The (1968), 109
Long, Chuck, 113
Lord of the Rings, The, trilogy (2001, 2002, 2003), 12, 78, 80, 81, 124
Lord of the Rings: The Fellowship of the Ring, The (2001), 100, 123, 124–125
Lord of the Rings: The Return of the King, The (2003), 100
Lord of the Rings: The Two Towers, The (2002), 47, 99–102
Lorre, Peter, 95
Love on the Run (1979), 84
"Lowering the Stakes: Prospects for a Historical Poetics of Cinema," 128
Lucas, George, 13, 19, 23, 56, 101, 137, 154

Lumière, Auguste and Louis, 4, 31
Lynch, David, 21

MacDonald, Scott, 50
MacFarquhar, Larissa, 45
Mack, Roy, 95
McKellan, Ian, 125
Magnificent Ambersons, The (1942), 90
Magnificent Seven, The (1960), 109, 120
Malle, Louis, 21
Mallrats (1995), 114
Malraux, André, 38
Maltin, Leonard, 106, 121–124
Manga, 72
Marilyn Manson, 88
Marshall, Rob, 5
Marx, Harpo, 122
*M*A*S*H* (1970), 111
Master and Commander: The Far Side of the World (2003), 9–11
Maupassant, Guy de, 133
Méliès, Georges, 4, 31
Metropolis (1927), 96
Meyer, Nicolas, 111, 113, 119
Mighty Manhattan: New York's Wonder City (1949), 95
Milestone, Lewis, 9
Milo, Sandra, 108
Mirisch, Walter, 109
Mischief Makers, The (1957), 85
Mis-en-scène, 4, 8, 10, 12
Mitchell, Glenn, 123
Mitchell, Margaret, 57
Mitchell, William, 63
Modern Times (1936), 91–94
Monsieur Verdoux (1947), 91–92
Monsoon Wedding (2002), 112
Monster's Ball (2001), 111, 116–117, 120
Montage, 4–10, 12
Monty Python's Flying Circus, 89
Moore, Michael, 23, 80, 86–89
Morgan, David, 89

Morrisette, Billy, 115
Motion Picture Association of America (MPAA), 70, 149, 151
"Movies Are a Mother to Me, The," 76
Multi Media Compact Disc, 17
Musicals Great Musicals (1996), 105
Mutiny on the Bounty (1962), 9–11
My Dinner with André (1981), 21
Myrick, Daniel, 22

Nair, Mira, 112
Napoléon (1927), 30
Nataka, Hideo, 141
National Lampoon's Animal House (1978), 102
Neely, Brad, 69
NetFlix, 24
New Biographical Dictionary of Film, The, 94
New Wave (Nouvelle Vague), 7, 37, 45, 46
New York Film Festival, 38
Nichols, Mike, 11–12, 113, 121
Nichols, Mike J., 155
Night at the Opera, A (1935), 122–123
Norrington, Stephen, 141
North by Northwest (1959), 115, 131

Obsessed with Vertigo: New Life for Hitchcock's Masterpiece (1997), 106
Oh! Brother, Where Art Thou? (2000), 80
Once Upon a Time in the West (1968), 46, 103, 145
On Sunset Boulevard: The Life and Times of Billy Wilder, 123
Original Aspect Ratio (OAR), x, 4, 14, 63, 79
Orman, Christopher, 71

Pan-and-scan, x, 4, 8, 44, 64
Panavision, 3–4
"Partie de campagne, Une," 133
Partie de campagne, Une (1936), 133
Passion of the Christ, The (2004), 23
Pathé-Baby, 30–32, 34, 39
Pekar, Harvey, 118
Pepe, Louis, 80–81
Perlman, Ron, 79, 114
Petersen, Wolfgang, 14
Phantom Edit, The (1999), 155
Phillips, Todd, 25
Photogénie, 128
Picture of Dorian Grey, The (1945), 141
Pink Flamingos (1972), 21
Pink Floyd, 67
Pinzon, Adrian, 60
Piracy, 20
Play It Again, Sam (1972)
"Poet and Peasant Overture, The," 95
Por Primera Vez (1967), 93
Porter, Cole, 94–95
Postman, The (1997), 70
Prince, Stephen, 122
Proyas, Alex, 95–97
Psycho (1960), 65
Pulcini, Robert, 118
Pulp Fiction (1994), xii, 22, 82, 103–104
Punisher, The (2004), 25
Puzo, Mario, 98, 119

"Q, The" (pseudonym), 68–69

Radloff, Toby, 118
Randall, Alice, 57–58
Ray, Billy, 113
Ray, Nicholas, 47
Ray, Robert, 128, 131, 134
Realism, 4–7, 10

Recording Industry Association of America (RIAA), 58, 73, 151, 156
Reiner, Rob, 77
Renegade Commentaries, 67–69
Renoir, Jean, 6, 41, 98–99, 133
Repo Man (1984), 21
Reservoir Dogs (1992), 12, 103
Return of the Secaucus 7, The (1980), 21
Richardson, Tony, 136
Richter, W.D., xi, 48, 82, 85
Ringu, 141
Ringu (1998), 141
Ripley, Alexandra, 57
Ritter, John, 117
Robertson, Todd ("Gut"), 61–65, 69
Robin Hood (1922), 47, 107
Robinson, David, 92–93
Rocky Horror Picture Show, The (1975), 44, 85
Roddenberry, Gene, 26, 56
Rogues of Sherwood Forest (1950), 47
Rohmer, Eric, 37
Rose, Charlie, 43, 80
Ross, Herbert, 90
Rouch, Jean, 38
Roud, Richard, 38
Routson, Jon, 156
Roven, Chuck, 113
Rowling, J.K., 72, 155

Sánchez, Eduardo, 22
Sandman, The, 97
Sarris, Andrew, 43
Saturday Night at the Movies, 8, 9
Saussure, Ferdinand de, 129
Sayles, John, 21
Scarface (1983), 83
Scarlett: The Sequel to Margaret Mitchell's "Gone With the Wind," 57
Schaefer, Roberto, 111
Schoedsack, Ernest, 110

Scorsese, Martin, 39, 50

Scotland, PA (2002), 115

Scott, Ridley, 16, 56

Searchers, The (1956), 47

Sharman, Jim, 44, 85

Shattered Glass (2003), 113

Shawshank Redemption, The (1994), 48

Sheen, Charlie, 112

Shelton, Ron, 115

Shore, Howard, 124

Show Girl in Hollywood (1930), 104

Showgirls (1995), 83

Sidney, George, 94

Sikov, Ed, 123–124

Silk Stockings (1957), 94

Silkwood (1983), 11

Singin' in the Rain (1952), xi, 76, 91, 104–105

Smile (1956) TV show, 93

Smith, James, 95

Smith, Kevin, 113–114

Soderbergh, Steven, 11, 22, 113, 119, 121

Sommers, Stephen, 25

Sonny Bono Copyright Term Extension Act, 147

Spielberg, Steven, 13

Stalag 17 (1953), 99

Star Is Born, A (1954), 110

Starsky & Hutch (2004), 25

Star Trek television and movie series, 26, 56, 85

Star Wars: A New Hope (1977), 19, 25, 44, 137, 154–155

Star Wars first trilogy, 45, 56, 85, 101

Star Wars I: The Phantom Menace (1999), 155

Star Wars II: Attack of the Clones (2002), 23

Stein, Patrick, 67

Stolen Kisses (1968), 84

Stone, Oliver, 112, 119

Storaro, Vittorio, 108

Strange Days (1995), 26

Stroheim, Erich von, 33

Sturges, John, 99, 109, 120, 124

Sundance Film Festival, 21

Sunset Boulevard (1950), 33, 105–106, 123

Super Density format, 17

Suppé, Franz von, 95

Suzuki, Kôji, 141

Swanson, Gloria, 33

Symphony in F (1940), 93

Tarantino, Quentin, xii, 12, 18–19, 22, 39–51, 75, 80, 82, 102, 103–104, 140, 142

Taurog, Norman, 5, 94

Tell Your Children (*Reefer Madness*) (1938), 138

That's Entertainment! (1974), 76, 91

39 Steps, The (1935), 77

This Is Spinal Tap (1984), 77

Thompson, Hunter, 140

Thomson, David, 94, 105

Thornton, Billy Bob, 116–117

Tolkien, J.R.R., 72, 101, 125

Tom Jones (1963), 136–137

Toubiana, Serge, 92–93

Tramp and the Dictator, The (2002), 93–94

Treasure of the Sierra Madre, The (1947), 106–107

Truffault, Philippe, 92

Truffaut, François, 37–38, 84–85

Truth About Charlie, The (2002), 83

Turan, Kenneth, 11

12 Monkeys, 81, 113

2600 Magazine, 150

Ulmer, Gregory, 129

Uricchio, William, 135

Vadim, Roger, 120

Van Helsing (2004), 25

Van Helsing: The London Assignment (2004), 25

Van Sant, Gus, 22

Verhoeven, Paul, 83

Vertigo (1959), 26, 106

Video Cassette Recorder (VCR), x, 13, 15–18, 29, 38, 39, 42–45, 48, 67, 138, 145

Video Home System (VHS), ix, 1, 17, 66

Vitaphone Corporation, 32–33

Wainwright, Loudon, 76

Wall Street (1987), 112

Walsh, Raoul, 137

Walters, Charles, 94

Warner Brothers, xi, 32–33, 81, 106

Warner Legends Collection: Flynn, Cagney, Bogart (2003), 106–107

Waters, John, 21

Wayne, John, 32

Wedding March, The (1928), 33

Weir, Peter, 9

Welles, Orson, 6, 90, 124

Wells, H.G., 96

Werner, Jeff, 98

Wertmuller, Lina, 108

Western Electric, 32

WETA Workshop, 125

What a Glorious Feeling: The Making of Singin' in the Rain (2002), 105

What Novels Can Do That Films Can't (and Vice Versa), 133

White Album, The, 71

Widescreen, 3–4, 8, 29, 44

Wilde, Oscar, 141

Wilder, Billy, 33, 99, 105, 123–124

Wilhelm, 137–138

Wind Done Gone, The, 57–58

Wise, Robert, 111, 113, 119

Wizard of Oz, The (1939), 8, 44, 47, 67, 71

Wizard People, Dear Reader (2004), 69

Woman in Paris, A (1923), 91–92

Wood, Sam, 122–123

World Intellectual Property Organization (WIPO), 149

Wyler, William, 6

Yahoo! Internet Life, 67–68

Yankee Doodle Dandy (1942), 106–107

Yearbook: An Animal House Reunion, The (1998), 102

Young Frankenstein (1974), 112

Zemeckis, Robert, 13–14, 19, 124

Zinnemann, Fred, 117

About the Author

AARON BARLOW teaches early American literature at Kutztown University. He has previously taught film studies at the Pratt Institute in New York City, and has written extensively on science fiction cinema.